MAYFLOWER
LIVES

MAYFLOWER LIVES

Pilgrims in a New World and the
Early American Experience

MARTYN WHITTOCK

PEGASUS BOOKS
NEW YORK LONDON

MAYFLOWER LIVES

Pegasus Books, Ltd.
148 W 37th Street, 13th Floor
New York, NY 10018

Copyright © 2019 Martyn Whittock

First Pegasus Books cloth edition August 2019

Interior design by Maria Fernandez

ISBN: 978-1-64313-132-0

10 9 8 7 6 5 4 3 2 1

Printed in the United States of America

Distributed by W. W. Norton & Company, Inc.

In fond memory of

Don Bramwell Myers (1929–2018).

Definitely one of the Saints.

CONTENTS

INTRODUCTION

The publication of this book coincides with the four hundredth anniversary of the voyage of the *Mayflower* to North America in 1620. Since that first historic landing at Plymouth Rock, in the winter of that year, the ship, its voyage, and its complex mixture of passengers have passed into myth and legend. Their voyage, trials and triumphs, settlement and interaction with the indigenous peoples of the New England coastlands have become integral to understanding the roots of American culture and identity. It is, of course, undeniable that their contribution is only one of the many streams of immigration that have flowed into the making of the modern United States. And their immigration "stream" is numerically tiny compared to the massive "tributaries" that flowed into North America in the 19th and 20th centuries, and which continue into the 21st century. Just about half of these 130 travelers to the New World died in the first winter of 1620–21, which sets both their numbers and hardships in sharp perspective.

Nevertheless, the Pilgrims have had an impact on popular consciousness that is in excess of their original numbers and original significance. As such, their legacy punches well above its original weight. A United States without the Pilgrims, without Thanksgiving and the Mayflower Compact, without their epic voyage and their passionate desire to create a new home in a new world, is significantly incomplete, emotionally as well as historically.

Furthermore, their story is an English one as well as an American one, for both before and after the journey they were subjects of the Stuart monarchy (whether they liked it or not). And they remained connected with a nation spiraling down to the British Civil Wars of the 1640s. The *Mayflower* story is, therefore, a transatlantic story and a uniting factor between two Atlantic communities that would eventually (in the next century) take separate but related paths of national development. But the *Mayflower* was part of both these national journeys.

In many ways the unique impact of these Mayflower Lives is encapsulated in the word *Pilgrims*, for these immigrants included many whose motivation went far beyond economic migration, as important as that was. These particular passengers—and later settlers—saw their goal as being much more than that. They believed that they were God's elect, set on building more than merely a new community beyond the reach of religious persecution. Their aims encompassed nothing less than the construction of a "New Jerusalem" in the "New World." It was this that contributed something very distinctive to how they understood their escape from religious persecution (many had been in exile in the Netherlands after facing problems in England), the upheavals and upsets of the journey, surviving New England winters, and the kind of community they should eventually create. This cannot be ignored, whether one interprets their arrival positively, as contributing something essential to the ethics and self-understanding encapsulated in the later American Dream, or negatively, as part of a European settlement that was to eventually lead to the destruction of the lives and culture of Native Americans (whether deliberately or as collateral damage caused by European diseases). There is something of the seeds of both these later experiences in aspects of the mind-set and the early impact of these settlers. What is clear is that the Pilgrims shine a strong light, or cast a long shadow (depending on the viewpoint of those reflecting on them), down the centuries.

The people who feature in *Mayflower Lives*, as on the original ship, were a mixture of so-called Saints (members of Puritan Separatist congregations) and Strangers (economic migrants). Together they made up a rather uneasy community on the ship and in the eventual settlement, and we need to remember both groups when exploring the adventure on which they embarked. Some of those we will meet were Saints, some were Strangers. And one of the latter was very much an outsider, who came to have an impact to rival any of the insiders. But together they give us an insight into this epic adventure.

Many books tell the story of the *Mayflower*, but the characteristic of this book is that it explores the motives, trials, tribulations, successes, and significance of this myth-making voyage and settlement through the interlocking lives of fourteen of those who were part of these events. Some were men; some were women; one was a little child who did not survive the first winter; one was a Native American. Their lives are dramatic and colorful. For example: Captain Jones was a successful sailor but one who had never previously crossed the Atlantic; John Howland fell overboard but survived; William Bradford wrote the definitive history of the settlement; Mary and Richard More were sent to America without family because their father thought them products of his wife's adulterous relationship; Stephen Hopkins had survived shipwreck and had served with John Smith (of Pocahontas fame); Tisquantum (Squanto) was a Native American who had escaped from kidnapping, spoke English, and assisted the colonists; Myles Standish and John Alden were allegedly love rivals, and Standish was a brave but, at times, brutal military man; Richard More was later excommunicated for "gross unchastity with another man's wife." Together they are part of this astonishing story.

As these individual stories build, we will increasingly see how these particular lives intersected and affected each other; whether it was by way of cooperation, or conflict; positively or negatively. Each life has been selected because it opens up a window into a particular aspect of the *Mayflower* experience. In this way we can explore wider issues, such as religious faith, relations with native peoples, politics, the fur trade, motherhood and family life, romance and sexual relationships, deviance and crime. Yet each wider theme is rooted in a personal "his-story" or "her-story." They have also been chosen so that, together, they move the story forward from journey, to settlement, to building a community. And where they intersect with other lives they provide their own individual perspective on the unfolding events. For these were lives bound together on one very small ship and one very small colony. Despite this, their interlocking small worlds give us insights into a distant past and a legacy that transcends their own individual experiences. It is biography with a difference, because these are Mayflower Lives.

Visiting Massachusetts in 2018 as part of the research for this book gave me a vivid insight into how this history is still apparent in the modern world. While waiting at passport control in Boston's Logan International Airport, I was amused to see a poster of a demurely dressed Puritan woman assuring me that "We thank thee for thy patience"! But the connection with the 17th century is even more tangible. It is still possible to touch the water from the spring near Truro, on Cape Cod, where Pilgrims first drank; stand on First Encounter Beach and imagine the flying arrows and musket shots; walk the street they knew in Plymouth; gaze out to sea from Cole's Hill, which still contains the bones of those who died that first winter; stand beside the graves of John and Priscilla Alden, and of Myles Standish, at Duxbury; see the grassy depression marking the cellar of their house there and stand beside the hearth of John Howland's excavated homestead at Rocky Nook. One can still look down at Plymouth Rock and wonder if it truly was where the Pilgrims first stepped ashore at the place the indigenous peoples knew as Patuxet. *Mayflower* history still resonates with modern experiences in the 21st-century landscape. Then, later that same summer, running into a friendly group of *Mayflower* descendants in St Wilfrid's Church, in Scrooby (where William Brewster was fined for refusing to attend services), brought home the living legacy of these remarkable people. And sitting on wooden pews from the 17th century there, and later visiting St Helena's Church, in nearby Austerfield (where William Bradford was baptized), reminded me once again of the remarkable journey that had taken these Pilgrims from the English countryside to eventually settle in North America. Their story is amazing.

Finally, a note about dates. When recording events that took place in British and colonial North American history, I have used the dates that were recorded at the time of the event, but with the year adjusted to start on January 1, for clarity. The latter point is important to remember, to avoid confusion. This is because until 1752, the civil or legal year in Britain and its overseas colonies began on March 25 (also known as Lady Day). This left the period of time from January 1 to March 24 in a rather ambiguous position. So, an event such as the birth of the *Mayflower* Pilgrim William Bradford on March 19 was technically, at the time, in the tail end of the year 1589, but any modern reader would assume it to have occurred in 1590 because the assumption now is that a year starts on January 1. So, while his birth date *can* be communicated as 1589 or as 1589/1590, *we* will just say that he was born in 1590 for simplicity.

To add to the confusion, until 1752 Britain and its growing overseas empire (including the Eastern Seaboard of North America) used the Julian calendar, which was ten days behind the Gregorian calendar used in much of continental Europe. Protestants were initially reluctant to accept the new calendar because its use had been decreed by the Catholic Pope Gregory XIII, in 1582. This means that when the *Mayflower* finally sailed from Plymouth, England, its crew and passengers considered it as happening on September 6; we would now call it September 16. When they wearily returned to Cape Cod—having failed to get south to the Hudson—and signed the Mayflower Compact, they did it on November 11; we would call it November 21. The "adjusted date" (adjusted to *our* calendar) is ten days later. For simplicity, though, we will use the dates that *they* used. So, as far as this book is concerned, they sailed on September 6 and signed the famous compact on November 11. This is worth bearing in mind, as adjusted dates can occasionally be found in some books and websites, which can sometimes cause confusion. Simplicity seems best: we use the dates a Pilgrim would recognize!

1

The Master's Story:
Christopher Jones,
Master of the *Mayflower*

In November 1620, a battered sailing ship wearily worked its way up the coast of what is today Massachusetts. Called the *Mayflower*, there was little about the ship and its passengers that indicated it might ever have a place in future history, myth, and legend. Indeed, everything pointed towards, at best, hardship and, at worst, disaster. As those on board looked out on the shoreline of Cape Cod, their anxieties mounted. Not only had the voyage from a very distant England been long and hard but this was not where they intended to be. Only two days earlier, on November 9, they had first sighted this same shore and then attempted to sail down the coast to their intended destination of the northern parts of the colony of Virginia. It was not to be. The strong winds, coastal shoals, and rising winter seas of the Atlantic, which had already battered the ship on its two-month-long journey to this "New World," contrived to thwart their plans. At last they had accepted the inevitable and turned back. Now they once more looked out on the same forbidding shoreline that they had spotted earlier. Here they paused their journey to take stock of their situation. Gray waves drove in against the beaches, which were fringed with dunes, rough sea grass, and woodland of pine and stunted oak growing down towards the shore. The ship strained at its anchor cable, and continual seasickness made the cramped, wet conditions on board all the more miserable. Already one passenger and one crewman had died on the journey (the passenger a mere three days before sighting land), and the future seemed far from certain for those who had made it this far.

For, if the intended destination of the colony of Virginia promised a tough but adventurous opportunity to build a new life on a new continent, the uncertainties of *this place* meant that it was impossible to predict what lay ahead. The experiences of the English settlement, established farther south in Virginia since 1607, indicated that there would be native tribes speaking unfamiliar languages and potentially posing a threat to those who landed from the ship. There would be strange trees, plants, and animals and none of the familiar domesticated crops and beasts of the fenced and parcelled-up English countryside or that around Leiden in the Netherlands, from where many on board had started their original journey. A safe anchorage would have to be found in the sand-silted bays beyond the hook of land that jutted out into the winter ocean. Timber would need cutting and shelters would have to be constructed to provide some protection from the falling temperatures of the fast-approaching New England winter. And it was rapidly becoming apparent that their European clothing was quite inadequate for the adventure. Already rotting from the salty damp-ness of the sea journey, it was ill suited to the cold of November that was penetrating the ship's timbers. Yet beyond the ship there was no existing settlement offering shelter, and the temperature was falling.

To add to their distress, all this was on top of a voyage that had been anything but plain sailing. In fact, things had gone wrong from the start. The *Mayflower* had originally left London with about sixty-five passengers in the middle of July 1620. From there she had sailed to

Southampton, Hampshire, to meet the *Speedwell*, which was bringing others from Leiden. The *Mayflower*'s master (captain), Christopher Jones, had then planned that the two ships would begin their Atlantic crossing by the end of July, but problems with the *Speedwell* (she had already been leaking on her voyage from Leiden to Southampton) threw out his plans, since repairs were needed once the *Speedwell* arrived in Southampton. Then, soon after leaving Southampton on August 5, the *Speedwell* began leaking once again. This forced *both* ships into the port of Dartmouth, Devon, for repairs, since Jones and the *Speedwell*'s captain were determined to keep the two vessels together for mutual support. They arrived in Dartmouth on Saturday, August 12. About nine days later, the two ships finally set off again. But to Jones's frustration, and that of the rest of the voyagers, the *Speedwell* again began to leak. Vital time was being lost, and the autumn was looming when they returned—this time to the Devon port of Plymouth. There the two captains and the senior passengers conferred and made the difficult decision to leave the *Speedwell* behind. Not surprisingly, some passengers had given up at this point and returned to Leiden on the ailing *Speedwell*.

Jones had had no choice but to take the remaining passengers on board the *Mayflower*. Grossly overcrowded with 102 passengers, including 3 pregnant women (one child was later born at sea), and about 30 crew, the solitary *Mayflower* finally departed from Plymouth on Wednesday, September 6. Along with the packed passengers were live animals, including goats, pigs, and chickens that were kept in pens on the drenched main deck. By this time the passengers had already been on board ship for nearly one and a half months; sleeping and living in thin-walled, low-ceilinged, dark, damp cabins. Now the ordeal continued as England fell away behind them into the sea mist of September. On good days they could go up on the top deck, but bad weather and the attendant rough seas drove them below once more into a fetid space that stank of vomit from perpetual seasickness and worse. The only toilet arrangements were wooden buckets that sloshed and spilled their foul contents as the ship heaved. Food, for those who could keep it down, consisted of hard tack, salted beef and fish, and cheese. For many, the waking day was occupied with praying and psalm singing; with services on Sunday that lasted the whole day. For others less godly there was nothing to do except talk, grumble, vomit, and hope the seas kept down. One of the crew passed his time taunting the most miserable of the sickly passengers with the promise that, if they died, he would be happy to throw their bodies overboard. However, in an event that some identified as the hand of God, this young seaman was the only member of the crew to fall sick and die on the journey, and it was his body that was thrown overboard.

Mercifully the first half of the voyage went well, apart from the unrelenting seasickness. But the trouble with the *Speedwell* had set back the sailing schedule, and nothing that Master Christopher Jones did could outrun the autumn weather. By October, the Atlantic storms caught them. At times the driving wind was so strong and the *Mayflower* so battered by the ocean that Jones was forced to let the ship drift before the driving sea. Then the main beam of the *Mayflower* (the timber running from one side of the hull to the other) cracked. Inspecting the damage, Jones was at his wits' end and considered turning back. But he faced criticism from some crew members who feared they would not be paid if they did so. At last, under Jones's direction, the ship's master carpenter managed to clamp the great timber together using a giant iron screw that some of the passengers had brought to assist in house construction. But it had been a close call!

All things considered, it was little wonder that after sixty-six days at sea, they had been blown off course from their originally intended destination of the Hudson River and so had first sighted land at Cape Cod.[1] And now they were back there again!

It was hardly surprising that grumbling on board the ship was growing into a threatening dissension and that tensions were rising between the disparate elements among the passengers and crew. But *disparate* hardly begins to describe them. Of the 102 passengers on board, some, as we shall shortly see, were there because their Puritan religious beliefs had set them at odds with an increasingly authoritarian Church of England, whose royal head—King James VI and I—was stamping his authority on the Church and kingdom under his rule. He was determined to bring to heel those dissenting communities who either sought greater austerity within the established Church or, worse still, attempted to set up worshipping communities outside its legal authority. After years of persecution and marginalization in King James's England, many of the so-called godly on the *Mayflower* had sought sanctuary in the Netherlands, where they had enjoyed greater religious freedom. But even there things had begun to turn sour, for religious warfare was intensifying in Europe and their sons were facing conscription into the armies of the Protestant Dutch state as it faced threats from its Catholic neighbors. In such a situation the possibility of starting afresh in the raw new lands of North America increased in its appeal as every year passed. Even its alien and unfamiliar nature added to, rather than detracted from, its appeal; for the godly passengers were deeply familiar with the history and experiences of another Chosen People: the Children of Israel. They too had been led by God out of the oppressive and sinful land of Egypt; had struggled through the wilderness for years; and had conquered a new home in the land of Canaan, after crossing the waters of the river Jordan. So, if God's people had once found their Promised Land in a place they'd had to conquer from the native peoples of Canaan, why should His new Chosen People not be similarly blessed as they sought out a new home, and built a New Jerusalem, in the New World? Consequently, the odds against them only served to strengthen their resolve to do as God had commanded. It is therefore perhaps not surprising that later history would remember such intrepid religious adventurers as Pilgrims. However, while their Puritan beliefs had set them at odds with the royally approved Church back home, this did not mean that they necessarily saw eye to eye with each other, or indeed with other dissenting groups. They might describe themselves as Saints, engaged on a mission to build a New Jerusalem on earth, but that did not mean that there was agreement among them over how such a new community should be constructed! And this was not the only cause of tension among the *Mayflower*'s passengers, because those on board also included Strangers. In order to make the venture financially viable, economic migrants had been allowed to join the trip. They brought money, skills, and resources to the mission but not the passionate and godly commitment that was a hallmark of the Saints. And then there was the crew. God alone knew where they stood on the path of salvation. From the manners and speech of some, it seemed that they did not stand well in this matter at all, while for others there perhaps was hope. But unity on board ship, there was not!

Not only were conditions appalling and personal relationships fraught but their very legal status was in doubt. Having gained permission from the English authorities to settle in Virginia, they had no proper legal right to establish a colony on this stretch of the New England coast. And, as godly and upright Christians, they knew that if their new home was to flourish, it was essential that they had right and title established by law, even if they had little regard for the Christian integrity and purity of the king and royal authority that issued it. If they were to become God's pilgrim people in this new Promised Land, they needed to establish order and decency among themselves and proper government as a community in a strange and alien environment. All this was now complicated by the fact that their present location was not where they had intended to be, and, consequently, they were about to establish a settlement in an area that lacked approval by English royal authority. The way forward was far from clear. So it was in this state that, on Saturday, November 11, the male passengers signed an agreement that would regulate their new settlement.[2] Of the Mayflower Compact we will hear more in due course, but it was a step forward in providing rules and regulations for the less than united community.

The ship was now anchored in a sheltered spot—later called Provincetown Harbor—protected from the Atlantic waves by the curving spit at the northern head of Cape Cod. As the *Mayflower*'s master, Christopher Jones, consulted what little documentation he had about this coastline and prepared to assist in the search for a suitable place on shore to settle for the winter, he must have been wondering how he had ever let himself get drawn into such a risky venture in the first place.

The backstory of Christopher Jones and the *Mayflower*

The backstory of Christopher Jones reminds us of how many unlikely factors came together in order to make the *Mayflower* voyage possible. It was a backstory that started well before the momentous events of 1620. Yet without these previous histories, what occurred in that crucial year would not have happened, for a wide range of Mayflower Lives were drawn together in order to create the voyage and eventual settlement. So, before we explore the motives and experiences of some of the other key individuals among both the Saints and Strangers on the voyage and in the settlement that followed, we need to appreciate something of the man and the ship that made it possible. For both Jones and the *Mayflower* had a backstory that existed before the events that thrust them into the full glare of history. They were both experienced, as seafarer and ship, before their American connection eclipsed all their previous activities. But those previous experiences flowed into the later events.

For such a crucial player, we cannot be absolutely certain of the origins of Christopher Jones. However, we are fairly certain that he was born in Harwich, Essex, in about 1570. Despite this, there appears to have been something of a lapse in the keeping of the baptismal records there between the spring of 1565 and the early summer of 1571.[3] Since it is obvious that children will have been born and baptized there in this time period, the loss of records indicates a problem in record keeping and document survival, not an absence of baptisms. From the fact that Christopher was later first recorded at, and was then active in, Harwich, and that both he and his family seem well established there, it is clear that this was where he was born.

Harwich was an important port in eastern England, which in the 16th century provided a base for trade across the North Sea to northwestern Europe and Scandinavia. The position of Harwich on the estuaries of both the river Stour and the river Orwell enhanced its status as a port. In addition, it was one of the few safe anchorages between the Thames and the Humber estuaries. As such, it provided Jones with the opportunity to gain experience in both shipping and trading, which would later be so valuable in 1620.

What we do know about the early life of Christopher Jones comes to us from the evidence of two weddings and a funeral. The first key event was the funeral. This occurred in Harwich in 1578, the year of his father's death (the funeral in question), when Christopher inherited from his father his interest in a local ship called the *Marie Fortune*. The family members were well established mariners, since Christopher's younger brother, Roger, also received the eighth part of a ship named the *Centurion*. Later, on Roger's death at sea in 1597, he left his older brother his astrolabe (a navigational instrument), which emphasizes his role as a mariner. Clearly, the Jones family was of some significant middling wealth, as evidenced in the part-ownership of the ships that appear in these inheritances. [4]

The next time that Christopher appears in the 16th-century records is 1593. This was the first of his two weddings. On December 23 of that year he married seventeen-year-old Sara Twitt, who also came from a family with strong maritime connections. The Twitt and Jones families were near neighbors, and the wedding nicely consolidated their financial interests. We have no way of knowing what Christopher and Sara thought of each other, but their marriage was a sound commercial proposition, since Sara Jones, née Twitt, soon inherited from her father a twelfth share in his ship, named *Apollo*, in 1599.

Christopher was doing well, because in 1601 he became a freeman of the Borough of Harwich. As a freeman he enjoyed a number of rights and privileges, including exemption from various tolls when moving goods in and out of the town. In most cases such freemen were also the only persons eligible to vote at parliamentary elections. When King James VI and I granted the town its Great Charter in 1604, Christopher was named as one of twenty-four of its leading citizens. As such, he is further recorded as assessing tax values on land and urban properties, and as a jury member. An intriguing insight into his upward mobility and its limits comes from 1605, when he was accused of illegally keeping hunting dogs. The relevance of this lies in the fact that this was prohibited for anyone lacking the status of a "gentleman" owning property worth forty shillings. Clearly, there were financial limits to what Christopher had achieved by this time, but this had not put a ceiling on his aspirations or his sense of status. His tenacity would later prove valuable when the *Mayflower* crossed to North America in 1620.

This brings us to that second wedding. This followed the early death of Sara, his first wife, in 1603, aged just twenty-seven years. Following Sara's death, Christopher quickly remarried. As with his first wife, this was also a financially advantageous maritime match. His new wife, Josian Gray, was the widow of a successful ship owner and merchant (Richard Gray), whose wealth had been enhanced by involvement with speculative ventures in the Caribbean. She was twenty-one and brought to the marriage substantial property and land. The marriage produced eight children. It also gave birth to a new phase in Christopher's shipping business, since his wealth was boosted by the new match. This is reflected in the fact that, by 1605, Christopher owned his own ship, named *Josian* after his young wife. At 240 tons, it was an above-average-sized merchant vessel.[5] Christopher was doing well.

In 1611 the family moved from Harwich, in Essex, to Rotherhithe, on the south bank of the river Thames. However, the family kept a close connection to their old home port, as, while Master Jones was away on his 1620 journey to America, he sent his heavily pregnant wife (carrying their sixth child) back to her family in Harwich. It was a thoughtful act, given that she would be carrying their latest child to full term on her own. But back to that move in 1611. Today Rotherhithe is part of the London borough of Southwark, but in 1611 it was an independent port and the location of a number of shipyards. To an ambitious seaman, such as Christopher Jones, it offered opportunities due to its close proximity to London and the trade of the Thames estuary. And, at last, around this period of time his story became intertwined with that of a ship which would loom large in the history of North America. For it was in 1611 that a salvage claim names him as the "Master" of the *Mayflower*. There is an earlier brief mention in the Port Books of 1609 also linking this ship to Harwich, so it looks as if he had acquired it before he moved to Rotherhithe. Jones was her master and part owner (he had a quarter share); he shared ownership of the ship with men named Christopher Nicholls, Robert Child, and Thomas Short.

Sailing on the *Mayflower*, he was involved in trade to continental Europe. Between 1610 and 1620 the Customs Books of the Exchequer show that most of his work involved the French wine trade. An exception was in 1614–15 when his voyages took him to northern Germany, shipping out English cloth and returning with European fabrics; he then sailed to Málaga, Spain, in 1615. But none of these journeys took him into the Atlantic. Neither he nor his ship gained any experience on that stormy ocean, so the voyage of 1620 was to test him and the ship to the limit. As we shall eventually see, both paid a heavy toll for the endeavor. It is clear that the *Mayflower* was a fairly old ship by the time she took part in the famous and difficult voyage of 1620.

Exploring, as we will, the lives of fourteen players (including Christopher Jones) reveals the dramatic events that led to the arrival and settlement of the Pilgrims in the New World. But the story cannot be told without saying more about another—inanimate—character, and that, of course, is the *Mayflower* herself. She was a freight galleon and was crewed by about thirty crew. What is astonishing is that nobody who recorded the events of the famous 1620 voyage actually mentioned the name of the ship involved! Poor *Mayflower* battled the Atlantic and the winter off Cape Cod in anonymity. William Bradford and Edward Winslow (key players in the Pilgrims' story) simply referred to her as "the bigger ship," "the larger ship," and the "vessel." It was only a document known as the Allotment of Lands, written at New Plymouth, New England, and dating from March 1623, that first mentions the name of this crucial player in these great events.[6] For us, though, the name of the ship is now so famous and so closely entangled with one particular historical event that it is difficult to think of any other ship by that name. But of course, in reality, there would have been many ships sharing the name, which, in time, became associated with just one vessel. We know of no fewer than twenty-six different ships called *Mayflower* that were operating out of English ports between 1588 and 1642.[7] One of these earlier ships had even fought for Queen Elizabeth I against the Spanish Armada in 1588. Confusingly, it even seems that a quite different *Mayflower* was involved in voyages to Plymouth Colony in 1629 and again in the 1630s. It seems to have been lost at sea on another such crossing in the winter of 1641–42. We know that this was not *the* Mayflower, because, as will be revealed, that historic vessel was broken up soon after 1624.

What we can say with certainty is that the *Mayflower* was not the right ship for the events of 1620. That summer she transported wine from Europe to London; in the autumn she carried the godly to a New World and the hopes of building a New Jerusalem. She was nothing if not a versatile vessel. But she was not up to the second of these voyages that year. From the slight references to her we can conclude that she was of a type of vessel that could cope with sailing the coasts of Europe but was ill suited to the Atlantic crossing. She had structures, called castles, at front and rear to give some protection to crew and passengers and provide some shelter to the main deck, but her construction would have made her extremely difficult to sail against the wind. This was particularly problematic given the North Atlantic's prevailing westerlies. These posed particular problems in the autumn and winter; it was in these unfavorable seasons that she sailed to America and stood off the New England coast in 1620–21. This unsuitability helps explain some of the unpleasant experiences recorded by those sailing and living on her. It is no surprise that the ship's voyage from England to America took more than two months; two months that ate away at the morale of the passengers on board. Given that the *Mayflower*'s return trip to London in April/May 1621 took less than half that time, we can be sure that the ship was poorly built for the westward journey but fared better when she sailed home again, with a following wind.[8]

She would have had three decks: a main deck, a gun deck, and a cargo hold. William Bradford, one of her passengers with whom we shall soon be acquainted, thought that she could carry somewhere in the region of 180 tons of cargo. On the *Mayflower*'s journey to America the cargo hold contained trade goods, supplies for the journey and the establishing of the colony, military equipment, tools and utensils, clothing and bedding.[9] We know she carried weapons, as Master Jones would eventually unload four small cannon in order to protect the newly established colony.[10] Another clue regarding the *Mayflower*'s weaponry lies in the fact that the ship's (unnamed) "master gunner" accompanied one of the expeditions ashore in December 1620 and died later that winter.[11]

Sadly, the *Mayflower* was to suffer greatly on her one and only trip to North America. Just four years after the epic voyage, three of the owners of the *Mayflower* applied to the Admiralty court for an evaluation of her worth. This occurred two years after Jones's death, in 1622. One of these part owners was his widow, Josian Jones, who had inherited her husband's share in the vessel. The ship was eventually described as being "in ruins," with a value of only £128 and laid up since the voyage of 1620–21.[12] It seems that the *Mayflower* had fallen victim to the demands and trials of that historic voyage. It was not only passengers and crew who had been exhausted by the experience. After that she was broken up and so vanishes from history.

But famous old ships leave a legacy of legends, and, in this case, these include claims that *Mayflower* timbers today prop up buildings as far apart as the Old Schoolroom in Abingdon, Berkshire, and an ancient barn in the village of Jordans, Buckinghamshire, where some have even claimed that they have seen a letter *M* carved into the timbers. All are sadly mistaken, because there is not the slightest piece of surviving evidence to tell us what happened to the timbers of the *Mayflower*.[13] Nobody at the time realized that the ship would become so retrospectively famous. The "connection" with Jordans has probably been invented due to its close proximity to the burial place of William Penn, founder of Pennsylvania (died 1718), in the cemetery of the Jordans Quaker meeting house.

So ended the existence of a ship that was an unlikely choice for its historic role and later iconic status. Neither Jones nor his ship had sailed the North Atlantic before they were contracted to move the mixture of Saints and Strangers across the ocean. He and the ship were clearly chosen for the contract because they were available at a low enough price, and were willing to accept the role because there had been a downturn in European shipping contracts. This is how an Essex (turned Rotherhithe-based) master—possessing only sailing experiences of European waters, and mastering a ship built primarily for those waters—became engaged in an enterprise that took him and his ship across the North Atlantic.

So it was that Master Christopher Jones and his co-owner Robert Child were approached by Merchant Adventurer Thomas Weston, who was looking for a ship to transport settlers to North America in order to start a new colony. Weston and an associate named Robert Cushman were acting as agents for Puritans (the later Pilgrims), who had left England due to religious persecution and who were living in exile in the Netherlands. Until 1622 Weston played a major role in organizing the movement of this party to America and in the later financing of the colony, until he finally pulled out of the venture in that year. His dealings with the colony will feature later in this book, but suffice it to say, his involvement was based on economics, not religious ideology, and he was clearly keen to make a profit from the venture. Later dealings reveal his lack of scruples and his willingness to set beliefs to one side if offered the possibility of making a quick profit; he was later accused of selling weaponry destined for New England to Turkish pirates![14] As a result of this contract, Jones and the *Mayflower* made their one and only journey across the Atlantic and back. Given this lack of experience, it is surprising how good a job they made of it. Remembering the apparently cut-price funding of the trip, we may therefore be less surprised at the way in which the other vessel similarly tasked (the *Speedwell*) failed the test when the journey had hardly begun. However, Christopher Jones had several crew members who had been to the New World before, because the fifty-year-old Jones was very aware of his limitations and sought to make up the deficit in his own Atlantic experience through his choice of senior members of the crew. For this reason he took on two master's mates who had previous experience sailing to the New World. The first of these was 45-year-old John Clarke, who had been a ship's pilot on a voyage to the English settlement at Jamestown, Virginia, in 1611. While in North America he had been taken prisoner by the Spanish and, as a prisoner, been taken first to Havana, Cuba, and then to Málaga, Spain. After repeated interrogations by the Spanish authorities, he was eventually released to return to England in 1616. In 1618 he was engaged in transporting cattle to Jamestown. Jones recognized the value of such a man and hired him for the *Mayflower*'s voyage. The same motivation led him to take on Robert Coppin (also as a master's mate), since he had some whaling experience in the North Atlantic.

However, there were also family connections influencing one of his appointments, as he employed John Alden, who was probably his cousin, as the ship's cooper in charge of storing provisions. But this was about more than just creating jobs for a relative. Jones knew that he needed someone he could trust in this vital role, because everyone's food and drink were stored within the barrels in the cooper's care. Consequently, it was Alden who had been sent on ahead to Southampton to buy provisions and store them in sealed barrels. Alden would eventually marry a passenger named Priscilla Mullins in the New World, after she nursed him back to health when he fell ill that first winter. He stayed in America when Christopher Jones eventually sailed home.

On one area the limited financing of the trip restricted Jones's choice, and that was in the area of medical support. The ship's surgeon, Giles Heale, was very young and inexperienced and only recently apprenticed as a London barber-surgeon. He had just gotten engaged, in May 1620, but the journey pulled him away from his fiancée for a year. Whether a bigger budget, leading to the employment of a more experienced surgeon, would have made any difference is now hard to decide, but the fact that half the crew and passengers would die that first winter may be traceable to the choice of such an inexperienced young man. In defense of his choice, Christopher Jones would, no doubt, have said that the budget only ran so far.

Other crew members included one surnamed Leaver, lost to history other than in a later record, which names him as one who rescued Pilgrims who had become lost in the woods in January 1621.

An insight into the rough and tough men Jones employed can be seen in the case of the Mayflower's boatswain, who was, in the words of William Bradford, "a proud young man [who] would often curse and scoff at the passengers. But when he grew weak, they had compassion on him and helped him."[15] So it was that Saints and Strangers were thrown together and made their unique community at sea and eventually on land.

We shall soon return, via another Mayflower Life, to the events in the Netherlands that led to the decision to sail to America, but it is frustrating to note that, in contrast to earlier records for the movement of Master Jones and his ship, there is no official English record that specifically relates to him and the *Mayflower* between 1616 and 1624. In short, the famous voyage was not even noticed by those port officials in England keeping records of the movement of ships. This absence might have been caused by the rather irregular way in which the Pilgrims were transferred from Leiden to New England, as we shall see. So much for the making of a legend! All *that* was to come later. Despite this, there is plenty of other evidence showing that it was in 1620 that a master and ship that were poorly suited to the task set off with a motley band of Saints and Strangers on a hazardous journey to the New World.

But why was North America, of all places, even considered as a viable option for the transplanting of people in order to create a new, godly society? Clearly, the Pilgrims were not the first seekers of a new life there.

When the *Mayflower* was chartered for its voyage in 1620, it became part of a transatlantic connection that was drawing Europe and North America ever closer together. Since 1492, when Christopher Columbus landed on the island later known to Europeans as Hispaniola, at the head of a Spanish expedition, the Old World and what Europeans soon described as the New World were drawn together. For Europeans it offered prospects of new land, resources, and wealth. In 1497 John Cabot sailed from Bristol, England, and became the first European since the Vikings to land on the coast of North America.[16] Soon the seas off Newfoundland and farther south were being visited by French and English fishermen and Basque whalers in pursuit of the plentiful fish and whale stocks to be found there.[17] This helps explain why the Pilgrims were later assisted by Native Americans who could speak English. It also explains how a disaster had hit these Native American tribes long before the conflicts that broke out with them in the 17th century. Alien diseases had cleared coastal communities before anyone's foot was placed on the legendary Plymouth Rock.[18] European fishermen visiting North America had inadvertently caused this.[19] As early as 1616, perhaps as many as 90 percent of the Wampanoag confederacy of Massachusetts had died in an epidemic. We will later see how the survivors decided to seek common cause with the Pilgrims against their traditional enemies, the Narragansett, who were relatively untouched by epidemic disease until 1623, when smallpox devastated them too.[20]

After the Spanish and Portuguese conquered land in the Americas, they were followed by the English, the French, and the Dutch. The *Mayflower* expedition itself was part of a wider English mix of private enterprise backed by royal power that was a feature of the English way of colonizing. In 1586, an English colony was established at Roanoke, in what is now North Carolina, but it was soon abandoned. In 1587 another attempt to kick-start this venture also met with failure and the disappearance of all the colonists. This became known as the Lost Colony and reminds us that life was difficult and dangerous in the New World for Europeans poorly prepared for its demands. This was a bitter reality which the later Pilgrims also experienced in their first winter of 1620–21. A similar failure occurred at Cuttyhunk, Massachusetts, in 1602, where the fort that was established there was swiftly abandoned. However, despite the disaster at Roanoke and the failure at Cuttyhunk, other ventures were more successful. The most famous of these was the Jamestown Colony, established in 1607 in Virginia, by the London (or Virginia) Company. It became the first permanent English settlement in North America. So it was to Virginia Colony that the *Mayflower* was headed in 1620 in the hope of a new life, driven by dissatisfaction with England and the Netherlands. It was a venture made possible through the ambitions of London middlemen, the low prices charged for the hiring of an ill-suited ship, and a master inexperienced in the Atlantic, because of a falloff in the European coastal carrying trade. Yet, to many of those on board, it was rather God's providence that had made all this possible and which would, they were assured, carry them through the tough times ahead.

In this they were not unique, but they were distinct because the simple reality was that most of those sailing to America before 1620 and afterwards were not intending to build a New Jerusalem of godliness. Most were after personal wealth or were intent on blocking the ambitions of a rival European power. This was a long way short of the Pilgrims' desire to establish a New Jerusalem. That alone makes 1620 significant. For, as the *Mayflower* strained at its anchor cable in the lee of Cape Cod in the rising winter winds of 1620, a combination of events had ensured that the new colony would not be located farther south, where most settlers were economic migrants. Instead, it would be in Massachusetts that the New Jerusalem would be built. Furthermore, when a boat set off on a mission to locate a safer anchorage—and would finally return with vital seed-corn found at a deserted Native American settlement—it would be commanded by Master Christopher Jones, a Stranger rather than a Saint. He had come a long way, by a complex route, from his original home in Harwich, Essex, to the sandy bays and dunes of Cape Cod. Behind him lay a poorly suited ship, with a far from unique name, that was full of weary, wet, and cold passengers. They were awaiting news, which they hoped the explorers would eventually bring back, of where to settle in the new land.

Master Christopher Jones after 1620

Over the five months of the winter of 1620–21, Jones and the *Mayflower*, with its ailing crew, would remain in the New World. They had originally planned to return to England as soon as the Pilgrims found a suitable settlement site, but the same illness that had begun to overcome the passengers had also affected the ship's crew. As a result, Jones and the *Mayflower* were trapped in North America until enough crew had recovered (though many died) to get the ship safely home to England. Eventually Christopher Jones returned from America in the summer of 1621, but his health had suffered due to the difficulties experienced over the previous severe winter in Massachusetts. He died in early March 1622, aged about fifty-two, having just returned from a voyage to France. He was buried in the churchyard of St. Mary the Virgin, in Rotherhithe, on March 5. The exact location of his grave is no longer known. So ended the life of one of the key figures in the story of the *Mayflower* voyage. We have described him as one of the Strangers, as there is simply no evidence that would categorically place him among the Saints. However, the rector at St. Mary's between 1611 and 1654 was the Rev. Thomas Gataker, who had Puritan leanings. So perhaps Master Christopher Jones was a closet Saint after all. We shall never know.

It is a curious irony that the lost grave of Christopher Jones at Rotherhithe and the lost grave of Pocahontas at Gravesend are a mere twenty-two miles apart. In these two graves we are reminded of the twists of history that entangled the Thames estuary with the New World of North America. And it is to more of the motives behind, and experiences on, that momentous 1620 sea journey to the New World that we now turn, as we explore it through one of its most famous Saints.

2

The Asylum Seeker's Story: William Bradford, a Saint Fleeing Babylon

Before we explore the life of William Bradford, we will take a few moments to examine the way that such a member of the *Mayflower* godly community viewed the world. For them, God was testing and refining his beloved people as they lived in the sinful "Babylon" of "the World." Like the Chosen People of the Old Testament, they had turned their back on "the slavery of Egypt" and were seeking out a Promised Land where they could establish a new community, a "New Jerusalem," of holy living.

Babylon . . . Egypt . . . these words, suggesting oppression and sin, echoed from the pages of the Old Testament and were picked up in the New Testament in the book of Revelation to inform those among the 17th-century godly who sought to understand the true nature of their contemporary society. For did not the book of Revelation, in the Geneva Bible translation that was loved by the English-speaking Saints from Switzerland to North America, warn that:

> *It is fallen, it is fallen, Babylon that great city, and is become the habitation of devils, and the hold of all foul spirits, and a cage of every unclean and hateful bird. For all nations have drunken of the wine of the wrath of her fornication, and the kings of the earth have committed fornication with her, and the merchants of the earth are waxed rich of the abundance of her pleasures.*

Faced with such a Babylon of sin, the godly should flee from the sinful communities within which they found themselves living, in order to escape the wrath of God. The command to do so was clear and unequivocal:

> *Go out of her, my people, that ye be not partakers of her sins, and that ye receive not of her plagues.* [1]

In 1620 there were many who saw sinful Babylon and Egyptian slavery firmly entrenched in contemporary lifestyles and also in the persecutions they faced. And, from their fervent belief that they lived in the End Times preceding the Second Coming of Christ and the Last Judgement, they interpreted the turmoil and uncertainties around them as clear proof that they lived in the days spoken of by Christ, when,

> *"Ye shall hear of wars, and rumours of wars"* and when *"nation shall rise against nation, and realm against realm, and there shall be famine, and pestilence, and earthquakes in divers places."* [2]

Consequently, they thought it essential to separate from such a place of imperfection and, instead, to build a new and chaste community, both to escape God's judgement that was coming on the world, and to be spared the spite of their enemies while they awaited the vindication that would come with the return of Christ.

Today we live in an age of economic migrants *and* asylum seekers and are well aware of both the push and pull factors that make people leave their homes and seek to carve out a new life for themselves and their families. This is nothing new. The Pilgrims who traveled to New England on the *Mayflower* included both sets of people. There were those among them who were seeking religious freedom to worship God as they believed correct and to form Christian communities governed in ways that they felt were more in accord with the Bible than other forms on offer at the time. Persecuted in England for these principles, they had sought freedom to practice their faith in the Netherlands and then launched out to create a new community—a New Jerusalem—in the New World of North America. They were seeking asylum, freedom from royal restraints and bishops' interventions; freedom to live unfettered. They were the Saints, the battered but unbowed asylum seekers of their day. For them, living in the world was always being in a place of exile away from heaven. But maybe, just maybe, there was somewhere out there where something of heaven might be built on earth while they awaited the final, eternal vindication of all their hopes, suffering, and beliefs.

On the other hand, there were those (and they too found a place on board the *Mayflower*) who simply hoped to carve out a better deal for themselves and a more generous slice of the pie in a new place where enterprise and hard work might reward the man and woman who possessed the raw courage needed to seize the opportunity with both hands. It would be a world away from existing landlords, restraints, and restrictions. A place where new opportunities beckoned to those prepared to take a risk and seize their chance. These were the Strangers, who were not part of the tight Puritan communities but whose monetary commitment to an enterprise and whose practical skills were necessary in order to make the venture viable and to get it off the ground—or, rather, onto the sea.

And, truth be known, the boundary between the two was sometimes hard to draw, since even among the godly there were those who were disillusioned with the economic opportunities of both England and the Netherlands and who looked to God to bless them materially as well as spiritually in the New World. There was, for such Saints, both the push of religious issues and economic stresses shoving them out from the known; and the pull of godly hope and economic opportunities calling them into the unknown.

The pilgrimage of William Bradford

One of the most dedicated of the Saints was William Bradford. We know more about him than about many of the other Pilgrim people, not only because of his prominence within his church community in the Netherlands but most importantly because in North America he rose to high prominence among the Saints.

In addition, his compilation, entitled *Of Plymouth Plantation*, is a key source of information for the years 1620–1650 in Plymouth Colony. This vital document was compiled by Bradford in two bursts of writing. The first occurred in about 1630 and retold the story as far as the Mayflower Compact in November 1620. It was a slim volume. Then, in 1645, he returned to the project and wrote about 80 percent of what now survives. This continued the story as far as 1650, plus some additional reflections that he wrote between 1648 and 1652.[3] As he wrote these final sections, Britain itself was being torn apart in civil wars, and there are echoes of this in his writings, as the ripples from that distant conflict affected the godly settlements in North America. We will later see how these ripples affected other Mayflower Lives. In Massachusetts, though, relief that Plymouth Colony had finally paid off its debts might have encouraged Bradford to once more pick up his pen and complete his account, which tells us so much about him and his community.

In exploring Bradford's life we get an intimate glimpse into why the religious Pilgrims embarked on their journey and how they organized their departure. We also see the way they established their New England community in the face of adversity. It is an epic tale of an epic life and venture. We will use this particular Mayflower Life to explore the first part of this epic story.

William Bradford was born in 1590 in Austerfield, in South Yorkshire. His farming family was relatively well off, of the social strata sometimes known as yeoman farmers. This meant that he benefitted from a fair level of basic education (he could certainly read confidently by the time he was about ten) and inherited an independent outlook consistent with the social status of an economically independent family. But by 1597 he was an orphan: his father died when William was just over one year old; he was sent to live with his grandfather when he was four (his mother had just remarried), but his grandfather died just two years later; William then returned to live with his mother and stepfather, only to have his mother die a year after that.[4]

This simple catalogue of grief and family tragedy reminds us that the England William Bradford inhabited had a death rate comparable to less economically developed countries in the 21st century. Death was no stranger, and life was fragile. We can only guess at the impact of this on a child. While he was by no means unique in his orphaned predicament, we can, perhaps, see in this sobering reminder of the passing nature of human existence the beginnings of a journey towards a personal faith in God that could carry a person through such heartaches, make sense of the fragility of human life, and offer a way through which a person might be prepared to meet God, in a world where death was an ever-present possibility.

Orphaned at seven years old, he moved home yet again. This time he went to live with his two uncles, Robert and Thomas Bradford. From his later literacy and reading, it is almost certain that he must have attended a local grammar school. But his uncles clearly also intended he should work beside them on the farm. That plan was not to work out as anyone had intended.

If his misfortunes did not already seem too much to bear, he had not been with his uncles long before he was struck down by a debilitating illness that rendered him unable to work in the fields of the farm. What was that illness? We would really like to know, but Bradford's later recollections of it were strangely vague. When the New England Puritan churchman Cotton Mather wrote his *Life of William Bradford* in 1702, he drew on Bradford's later recollections but could not get beyond a general sense of crippling ill health that struck down the boy:

> *Soon a long sickness kept him, as he would afterwards thankfully say, from the vanities of youth, and made him the fitter for what he was afterwards to undergo.*[5]

Over five hundred years later it is rather difficult diagnosing an illness that struck down a child sometime around the year 1600. But one wonders if Bradford's mysterious illness that kept him isolated in his room for months was, in fact, a personal breakdown of some kind. The boy had reasons enough for a mental crisis and a meltdown. However, whether it was caused by a psychological crisis or a physical illness, the end product was much the same. A child who had become cast adrift from some of his closest relatives due to sudden and repeated mortalities was now locked in on himself to reflect on his life . . . and perhaps on death . . .

What is absolutely certain is that, closeted indoors with little to do, the boy took to reading. And he read voraciously, because he was intelligent and because there was nothing else to do. The books he read would change him. Firstly, he read what we now call the Geneva Bible.[6] For a member of a God-fearing yeoman farming family in the twilight of the reign of Queen Elizabeth I (she died in 1603, to be succeed by King James VI and I),[7] the Bible in English had been available since the middle of the 16th century. Here the Word of God could be explored, pondered, and reflected on. Although the Authorized King James Version of the Bible, of 1611, would eventually take the English-speaking world by storm, among many God-fearing families it was the version known as the Geneva Bible that was their spiritual staple for much of the 17th century.[8] Produced without official sanction in Switzerland (hence its name) by English Protestant exiles escaping the persecutions of "Bloody" Queen Mary in the 1550s, it was famous for being the first English Bible with its chapters divided into verses. But, in addition, it was a study Bible because it also contained marginal notes to assist with reading it. And these marginal notes were explosive!

They revealed the reforming and Calvinist outlook of its Protestant authors. These marginal notes were written by men (and it was always men) whose faith was inspired by the belief that since eternity God had decreed some to salvation and others to damnation; that those saved were a minority in a world of lost sinners; that all practices of the Church that were not explicitly found in the Bible should be stripped away; that the Church should be purified (hence "Puritan"); and that England was like a new Israel, a Chosen People of God, called to do His will on earth. For those whose prayers and personal study of the Bible had convinced them that *they* were members of the godly saved minority (God's elect "Saints"), this was dynamic and life changing. Those marginal notes inspired the godly in England and irritated royal authorities, most notably King James after 1603 (who hated its anti-monarchy comments) and English Church authorities (who objected to its calls for stripping ritual and Church hierarchies out of the Church of England).

It was this material that William Bradford was reading in his room. The young boy was becoming radicalized! It seems that he also read a book known as the *Book of Martyrs* by John Fox. Full of tales of Protestants who had died for their faith under both Henry VIII and Mary Tudor ("Bloody Mary"), its subtext was that Protestant England was a Chosen People and that in a world of conflict and the persecution of the godly, the Saints of God must be willing to sacrifice themselves in order to achieve personal salvation and for the transformation of their communities. It was heady stuff, massively popular among Protestant English men and women, and it only added to the cocktail of powerful words and images forming in the head of a child not yet twelve, closeted inside after a set of personal crises.

The end product of all this was that William Bradford began to question the validity of the way God was worshipped in the Church of England. By the time he was twelve years old he was becoming one of a vociferous and controversial minority within that Church who felt that its break from the Roman Catholic Church in the 16th century had not been radical enough and left too much ritual, too much formality, too much hierarchy (for which read *bishops*) in the English

Church. Looking to more fully "reformed" churches for inspiration, such as that in Geneva, Switzerland, these Puritans called for sweeping changes that would create a simpler, "purer," and (in their view) more godly Church, stripped of what they considered its surviving Catholic residues. They themselves strove to live in such a way in their personal lives: with a distrust of the overly ornate and fancy, and a love of the stripped down, the more simplified and unadorned. However, this should not be overstressed, since they actually dressed rather more fashionably and less uniformly than they appear in modern images of them. Without any sense of hyperbole they described themselves as "the godly" and "the Saints." Others used the term *Puritan*, and so do we as a useful label, but they did not use it of themselves. But the term was a reasonable one, for they were dedicated to purity. And it was purity that came at a price, because personal self-discipline, Bible study, and prayer, were set in conflict with the drinking, gambling, gaming, and whoring of the world. Well, that was their perspective on things. Others disagreed. And these others included King James, after 1603, most of his bishops, and the two uncles of William Bradford. The evidence of access to the Geneva Bible and the *Book of Martyrs* in their home suggests they were solid Protestants, but they were certainly not going to push the matter as far as their young nephew was intending to. If they and he were on a related religious journey, they had gotten off several stops earlier. But William was intent on taking the ride to its terminus. They had gotten off. He was still journeying.

When he was just twelve years old, a friend told him about a group that was meeting in the nearby village of Scrooby, Nottinghamshire, in an area that was so notable for its independence of religious thought that it has been dubbed "The Pilgrim Quadrilateral."[9] It was just three miles from Austerfield to Scrooby. It could be walked in under one hour. It was just next door; but it was a world away from the mainline prayer book Anglicanism of the Church of England services in Austerfield. In Scrooby a group of the godly was meeting for extempore prayer, Bible study, and discussion. They met at the home of William Brewster (another of our Mayflower Lives), and their spiritual leader was the Rev. Richard Clyfton. That William Bradford was advised to try them suggests that he had already made himself known as one precociously in pursuit of holiness. That he had a friend of similar temperament suggests that he was not the only one who had, in his own later words, turned his back on the "vanities of youth." He himself gives us only a little insight into his own thoughts about his neighbors at Austerfield, in his *Of Plymouth Plantation*, just remarking that godly people were "both scoffed and scorned by the profane multitude."[10] However, later writers were pretty clear about what Bradford thought about those he was leaving behind in Austerfield. As Cotton Mather reminds us,

> *. . . the people* [of Austerfield] *were as unacquainted with the bible, as the Jews do seem to have been with part of it in the days of Josiah a most ignorant and licentious people, and like unto their priest.*[11]

No ambiguity there! It was such strength of feeling that caused him to throw in his lot with the community at Scrooby. And that community itself was lurching even further to what we might now call the Protestant left. For, in 1606, the Rev. Clyfton formed this little fellowship into a separate church *outside* the control of the bishops, Church courts, doctrines, and practices of the Church of England. This was a revolutionary step, since it was illegal to do this and brought down on their heads the weight of the law. Bradford had thrown in his lot with a radicalized group that was at odds with the prevailing norms of their society. No wonder, as Cotton Mather later recorded it, Bradford faced "the wrath of his uncles." But the die was cast.

In the 17th century there were, to put it simply, two types of Puritans. Those who wanted changes to the Church of England but who still intended to stay *within it* as an umbrella organization we now remember as non-separating Puritans. Those who considered it beyond repair and *wanted out* we now call separating Puritans or Congregationalists. At the time, these latter groups were also known as Brownists. We will generally call them Separatists. Technically, only those who stayed within the established Church were Puritans, but the term is often used for both groups, as they shared much in common (despite their differences), and so we too will use it as a term for both related groups.

Even further to the left were yet more radical groups who rejected infant baptism and would one day become independent Baptist churches. At the time their enemies called them Anabaptists, which was like calling someone a Red in the 1950s. Later there would be Quakers and others even further to the left, but that is getting ahead of the story, for we will meet these—and see some of them hanged in New England—later.

It would eventually be non-separating Puritans who would play key roles in establishing the Massachusetts Bay Colony in 1629–1630, then Connecticut Colony in 1636, and finally the New Haven Colony in 1638.

William Bradford, however, had joined a group of separating Puritans, and he was now on a collision course with the royal and the Church authorities in England as a result of this decision. The leader of this Scrooby group of separating Puritans would eventually be the Rev. John Robinson. Bradford later remembered him as "that famous and worthy man." Together with William Brewster he organized and ran the now independent group. Both men were to have a major influence on Bradford. When later, in 1643, Brewster finally died in the New World, William Bradford would amend his earlier record of his decision to join the Scrooby congregation with the fond memory that Brewster was "a reverend man." Even today the change in ink can still be made out on that vellum page in the original document *Of Plymouth Plantation*,[12] and it bears witness to the fondness he felt for the older man. Regarding the Rev. Robinson, he later led the group in the Netherlands and played a major role in the emigration of large numbers of them to North America in 1620. But that is getting ahead of the story.

Things heated up after 1607 when the archbishop of York was made aware of the illegal gathering in Scrooby. Some members ended up in prison. Others had their houses watched. As persecution increased, they began to put together plans to emigrate to the Netherlands. In the more tolerant Protestant society of Amsterdam they would be free to meet unmolested, and there was already a tradition of welcoming émigrés from England. It seemed like a good plan, but things did not go well.

Their first attempt to leave England saw them double-crossed by the sea captain they had hired, and in the Lincolnshire port of Boston, they found themselves denounced and their leaders thrown into prison for illegally attempting to leave the country. The next attempt was only partially successful. Meeting a Dutch ship on the southern shore of the Humber estuary, near Grimsby, they had only partly loaded the ship when the local militia turned up intent on disrupting the illegal exit. The ship escaped but left behind all the women and children, along with some of the men. It was months before all were finally reunited in Amsterdam, in 1608. William Bradford was now eighteen years old. He had come a long way since the days of interrogating the Bible in his room back in Austerfield, but he still had much further to go.

Sadly, Amsterdam was not the New Jerusalem. The Scrooby community had little money and had to live in poor-quality housing and settle for poorly paid work. William Bradford, without family, moved in with the family of William Brewster. They might have been religiously free, but they were still aliens in a strange land. However, this was not the only problem they faced. Free from the control of English bishops, in a context of relative spiritual freedom to worship and organize their communities as they wished, some of the English groups descended into bitter internal strife. One community from Gainsborough, Lincolnshire, who had been friends and allies of Bradford's Scrooby fellowship back in England, rejected infant baptism and became Baptists. William Bradford was later to recall that they fell "into some errours" and "buried themselves and their names."[13] Clearly, he regarded them as lost from fellowship as from memory. Other groups broke up in personal scandals.

It was a shrewd Rev. Robinson who decided to shift their base to nearby Leiden, in 1609, in an attempt to escape the Amsterdam hothouse of friction and fraction. Here they created a little community in the area known as De Groene Poort (the Green Alley) near the main church of the town, the Pieterskerk (Peter's Church). William

Bradford, still living with the Brewster family, resided in a poor neighborhood known as Stink Alley! It was a rather down-at-the-heels area, of smelly workshops and canals polluted with sewage and industrial waste.[14]Nevertheless, skills in textile manufacturing helped the newcomers make a living and settle into the life of the town. Here, perhaps, they could build their own little version of the New Jerusalem, within which Bradford was becoming a leading member.

In 1611 Bradford turned twenty-one and came into an inheritance from home, which improved his financial position. He bought a small house and became a citizen of Leiden in 1612. He was, by that time, the owner of his own workshop as a corduroy or fustian worker within the cloth trade. Things were looking up. In 1613 he married Dorothy May, the daughter of a fairly prosperous English family that was also living in Leiden. William was twenty-three years old; Dorothy was just sixteen. The Leiden records (which surname him as "Braetfort" and her as "Mayer") state that she had been living in the town for five years, in the area known as Nieuwendijk. William was alone when the banns were read (for he was over twenty-one and had no parents), whereas Dorothy heard them in the company of her father.[15]She and her family were originally, so the records state, from Wisbech, Cambridgeshire, in England.

In 1617 their son was born, and they named him John. Looking back from New England, William Bradford remembered this time as "a comfortable condition, enjoying much sweet and delightful society and spiritual comfort."[16] Perhaps this was, indeed, the New Jerusalem. William was clearly happy. But trouble was brewing. The New Jerusalem would soon show itself to lack the happiness and tranquility of its first appearance.

The problems began stacking up. The economic rewards for English immigrant cloth workers were low. They saw their children working long hours for little remuneration. Their children were at risk of losing their English identity as they morphed into Netherlanders. Their sons might be forced to serve in the army of the Netherlands at a time when Europe was spiraling down into a new cycle of religious wars. The Dutch, though Protestants, did not keep the Sabbath strictly, as the

English godly wished to keep it. Instead, there were games and feasting on a Sunday and children were expected to join in, even to enjoy these events. This was as worrying in its attraction to young minds as it was offensive to the older generation. The godly from Scrooby began to wonder if a better, holier life could be built somewhere else. Then there was the nagging feeling that to build a New Jerusalem one really needed a place that was not already fully established; a place where a new world might be carved out of the wilderness. As students of the Old Testament, they felt the draw of the idea of crossing "a river Jordan" and establishing a Promised Land in a wild Canaan. They began to fall in love with a dream of America. The Netherlands was a center of publishing, and some of the earliest accounts of the New World, along with early maps of its eastern shores and islands, were coming off the printing presses there. America was becoming known even as its mysteries were being extolled. It was a 17th-century "known unknown." Its appeal was magnetic. Bradford felt it, even though he *seemed* settled in Leiden. For, he pondered, beyond the sea (a rather wide version of the river Jordan, it must be admitted) lay "those vast and unpeopled countries of America, which are fruitful and fit for habitation" where "only savage and brutish men" live (so, not quite so "unpeopled"), who are little different, he opined, to wild animals![17] It was both exciting and frightening. It quickened the imagination. It was America. The Scrooby community—now settled, or perhaps unsettled—in Leiden began to consider and discuss the practicalities of moving there.

To add to these unsettling thoughts, the Scrooby godly had also brought trouble on themselves. They just could not stop meddling in English affairs. In 1618, William Brewster embarked on some godly printing. He was assisted in this venture by a 23-year-old named Edward Winslow (another Mayflower Life with whom we shall soon become better acquainted). Together they produced a pamphlet criticizing King James and the bishops. This was an age of pamphlets, with tracts demanding this, extolling that, proclaiming liberties and denouncing abuses. This was just one pamphlet among many. But it came back to bite them. Royal agents began the hunt for those responsible for printing the leaflet. It did not take long to trace the bread crumbs, as it were, back to Leiden. Trouble had come looking for William Brewster. As a result he had to go into hiding. It was not a good moment to lose him, as the community had begun planning their emigration to America and could not afford to lose his wisdom and experience at this vital time. In his youth he had acted as a trainee diplomat in the service of one of Elizabeth I's secretaries of state. Consequently, Brewster had knowledge and skills necessary to negotiating the right to settle in the North American coastal areas that were claimed by the British crown. This experience and networking were now lost to his community as he made himself scarce. It was a pity that the trainee diplomat had not been a little more diplomatic at such a sensitive time. But he was also of the self-proclaimed godly, and the two could sometimes cancel each other out, even in one as wise and reflective as William Brewster.

By 1619, the Leiden Pilgrims were well advanced in negotiations with a group called the Virginia Company regarding the possibility of emigrating to America. This company—formed in 1606—had originally involved the combined efforts of noblemen based in London and also in Plymouth (the Devon sea port, not the Massachusetts one) and Bristol to underwrite colonization in America in the hope of making a substantial profit from the venture. After all, the Spanish had profited handsomely from their adventurers in Central and South America and their ruthless exploitation of native communities and natural resources. Convoys of treasure ships laden with gold had long been the envy of the English crown (which was now the British crown, after the accession of the Scottish King James) and its dubious coterie of shady privateers and well-connected adventurers looking for rich pickings to rival the success of Spain. Things, though, had been a bit disappointing and had not quite lived up to the dream. A failed colonization in Maine and the less than thrilling profits from Jamestown, following its settlement in 1607, had persuaded the Virginia Company to do some subcontracting.[18] This lessened the risk (to the Virginia Company, that is) while opening up the possibility of new ventures in new areas of the North American eastern coastline. Known as particular-plantations, these temporary patents or charters empowered settlers to found colonies in agreed areas, with the stipulation that for a specified time period (such as five or seven years) profits would be shared with the Virginia Company. After this time period, the colony (if it survived) could apply for a fresh charter, which gave the settlers permanent title to the land being colonized. This was a neat arrangement, which reduced the risk to the Virginia Company, while at the same time offering the company the possibility of reaping the profitable benefits that accrued from the exploitation of the furs, codfish, timber, and other natural resources of America. The Virginia Company saw it as a win-win option. Time might cause them to question this positive assessment. It certainly caused the Pilgrims to do so, but that was only with the benefit of hindsight.

In the springtime of 1619, William Bradford sold his house, a clear indication of how far the negotiations had progressed. He and Dorothy were freeing up the liquidity of their assets in order to sink them into the American adventure. In June 1619 the Leiden Pilgrims' representatives—John Carver and Robert Cushman—signed the deal for a patent with the Virginia Company representatives in London. William Brewster, we will remember, was in hiding. Money, though, was still an issue. It was one thing getting the legal right to found a colony. It was quite another paying for it. Enter Thomas Weston. He represented a group of businessmen known as the Adventurers. Though not quite as enthusiastic in their religious inclinations as the Leiden Saints, they were still sympathetic to their Puritan character and the idea of establishing godly settlements in America. In early 1620 they offered the deal that promised to turn godly hopes into realities. Having secured yet another patent for a particular-plantation (this time specifying the location of a colony at the mouth of the Hudson River), the Adventurers proposed the formation of a joint-stock company. The Adventurers would provide most of the up-front cash to finance the venture; the enterprising colonists would, over seven years, work four days a week for the company, two for themselves, and keep Sabbath on the seventh day. After seven years the settlers would gain free tenure of their houses and land plots in the New World; in short, legal title to the land. Of the total population of Rev. Robinson's congregation of over

300, somewhere in the region of 125 were planning to join the adventure of sailing to America, including William and Dorothy Bradford. The spiritual needs of the emigrants would be overseen by William Brewster, while Rev. Robinson would stay with those remaining in Leiden, for the time being at least.

Then things started to go badly wrong. First, Thomas Weston demanded that the colonists would have to work six days a week, since a failure to secure a fishing monopoly meant that the financial benefits that could have accrued from a fishing deal were now out of the equation. Rev. Robinson and the rest of the congregation were horrified, but the inexperienced Robert Cushman had already agreed to the demand. The Leiden congregation members were losing room to maneuver. In fact, they were being taken by sharp operators in London.

Second, Weston had not secured any transport! This came out in June 1620. It was an eleventh-hour crisis; they had no ship. Weston began a hunt for a vessel that would eventually lead him to Master Christopher Jones and the *Mayflower*. Those in Leiden decided to purchase a second ship, the *Speedwell*, which would mean they had a vessel of their own when the ship chartered by Weston returned to England. The *Speedwell* was a third the size of the *Mayflower*.[19] The master and crew hired to sail the *Speedwell* agreed to stay for at least one year in America. The settlers would, therefore, not be stranded in their new home.

Then, there was a third problem. The Adventurers insisted on adding non-separating emigrants from London to the mix. These Strangers were something of an unknown quantity. A few were linked to the Leiden congregation, but the rest were truly strangers in every sense of the word. For people such as William Bradford, who had become part of a tightly knit community united by common ideology and experiences, this was an alarming dilution of the godly enterprise. The matter was made worse by the Adventurers' further insistence that a man named Christopher Martin would be the purchasing agent, alongside Carver and Cushman, tasked with equipping the ship. Irascible and willful, he refused to coordinate his purchasing in Southampton with the purchasing being overseen by Carver and Cushman in

London and Canterbury. It was clear that the imposition of Strangers threatened to undermine the whole enterprise. Would Babylon never cease from worming its way into the New Jerusalem?

It was thus, with rather mixed feelings, that the Leiden emigrants gathered at Delfshaven late in July 1620 to take ship for England on the *Speedwell*. William Bradford later recorded how, before they departed, they spent a day in prayer and fasting as Rev. Robinson preached from the Old Testament book of Ezra on the need to be humble before God in order to gain his guidance.[20] Then they set out. Turning their backs on what was familiar and secure, they headed into the unknown, for, in Bradford's words,

> *. . . they knew they were pilgrims, and looked not much on those things, but lift up their eyes to the heavens, their dearest country, and quieted their spirits.*[21]

And so they left, on about July 22, and turned their backs on the Netherlands, which had been their home for twelve years. There were tears on "watery cheeks" and many prayers. For William and Dorothy there was an added dimension to the emotions of the departure. They had decided to leave their three-year-old son, John Bradford, behind in the Netherlands. Their intention was that he would rejoin them when others of the Leiden congregation joined them after the initial colony was established. The parting must have been very hard. We shall see how it might have been an ingredient in the later fate of Dorothy Bradford in the New World. According to Bradford, even the curious watching Dutch "strangers" cried to witness such a moving leave-taking. For better or for worse, the Pilgrims were started on their momentous journey.

From Delfshaven the *Speedwell* sailed to Southampton, where it made its rendezvous with the *Mayflower*. The Leiden contingent was reunited with William Brewster, who had been in hiding, and with their agents, Carver and Cushman, who had been negotiating with the Adventurers and provisioning the ship. A couple, William and Susanna White (whose lives we will next explore), might have departed from

Leiden or joined the Leideners at Southampton; the matter is not entirely clear. They met up with other Puritans (sort-of Strangers, at least to the Leideners) who had bought into the venture, and they also reluctantly met what we might now call the full-blooded Strangers (those who had no connections with them and whose religious affiliations were uncertain). These included the Mullins family, the Billington family, and the unaccompanied More children (all of whom we will meet again in due course). Some of these would bring peculiar challenges; the Billingtons were, in Bradford's opinion, shockingly profane in their speech and behavior. They also met Christopher Martin, who seemed to have nothing but contempt for the Pilgrims traveling with him. This was particularly distressing, since the Adventurers had demanded he be in charge of the passengers consigned to the *Mayflower*. Clearly, the New Jerusalem was going to be a rather mixed community, to put it mildly. At Southampton they also met Captain Myles Standish, who was to oversee military matters, and Rose, his wife.

We will soon experience more of the fateful journey across the Atlantic through the lives of others of the passengers, but suffice it to say at this point that a delayed start and the leaking that had dogged the *Speedwell* meant that it was not until Wednesday, September 6, 1620 that they eventually left England after being forced to put into Dartmouth and Plymouth, both in Devon. And then it was on board *one ship* (the *Mayflower*), since the *Speedwell* had to be abandoned, along with a number of erstwhile Pilgrims who had decided that enough was enough. Among those who bailed out at the last moment, before they finally left Plymouth, was Robert Cushman, who had been crushed by the preparations for the venture and the stress of working with the bullying and aggressive Christopher Martin. How many Leideners were there among the 102 passengers who eventually sailed? Research has suggested that about 40 percent of those on board the *Mayflower* were from Bradford's congregation, with twenty-eight out of the sixty-nine adults on the *Mayflower* being congregational members from Leiden.[22] Other research has put the percentage slightly higher, at about 50 percent, with about fifty (adults, young adults, children) of the total passenger number of 102 being Leideners.[23]

We will soon take our leave of William Bradford for a while, before meeting him again in the accounts of the lives of other Pilgrims. And, consequently, we will pick up the story of the voyage and the exploration of Cape Cod through the experiences of others. But, before we leave William Bradford, we can signpost some of the places where we will, as it were, run into him again. He was one of the signers of the famous Mayflower Compact, which created a formal community from the disparate Saints and Strangers. He would go on to see the new community established in New England and, after surviving that first terrible winter of 1620–21, develop into the plantation of New Plymouth. Bradford was a part of each of the formative moments in its early life, and we will meet him again as we see the lives of other Mayflower Lives mixed and entangled with his own. And we will hear his voice again as his record, *Of Plymouth Plantation*, bears witness to so many of these key formative events in the lives of others. Bradford was a member of the party that eventually began the exploration of Cape Cod and its environs, in order to find a place for permanent settlement; we will meet him up in the air (quite literally!) when he was caught in a deer trap left by Native Americans during early explorations; he was there at the First Encounter, when the first sighting of Native Americans was followed by a short, sharp battle; he survived a strange illness that struck him unexpectedly in January 1621 and a house fire three days later that almost cost the ailing Bradford his life; he survived that first terrible winter of 1620–21 when half those who had traveled on the *Mayflower* died; he was present at the key meetings with local Native Americans that led to a treaty of friendship with Massasoit of the Pokanokets (one of the tribal groups that make up the modern-day Wampanoag Nation).

William Bradford was already a leading member of the godly community before the Pilgrims ever left Leiden, but his role and stature grew in New England to a remarkable degree. In April 1621 he was chosen as the second governor of the colony following the sudden death of John Carver, the first governor. He held this position off and on until just before his death in 1657. It was under Bradford that land was eventually apportioned out in 1623, after a period of working it in common. In the same way as he oversaw the Division of Land, he also oversaw the Division of Cattle in 1627, when the colony was finally able to restructure its debt to the Adventurers. In that year, fifty-three of the so-called Plymouth freemen, who became known as The Purchasers, agreed to buy out their Adventurer creditors over a period of several years. Ever since the *Mayflower* had returned to England empty in 1621, those financing the venture had been losing money; even when goods started to be shipped back it was clear that the colony was not going to be the lucrative project they had hoped it would be.[24] At about the same time The Purchasers made their agreement, twelve so-called Undertakers agreed to pay off all of the Plymouth Colony's debts in return for trade benefits in fish and fur trading. Bradford was among them. In 1630 a change in the legal status of the colony meant that the patent for the whole colony (the Warwick Charter or Patent) was made out in Bradford's name. This replaced the second Peirce Patent, of 1621, which had authorized their settlement, in the (revised location) of Plymouth, for seven years. By the Warwick document they finally became the legal owners of Plymouth Colony. It could have been an opportunity for personal power and wealth for Bradford, but he was just not that kind of man. Instead, he shared his rights with all those surviving from the original *Mayflower* voyage (the "First Comers"), and then, in 1641, he persuaded them to share this right with all the freemen of the colony. When, in 1648, the last of the debts to the Adventurers was finally paid off, it was because Bradford and four others[25] had sold houses and much land in order to finally free the colony. It was an act of one who took his godly responsibilities seriously. It was Bradford who presided over the first capital punishment in 1630, following a murder in the colony. By this time others of the Leiden community had come over. His son, John, whom he had left in the Netherlands, eventually joined his father and the New England settlers. John died in Norwich, Connecticut, some time before 1676.

However, one person who did not see or share in any of William's achievements was Dorothy Bradford. When William Bradford returned from an expedition exploring the bay behind Cape Cod, in December 1620, he found that she had fallen from the deck of the

Mayflower and drowned in the freezing cold waters of the sheltered anchorage. Her burial place, as with so many who died early in the history of the colony, is unknown. It might not even have been marked when it was dug in the sandy soil of the western shore of the cape. All William wrote of this in his record of the colony was a later note that she died soon after arrival. It was left to a later historian, the New England Puritan Cotton Mather, in 1702, to add the detail that she had fallen overboard and drowned. Does Bradford's sparse record of his wife's tragic death simply reveal the tough attitude of a man who had disciplined his feelings in order to survive in the American wilderness? Or was there something more? Was there a hint that Dorothy had succumbed to despair in that dark, cold winter as she'd gazed at the bleakness of the shoreline beyond the *Mayflower*, deeply depressed due to separation from her little child? Did Dorothy Bradford step over the side and plunge into the cold, dark water? We shall never know, and there is no hint of suicide in the meager surviving records, but this has not stopped speculation.[26] However, it must remain a mystery.

What is indisputable is that, in 1623, William Bradford—now governor of New Plymouth—married a second time. This time his spouse was a widow named Alice Carpenter Southworth, who had been a member of the original Leiden congregation and who had arrived in New England on a ship called the *Anne* just a few weeks earlier. Their wedding, when it occurred, was even attended by the Native American chief, the *sachem* (leader) Massasoit of the Pokanokets. It was a far cry from that first wedding in Leiden, between William and Dorothy. Alice and William eventually had three children, and the woman, who through that wedding became Alice Bradford, finally died in Plymouth in 1670. William himself had died earlier, in 1657, at Plymouth, aged sixty-seven.

The literary afterlife of William Bradford

We have heard something already about Bradford's compilation, *Of Plymouth Plantation*. It was handwritten on vellum (calf skin), with poorly numbered pages (Bradford never quite got the hang of consistent numbering), variable and inconsistent spelling, abbreviated or contracted words. It was not the easiest read in the state in which it was left at his death.[27] Yet its words form the raw first draft of what was to become almost mythical in the formation of the United States of America. And raw they are, both in the immediacy of the experiences so memorably phrased, and in his endearing desire to include everything that might be historically useful: from copies of letters and lengthy official documents, to the exercises that record his own later attempts to learn Hebrew in the last seven years of his life (the better to explore the Old Testament). In its original state it is something of a yard sale of antique stuff, poorly numbered, mixed together and challenging to penetrate at times. But what a yard: the beginnings of New England! And what a sale: for what is on offer (when the extraneous bits and occasional lengthy digressions are set to one side) is an insight into an heroic age, a time of almost mythical struggle. When read in an edited modern edition, the engaging story leaps out from the page.[28]

The manuscript itself had an afterlife almost as dramatic as that of its author. Lovingly kept within Bradford's family in New England, it was borrowed and copied by later 17th-century Puritan historians such as Increase Mather and Cotton Mather. Then it was borrowed and kept by Thomas Prince as he collected early Americana to form the New England Library, after 1718, in the Old South Church, Boston. It was stolen by the British, following the Siege of Boston during the Revolutionary War, only to be rediscovered by American historians in 1855, squirreled away in the library of the bishop of London at Fulham Palace. It was then transcribed and finally published in 1856, before being returned to the United States, in 1897, to thereafter reside in the state library in the State House in Boston. Quite a journey, and one that involved twice crossing the Atlantic Ocean, a journey that William Bradford experienced only once.

William Bradford's words will paint verbal pictures of life in the colony as we trace its later history through other lives. In the 1690s the New England Puritan Cotton Mather used Bradford's record of the founding of Plymouth as he wrote his own account of the origins of New England, entitled *Magnalia Christi Americana* (*Glorious Works of Christ in America*), in which he praised William Bradford as "our Moses." The Geneva Bible, from which this New England Moses drew inspiration, can still be seen at Pilgrim Hall Museum, Plymouth, as can the "great chair" he would have sat in as he pondered the colony he had come to lead. The troubled boy from Austerfield had come a very long way. It was a journey to great achievement and fame. But it had not been an easy journey, as befitting one who described himself as a Pilgrim. As Emmanuel Altham, a visitor to Plymouth, expressed it in 1624,

> *They are honest and careful men. However, they have had many crosses; yet now they will flourish, God blessing them, which God grant.* [29]

William Bradford would have said "Amen" to that.

3

The Mother's Story:
Susanna White, Mother of the
First Baby Born in New England

Pregnancy and childbirth in the 17th century were no easy matter. They never are. But the hygiene and medical knowledge of the 1620s did little to enhance the chances of survival for mothers and babies. Complications often meant death. And that was before one factors in the experiences of a two-month Atlantic sea crossing. While Master Christopher Jones was away, he sent his heavily pregnant wife (carrying their sixth child) back to her family in Harwich for care during her confinement. But there was no such escape to a more caring environment for any passenger whose pregnancy had started before embarking on the journey itself. Susanna White had picked a particularly tough moment to be pregnant. But of course, in the sexual politics of even the most relaxed Puritan household, the choice was not hers in the first place. And we will look at that too, for in this *Mayflower Life* we will begin to explore something of what it was like to be a woman and a mother on the *Mayflower* and in the new community being forged in New England. This is therefore the mother's story and also something of the woman's story. . . .

The backstory of Susanna White before she boarded the *Mayflower* is not exactly clear. This is hardly surprising. For one thing, she was a woman, and in the society of early 17th-century England, the Netherlands, and New England, women tended to leave less of a trail of evidence behind them than did men. And the bread crumbs of evidence they left on their journey through life were, therefore, all the more likely to be picked up and consumed by the passing "birds" of time—chance and the vagaries of survival. There was less evidence to start with, so it is not surprising that less has survived over five centuries. She is usually identified as being from the Leiden congregation of the godly.[1] There have been some suggestions, though, that she and her husband boarded at London as part of the group of merchants who joined the venture there. In William Bradford's *Of Plymouth Plantation*, the name Mr. William White appears among those listed as joining at London. There definitely were two William Whites living in Leiden, but they appear to have remained there. The matter is made more difficult by the fact that the combination of names was a fairly common one at the time.[2] However, the speed with which Susanna remarried the leading Leidener, Edward Winslow, in May 1621 following the death of her first husband seems to indicate not only that she was one of the Saints but also points to her being someone known to Winslow from the Leiden days. The matter must remain open to question, but even if she originated in London, she could still have been numbered among those members of the Separatist godly known to the Leiden congregation, even though not actually residing in Leiden in 1620. There is certainly no need to class her as one of the non-separating Strangers. Recent research seemingly corroborates this identification of her as one of the Separatist Saints, suggesting that she was probably born in Scrooby (the English home base of the Leiden congregation) in about 1592, as Susanna Jackson. If so, her father was the Richard Jackson whose name appeared, alongside that of William Brewster, on an arrest warrant in 1607 for the offense of Brownism, being what we would now call Separatists.[3] Joining a Separatist congregation in Amsterdam, they would have been one of the small number of non-Leiden Separatists who elected to join the expedition to North America. This might have been because they were related to William Bradford's wife, Dorothy.

What is beyond dispute is that Susanna boarded the ship in the company of her husband, William, their son, named Resolved, and two servants. This unusual name is another clue that she came from within the ranks of the Saints. Names such as Resolved, Remember, Wrestling, Love, Humility, are all found within the families of the godly community of the Mayflower settlement. While these earnest names are not a sure proof of godly origins, they point very much in that direction and are certainly found among leading families involved in the New World adventure. Resolved was born in about 1615 and went on to marry twice in the New World (in 1640 and again in 1674). He would have been about five years old when Susanna and her husband took him there. That she was pregnant with her second child, five years after the birth of her first child, is in keeping with the average gap between births that we can see among a number of early New England families; as we shall see, it suggests some measure of abstinence as a form of birth control, since regular marital sex was promoted among a community that was far from the later prudish image of Puritans.

We would love to know what Susanna was thinking when she left Delfthaven on Saturday, July 22, 1620, on the *Speedwell*. She was already some five months pregnant. Even given her faith in God and the certainty that providence had guided the group so far in the difficult route to leaving the Netherlands, she must have felt some apprehension. But at least there was the consolation that, God willing, they would be in the New World by early in September. For, after meeting with their second ship, the *Mayflower*, which had been chartered in England, the plan was to be on their way by early in August at the latest. Then a month's sea journey would see them in their new home along the Hudson River, in what is today New York but was then on the northernmost edges of the colony of Virginia. But the best-laid plans of mice and men, and of emigrant Pilgrims, go awry. . . .

As we have already seen, things had gone wrong from the start for the *Speedwell* and the Leiden community (including Susanna White) traveling on it. Leaking from the word go, the ship was clearly unprepared for the Atlantic Ocean. Later some among the Leiden Saints would accuse the *Speedwell*'s master of deliberately badly rigging the ship so as to open its seams and let in water, in order to cheat the passengers by avoiding the ocean crossing and the crew's commitment to spend a year in North America with the colonists. After the despairing passengers abandoned it, the ship was later sold and then, when rigged correctly, it was fit for what then turned out to be successful further use.[4] However, none of them had evidence of this at the time, and, whatever insights hindsight might provide, women such as Susanna White were in no position to doubt the proficiency of the sailors, even if later some of their menfolk were to do so.

All they knew at the time was that for a week they were forced to kick their heels in Southampton as repairs were carried out on the leaking *Speedwell*. But there was no need to panic, and we can imagine Susanna and her Christian sisters in silent prayer alongside their praying husbands, listening to the expounding of the scriptures by the male members of the group, in which their journey was compared with God's Chosen People, the Israelites, as they left Egypt and journeyed to their eventual home in the Promised Land beyond the river Jordan. Like that journey—which the sins of God's original people had caused to be prolonged for forty years in the wilderness—the journey from Delfthaven had not gone smoothly. Now in Southampton there was time for personal reflection and seeking out and repenting of any personal sins that had caused this delay on a journey to a new Promised Land in the New World.

However, the trials and testings of this new Chosen People were only just starting. Soon after leaving Southampton, on Saturday, August 5, poor *Speedwell* began leaking once again, and it was necessary to put into another port to try to remedy the problem. So it was that they arrived in Dartmouth, Devon, on Saturday, August 12, for another week of prayers and, we may be sure, seeking God, while the ship's leaking seams were examined and worked on. Sometime about the date of Monday, August 21 the two ships finally set off again. But, to the frustration of the voyagers, the *Speedwell* again began to leak. After sailing some three hundred miles into the Atlantic, they were forced back to yet another Devon port. This time it was to Plymouth, which by happenstance shared a name with the New World area in which the travelers would eventually settle.[5] By a strange coincidence, that North American location was known by the name even before the *Mayflower* Pilgrims landed there. Captain John Smith, the famous member of the colony at Jamestown, Virginia, had previously explored parts of Cape Cod Bay and is usually credited with naming the region New Plimoth or New Plimouth.[6] Today, though, it is often assumed that Plymouth, Massachusetts, was so named because Plymouth, England, was the last port used by the *Mayflower* in 1620. Truth is odder and more coincidental than this apparently intuitive fiction. The truth was more providential.

The ways of God must have seemed strange but very real to the Puritan emigrants in that unexpected sharing of place names separated by the great gray ocean. But, of course, in the early autumn of 1620 they did not know they would eventually settle across the bay from Cape Cod. They were headed to the Hudson and the northern parts of what was then the colony of Virginia. Only time—by way of a long, tough crossing—and later change of plans would finally reveal this aspect of God's providence for his godly people.

In the Devon port of Plymouth, those whose nerve held crowded onto the *Mayflower*, while those who could take no more of the journey abandoned the mission and either stayed in England or returned to Delfthaven, via London, on the *Speedwell*. A number of those with young children were advised by those continuing the journey to opt out of the adventure at this point, being, in the words of William Bradford, "least useful and most unfit to bear the brunt of this hard venture."[7] Not everyone, though, responded to the warning, since the parents of little Samuel Eaton, under a year old and therefore still being breastfed, continued with the journey. This little one—described by

William Bradford as a "sucking child"—survived the voyage and died at Middleboro, Massachusetts, in 1684, aged about sixty-four. His mother, though, died soon after arriving at Cape Cod.

Pregnancy and pilgrimage

For the three pregnant women on board—Elizabeth Hopkins, Susanna White, and Mary Allerton—the delays they had experienced posed serious problems. They should have arrived in their New World home early in September, in which case none of them would have been in the final stages of pregnancy while at sea. But the leaking *Speedwell*—whether a sad testimony to its poor state or a bitter testimony to the machinations of men—had thrown the traveling plans out by many weeks. As a result, it was not until Wednesday, September 6, that the *Mayflower* finally set sail for North America, from old Plymouth to New Plymouth. The die was cast and Susanna was still aboard as the *Mayflower* cut its way through the heaving gray waters of the Western Approaches and out into the Atlantic towards what lay beyond.

Any pregnant woman looking toward the New World might have felt anxious about matters of health. In an age before germ theory, strange air and an unusual environment carried the threat of new diseases. The possible effects of this strange air and water on a body unaccustomed to it were an alarming thought in 1620. And it was one that particularly worried those considering movement to an environment as strange and exotic as North America.[8] As William Bradford wrote, concerning the anxieties of those facing the New World,

> *The change of air, diet and drinking of water, would infect their bodies with sore sicknesses and grievous diseases.*[9]

This was not a fear of pathogens but the still more alarming fear that something about the very strangeness might itself prove lethal. The air itself could threaten the health and lives of those who breathed its unaccustomed vapors. But before that risk was faced, the Atlantic Ocean beckoned, and it was not gentle in its welcome.

The sea journey was very hard. William Bradford says very little about it in his manuscript, *Of Plymouth Plantation*, except that the ship faced crosswinds and many storms, which caused water to flow into the vessel and which also caused structural damage to the ship. These storms were so bad at times that the crew was forced to draw in the sails and just let the ship run before the wind and the tempestuous seas. For Susanna and the other passengers this meant that they were trapped below decks in the dark, confined spaces they had erected for themselves and in which they had gathered their meager belongings. And all the while, as the sea broke over the sides and flowed across the decks, salt water poured down through gratings and around the edge of hatches. What was clear was that it was too dangerous to go up on deck to take fresh air at these times, as was seen in the experience of one passenger (whom we will later meet in another Mayflower Life) who was washed overboard—but survived!

However, we can augment this frustratingly thin evidence from Bradford with some careful reading of another key document. This is a letter written in 1621 by Edward Winslow—a leading Leidener and a leading member of the colony at New Plymouth—and sent back to London with a number of other documents reporting on life in the newly founded colony. It was printed in 1622 under the far from catchy title of *A Relation or Journal of the English Plantation settled at Plymouth*, and today is often referred to as *Mourt's Relation*, probably named for the man responsible for its printing in England.[10] This letter gives advice to those coming on other ships; reading between the lines, we can see lessons learned from experiences on the first voyage. The reference to a good "bread-room" within which to put biscuits suggests that soggy ship's biscuits soon became tiresome on the original journey. Similarly, the advice to improve the robustness of containers for beer and water was undoubtedly prompted by soiling of drink on the *Mayflower* by seawater or leakage from barrels insufficiently bound with iron hoops. We can be sure that Susanna experienced the nausea caused by poorly preserved meat, since specific advice was given to newcomers to make preservation more effective and to involve the sailors in the process, since they were better at it. Hunger too would have plagued her on the overly extended original voyage, as the next travelers were advised to bring good quantities of meal (hard pressed and rammed down into barrels to maximize the amount carried), since they would need it on the voyage as well as when they arrived in North America. But eating it on the way was acceptable, since, after initially settling into their new homes, they would be wise to rely on planting native corn rather than relying on planting ill-suited English grains. The cramped conditions on board ship that Susanna experienced (with temporary partitions erected to give a little privacy and protection for possessions) could be ameliorated a little, the letter suggests, by building more spacious cabins on future trips. Such improvised constructions would improve comfort and assist storage. Susanna would, likewise, have benefitted if the original voyage had carried more of the lemon juice advised to be carried in future by the writer of *Mourt's Relation*, along with aniseed water to mix with hot water. Although nobody as yet had connected scurvy with lack of vitamin C, the health-giving property of citrus juice was already being appreciated. In the autumn of 1620, Susanna and the other passengers would have much appreciated not only its health-promoting character but also the way it soothed sore throats and cleared the thickness of the mouth and bad breath that accumulated from weeks of poor diet, rancid meat, and increasingly foul water supplies as the wooden ladles scraped the bottom of barrels growing green with age. Good advice for future emigrants, but Susanna had been one of the godly pioneers on the first Pilgrim voyage, and all the shortcomings of that sailing had impacted on her and on her fellow passengers. This made conditions on the *Mayflower* hard for everyone.

It was, though, an especially difficult environment in which to give birth. But this was the location in which one of the women—Elizabeth Hopkins—found herself during the autumn of 1620. She was the wife of Stephen Hopkins, who was one of the so-called Strangers recruited by the London Adventurers to assist in the governance of the new colony (and a Mayflower Life we will get to know better in due course). Elizabeth was pregnant when she boarded the *Mayflower* in London, although she imagined that her child would be born on land in North America, not on a rolling ship, buffeted by Atlantic westerly gales and with seawater penetrating the timber sides and hatches of the vessel. Had the ship not been so delayed in its departure from England, the birth would have occurred about two months after the adventurers had arrived in North America. However, as we have seen, that was not to be, so her baby was delivered in the dark berth of a between-decks compartment, by the juddering light of a lamp, as the ship heaved in the mid-Atlantic. It is perhaps not surprising that the little boy was named Oceanus (Latin for *ocean*). Oceanus Hopkins was the only baby born on the actual voyage. And he is the reason why 102 passengers embarked and 102 reached the new world; for his birth replaced the life of passenger William Butten, one of the young servants, who died shortly before the *Mayflower* reached Cape Cod. Little Oceanus survived the first winter, anchored off Cape Cod and then in the ramshackle settlement that was hurriedly put up at New Plymouth in the New Year of 1621. But he did not survive long. By 1627 he was dead. We know this because his name does not appear in the list accompanying the Division of Cattle that occurred that year. He had not survived to see his seventh birthday, but the site of his grave is unknown. His short life is a testament to the tough years that accompanied the early settlement and, sadly, is also consistent with the infant mortality rate among 17th-century European and North American communities. The beginning of life was precarious, and for many it was also the end of life. Other little ones died well before the six short years accrued by Oceanus, the little sea-born and sea-borne Pilgrim.

One of the other heavily pregnant women on board was a little more fortunate than Elizabeth Hopkins, with her dark, low-cabined place of confinement. Susanna White finally gave birth to a son, who was named Peregrine, late in November 1620.[11] This birth occurred while the *Mayflower* was anchored in the shelter of Cape Cod. His name was illustrative of a saintly mind-set, for it means 'wanderer' or 'pilgrim.' Due to the ship's late arrival, there was no cozy New England home ready for the birth. Instead, the damp walls of the ship echoed to the cries of the first little *Mayflower* Pilgrim to be born in the New World.

Susanna was not alone in coming full term while still on the ship, for Mary Allerton gave birth to a stillborn son in Plymouth Harbor (the *Mayflower* having previously shifted its mooring place) on Friday, December 22, 1620. Mary herself died during the cold depths of the first winter, in late February 1621.

As the newest *Mayflower* Pilgrim, baby Peregrine White was a little piece of North American history. Today it is moving to stand beside the actual cradle that was used for him and is now on display in Pilgrim Hall Museum, in Plymouth. It is the first cradle used for the first recorded English-American baby. But firsts were about to run in the family, by way of a tragedy.

Susanna's husband, William, died on Wednesday, February 21, 1621. Like Mary Allerton, this was also in the middle of the first terrible winter in the New World, which claimed the lives of about half of those who had arrived in November. We can only assume that after crossing the sea, a combination of exhaustion, cold, and little food so weakened his health that infection, scurvy, or sudden physical strain was capable of carrying him off. William Bradford later blamed the many deaths early in the colony's history on the poor provisioning of the expedition by the penny-pinching Adventurer Thomas Weston. In the New World, William White had hoped to find a home but, instead, had only found a grave. It was a terrible blow to Susanna. She was now left with the care of two children: five-year-old Resolved and three-month-old Peregrine. And the New England winter was far from over; death had taken William well before spring brought the prospect of warmer weather and the hope that pressures on the little colony might at last be eased somewhat. It must have been a daunting challenge, yet she could draw on a deep reservoir of faith to strengthen her in her hour of trial.

The newly widowed Susanna was one of only four adult women among the Pilgrims who survived that first winter in North America. The others were Eleanor (or Ellen) Billington, Mary Brewster, and Elizabeth Hopkins. No fewer than fourteen out of the eighteen wives who had embarked on the *Mayflower* in September 1620 died after the ship reached their new home in North America. The winter took a terrible toll, and many widowers and orphans were now facing life without a wife or mother. As we shall later see, it was these four women, plus their daughters and the servants (female and male), who prepared the first Thanksgiving feast in the autumn of 1621.[12] But that joyful occasion was months away in the late winter/early spring of the year. Then, the situation looked desperate, especially for a newly widowed woman with two little children. And she stood out in this position, for Susanna was the only surviving widow from the many families who had suffered during that first winter.

New World . . . new husband and family

Then her position was transformed. She was not the only one to be bereaved over that first terrible winter of 1620–21. Another Leiden Pilgrim, the 26-year-old Edward Winslow, had also lost his spouse. Edward Winslow's wife, Elizabeth, had died on March 24, one of the last to die that winter. Like William White and these other Pilgrims, she was laid to rest in the Cole's Hill Burial Ground, in Plymouth. Just one and a half months later, on Saturday, May 12, Edward Winslow (another of our Mayflower Lives) and Susanna White became the first couple to marry in Plymouth Colony. Another first for a remarkable woman. It seems unseemly haste on the part of Edward, to have a bereavement of just forty-eight days. But there were practical as well as emotional factors driving forward such a rapid remarriage. For a start, Susanna had two little children in need of additional support and protection. We do not diminish her grit and courage by suggesting that such an early widowhood was as exhausting as it was distressing and that she looked rapidly to remarry. There was plenty of reason for looking for a new husband. And Edward too had a dependent. Little Margaret Winslow was probably only about three years old when her mother died, leaving her in the care of a father who had much on his mind as one of the leading men in the newly established colony. Both he and Susanna faced very practical as well as deep emotional needs following the loss of a husband and a wife. Shared faith, shared history, mutual respect, and, no doubt, physical as well as emotional attraction drew them together. And there is plenty of evidence for loving physical union enhancing partnership in the godly marriages. These were not austere prudes or plaster saints. We might not find much romance (of course, we occasionally might) but it is perfectly reasonable to imagine a mixture of mutual affection and desire alongside an assessment of real practical issues. From such a coming together, love could develop powerfully, even if it was not the initial driving force in an age unaccustomed to the concept of romantic love. In a marvelous piece of detective work, it has been shown that when, in 1651, Edward had a portrait of himself painted in London, the letter that he is holding can be read in part. The last three lines read simply, "from your loving wife, Susanna."[13] We may safely assume that as early as 1621, they very much liked each other, and the pressing needs suggested that this was basis enough for a godly partnership. Well, godly in terms of their beliefs, but surprisingly civil as an arrangement.

The wedding was a civil ceremony, conducted by the newly appointed second governor, William Bradford. This was just as Edward and Susanna wanted it, since the Leiden Separatists did not consider marriage a sacrament. Unlike members of the Church of England (and also the Roman Catholic Church), they regarded it as a legal secular arrangement, performed before secular authorities appointed by the state. When William Bradford recorded their historic marriage, he noted that it was done in the manner of the Netherlands, at Leiden. But this did not mean they were denigrating marriage. Far from it. Susanna and Edward, like all their community, had a high regard for marriage and for family. It was God-given and essentially the normal pattern of human existence as far as they were concerned. For them celibacy was an aberration, and only for those called by God to it and equipped with grace to pursue it. It was certainly not a higher calling, below which lesser mortals (who could not discipline their emotional and sexual needs and desires) operated. The godly, like Susanna and Edward, did not see it that way at all. New England Saints, like those in old England, regarded the family as a small world, a community in miniature, that mirrored wider society. It was a little commonwealth.

And like the bigger commonwealth, it assisted its members to understand and worship God; it maintained order (and, boy, that was challenged by dysfunctional colonial families, as we shall see); and it provided comfort for its members.[14] It could be complex, of course, as it was for Susanna and Edward as they welded together two different family units.

Edward adopted Susanna's boys as his own sons. He and Susanna went on to have five children together (three boys, one girl, and one whose gender is unknown). Only two of these—Josiah and Elizabeth—were to outlive their parents.[15] Edward's daughter Margaret, by his first wife, died the same year as her father: in 1655. The longest lived of the children raised by Susanna and Edward was Peregrine, the first baby born in Plymouth Colony. Much revered as the first child born in New England, he served in various administrative positions, as well as within the colony's militia. He finally died in 1704 at the impressively old age of eighty-four, at Marshfield, near Plymouth. In that year the *Boston Newsletter* rather judgmentally noted in his obituary, "Altho' he was in the former part of his Life extravagant; yet was much Reform'd in his last years; and died hopefully."[16] Clearly, Susanna's second son had been a bit of a wild youth, at least by the standards of his godly observers. By 1704, New England was another world, compared with his place of birth, way back in 1620.

Their total of eight children was fairly average for colonial-era Plymouth, where between seven and ten children was the norm. As with that wider sample, Susanna's children were usually born at about two-year intervals—again, perhaps suggestive of some kind of birth control (presumably abstinence or perhaps some artificial form) practiced by Edward and Susanna, as earlier we suggested it was practiced by William and her, as evidenced in the gap between the births of Resolved and Peregrine. There does seem to be a discernible pattern here.[17] Their loss of three of the eight in childhood was actually worse than a colonial-era average of about one in ten and probably reflects the tough life in the first few years of the colony. Those who survived generally confound our modern expectations of 17th-century life spans by their longevity, living to seventy-two (Resolved), eighty-four

(Peregrine), fifty-three (Josiah), sixty-seven (Elizabeth), thirty-seven (Margaret, Edward's child by his first wife). And they were not unique, since death at seventy for a man and a little younger for women was not uncommon for those who survived the perilous early years of childhood, although giving birth could severely reduce a woman's chance of achieving that ripe old age.

After her remarriage, Susanna found herself once again in the position of running the household under the authority of a husband. It was summed up in the Puritan descriptor *goodwife*, often abbreviated to *goody*. In time, though, she achieved the more elevated social position that earned her the more exalted title of mistress. She knew that Edward (as William before him) was undoubtedly the master. She was descended from Eve, who had been tempted and who had, in turn, tempted her husband, while he was descended from Adam, who had been established as head of the woman, Eve. The man would lead the family in daily reading of the Bible, in discussing its teaching as expounded on the Sabbath, and in prayer. He was also the one who would administer discipline when it was required. However, in the New World, although she considered her husband her "head" and head of the extended household of family and servants, she soon knew the kind of partnership marriage that became a hallmark of colonial life on a new frontier. While she took day-to-day control over the household affairs, she was involved in far more than simply supervising the preserving of meat, the preparing of meals, the cleanliness and efficiency of the household. She was also a partner with her husband. With mutually important duties, Susanna was taught (as was Edward) to build a respectful partnership. They knew from their church's teaching that it did not exist just for procreation; it also existed for companionship. If anything, companionship was perhaps even more important than procreation.[18] And it was not just a remedy for fornication. In fact, there was godly teaching, on the record as it were, that marital love should be "the most dear, intimate, precious and entire that the heart can have toward a creature."[19] Their non-separating Anglican neighbors regarded them as very edgy, if not downright alarming, to place such an emphasis, as it elevated the role of sexual intimacy from mere procreation to joyful expression of love. Susanna and Edward looked forward to a marriage where the physical intimacy of sex played an honorable role.

Although Susanna and Edward subscribed to a belief in original sin that identified misplaced seeking after pleasure as a hallmark of the fallen condition of human beings alienated from God and in urgent need of grace to affect salvation, we should not regard them as stern killjoys. There is evidence that Puritan ideas of marriage generally stressed the quality of lovemaking as well as its regularity. Since God had ordained sex within marriage as a key way by which that love should be expressed and sustained, it should be good sex![20] It should be, in the words of a contemporary preacher, "the crown of all our bliss"; one modern historian has gone so far as to state that for the godly, "Married sex was not only legitimate . . . it was meant to be exuberant."[21] The godly were not always consistent in these (what we might call progressive) attitudes towards sex within marriage, but they certainly challenged many hitherto entrenched ideas—and also many of our 21st-century views concerning the Puritan mind-set.[22]

This did not mean, of course, that they had a lax attitude towards sex. Premarital sex was considered a sin, and many were prosecuted for it.[23] Homosexuality was utterly condemned. And there is an example, as we shall later see, of an execution in Plymouth Colony for bestiality.

While the feminine was regarded as divinely and naturally subordinate to the male, this was not as straightforward as it might appear at first glance. In the church and family Bible study, the dominant image of Christ and the Church—Christ and the believer—was that of bridegroom and bride. Though the impact of this teaching might be fended off by aspects of masculine desire to dominate—or its implications downplayed by some preachers—it could have an unconscious effect, since Christ (the husband equivalent) was not a tyrant, and the bride role (the Church/believer equivalent) demanded obedience and submission to God by all, regardless of gender. This both raised, in theory at least, the concept of the feminine and toned down, in theory at least, masculine desires to dominate and assert self. Clearly, there might actually be "feminine virtues" (humility, obedience) that a man

could, should, emulate. And the example of Christ could, should, ame-
liorate the worst excesses of male authority. Well, that at least was the
theory. There is plenty of evidence to suggest that this did not happen,
but the (often preached) message must be held responsible for some, at
least, of the more positive Puritan views of marriage. And it might, at
times, have influenced male behavior within the privacy of the home.
The evidence suggests that while this had little or no effect on the
political ordering of the colony (women were certainly subordinate to
men), it could have some impact within the family, where it was taught
that each spouse should aim to be more loveable in their conduct.

A slightly higher status (compared with England) for women such as
Susanna was also prompted by demographics, since in New England by
the 1630s, men seemed to have outnumbered women by a ratio of three
to two. This, allied to a labor shortage, made it more difficult to take
women for granted, and women were quick to seize the opportunity for
greater economic activity. This improved status was accelerated by the
theology that souls have no genders and what mattered was the ability
to express a conversion experience. A woman was as capable of doing
that as a man. As the years rolled by after 1621, the increasing number
of women admitted to Church membership, while their husbands were
not, greatly unsettled the status quo. For as well as promoting the idea
of the female Saint, it meant that Church politics became skewed, as
congregations might consist of a high proportion of women. We will
see how this impacted on life in the churches in New England in due
course, but suffice it to say that the godly theology of salvation could
(unintentionally) go a long way towards mitigating the sinful legacy
of Eve. But this should not be overstressed, for across New England,
as in Europe generally, at times of social and economic stress it was
thought that the devil was more likely to assume the shape of a woman
than a man. As we will finally see, when we examine the evidence of
what occurred at Salem in the 1690s, this did not mean that men were
not accused of witchcraft. However, it did leave women particularly
vulnerable as targets of the accusations, and it is surely no coincidence
that the adolescents behind these terrible events were all girls. This
combination of gender and age ensured their lack of power in normal

circumstances, and might have encouraged their sudden and unaccustomed acquisition of terrible power over life and death in the appalling events that occurred at Salem. Clearly, we should not overstress the existence of empowered women in the normal run of things.

What was certainly the case was that in the home constructed by Susanna and Edward there was little room for privacy, and the little commonwealth of the family lived pretty much on top of each other. A private time was not very easy to devise, and for most it was conceptually alien; they were a community, an "us." Most of the homes that were finally raised in 1621, as thereafter in New Plymouth, were both small and overcrowded. Most early homes had just one large room in which could be found the hearth with its chimney, a bed, wooden trunks, a table, and the folded mattresses that served as beds for children and servants. Mats on the floor kept down the dust, though as herds grew larger, cattle blood might be stamped into the floor to harden the earth. The most luxurious homes consisted of no more than three rooms in total. Even in these, the bedroom might sleep parents, children, and their servants, not to mention visitors. The room that served as the kitchen also acted as the general communal area for activities as diverse as textile production and candle making, family Bible study and communal prayer. Outside, the walls would be protected by clapboard, but inside it was plain wattle and daub. The life of a house might be as short as ten years, although after 1627 the shift from thatch to wooden shingles reduced the hazard of roof fires (caused by floating embers descending from the chimney) somewhat. An Englishman's home might be his castle, but in Plymouth it was a very small and rather roughly constructed castle—and a busy and bustling one at that. Life was materially rougher and poorer there than in comparable homes in England or even in the rather mean alleys of Leiden.[24]

When Susanna and Edward built their first home it was one of a number on the single street leading uphill from the shoreline that they called First Street but which today is Leyden Street in Plymouth. The modern visitor to Plymouth, standing on the shoreline, can still look up the street that Susanna knew: Cole's Hill (where so many early Pilgrims were buried) lies to the right of the lower part of it; the land falls away to Town Brook on the left; at the top (the view now partly obscured by the location of First Parish Plymouth Church) is Burial Hill, where a fort was constructed. On the modern street, not a single house dates from the 17th century, but their house plots preserve the sizes and arrangement of homes that Susanna knew.[25]

Susanna's role in the house that was established in Plymouth would primarily have focused on the home area, including all that took place in the garden and orchard and all that was stored in the barn. At first the only livestock would have been chickens and perhaps pigs. These had been small enough to pack into the already overcrowded *Mayflower* in the autumn of 1620, and we have some clues that point to their presence. As we will see in due course, it was chicken broth that Susanna's husband, Edward Winslow, gave to the Native American *sachem* Massasoit when he was seriously ill early in 1622. Then, when a man named Emmanuel Altham visited the colony in 1623, he noted that there were six goats (apparently new arrivals), fifty pigs, and lots of chickens. Such small farmyard animals came within the purview of wives such as Susanna. Her children, along with all those in the colony, were pressed into active service on the family plots as soon as they were able to assist, and they too would have fed and watered the animals in the newly erected barns, pens, and about the yard. Her husband, as with all men, had his primary focus of activity on the fields and also on stock management of larger animals once cattle arrived from England on the supply ship *Anne* in 1623 (with three cows), and then on the ship *Jacob* a year later in 1624 (with four heifers).[26] By 1627 the herd had increased to sixteen cattle and twenty-two goats, plus a "Red Cow" and its two calves, which belonged to the poor in the colony. By 1628 there were sheep too. Susanna's husband also had the pressing issues of the colony's administration and politics to attend to.

As one of New Plymouth's leading families, Susanna, Edward, and their children occupied one of the larger homes and land plots in the colony. And they were soon on the move from the original settlement site. Together, goodwife Susanna and her husband founded one of Plymouth's daughter settlements, Marshfield, in 1632, about twelve miles north of Plymouth. Situated near the coast, it was separated from the sea by salt marshes, hence its name. The settlement that eventually was called Marshfield had started off as the fishing enterprise known as Green's Harbor as early as 1623. When a separate township was established there in 1632, it became known as Rexhame for a while and then, finally, Marshfield (the name it carries today). It was officially declared a separate town from Plymouth in 1640. Under the Winslows' supervision, Marshfield became the center of cattle rearing in the colony. It was soon after visiting Marshfield, in 1662, that the Native American *sachem* Wamsutta, known to the English as Alexander, died. His brother, Metacomet or Metacom (known to the English as Philip) became convinced that he had been poisoned.[27] And so, Susanna's home at Marshfield (by then the base of Josiah, her son) became entangled in the complex events that would eventually lead to the worst episode of intercommunal violence in the history of New England.

The Winslow land holding was augmented by the four acres allocated to the deceased William White (in effect, to his widow) at the 1623 Division of Land. This plot lay behind the fort that had been constructed at Plymouth. The allocation was due to the fact that he had been one of the original Pilgrims, even though dead at the time of this land allocation. It was a mark of solidarity between Pilgrims living and dead and their surviving dependents. Now goodwife Susanna was very much mistress Susanna Winslow.

Susanna's second husband greatly prospered after their marriage. He went on to become three-time governor of Plymouth Colony in the 1630s and '40s and was assistant to the governor most other years. His only surviving son by Susanna, Josiah, became the thirteenth governor of Plymouth Colony in the 1670s. In another first for Susanna, this son was the very first native-born governor of an American colony. He is also famous—we might say infamous—for being party to allowing an acrimonious situation with Native Americans to spiral out of control into the appallingly bloody conflict known as King Philip's War (1675–1678). For this reason we shall meet him again too in our developing story. But to return to Susanna.

We know little in detail about her personal life in Plymouth after her marriage to Edward Winslow in 1621. Although he visited England several times (in 1623, 1624, 1635, and 1646) on Plymouth or Massachusetts Colony business, there is no evidence that Susanna left New England with him. When Edward eventually died, in 1655 in the West Indies on a mission for Oliver Cromwell's government, he had been apart from Susanna for almost ten years.[28] If mutual attraction had drawn them together and love had cemented their relationship, it was business in support of the godly colony that kept them apart. Clearly, Susanna had not married a man who would be her close companion for life. We do not know exactly when she died. It seems that she passed away sometime between December 18, 1654, the date of Edward Winslow's will, and July 2, 1675, the date of their son Josiah Winslow's will. After Edward Winslow died, in 1655, Susanna was supported by one third of his estate in and around Marshfield until her eventual death.[29] By that time she had become the relatively wealthy widow of one of the foremost citizens of Plymouth Colony and the mother of a man who was also a leading—and highly influential—figure in the colony. It was a far cry from the desperate situation she had faced in February 1621, when widowed with two small children.

Susanna White's first son, by William White, the little *Mayflower* Pilgrim named Resolved, died sometime after 1690. In that year, somebody wrote into the manuscript copy of William Bradford's *Of Plymouth Plantation* the record "Two persons [still] living that came over in the first ship . . ." These were then named as Resolved White and Mary Cushman. Resolved appears to have died shortly after that note was written.[30] By that time New Plymouth had become united with the settlements of Massachusetts Bay, Martha's Vineyard, Nantucket, and what is now, broadly, Maine, New Brunswick, and Nova Scotia, to form the Province of Massachusetts Bay, under British royal supervision. By that time, godly government of the area was over and the British crown was firmly in control. It ended an era. From his time on the *Mayflower*, to his death in the newly relaunched colony, Resolved's life bracketed the history of the settlement of New England. Susanna's first child and survivor of the *Mayflower*'s epic journey was, as it were, a human bookend for a momentous period in the European settlement of North America.

4

The Adventurer's Story: Stephen Hopkins, Survivor of Shipwreck and with Unique New World Experience

We have seen how Elizabeth Hopkins gave birth to the only child born on the actual voyage of the *Mayflower* between England and Cape Cod. Little Oceanus Hopkins was son of Elizabeth and Stephen Hopkins. We know little else about Elizabeth, but we know much more about the life and adventures of her husband.[1] This is Stephen's story.

Stephen Hopkins was one of the so-called Strangers, those not personally known to the Leiden congregation. He stood out in many ways from the other Strangers because he was the only *Mayflower* passenger with any detailed prior experience of America, having been shipwrecked in Bermuda in 1609, on a ship called the *Sea Venture*, which was part of the third supply mission to the Jamestown Colony, in Virginia. As we shall see, he just missed serving under the famous

Captain John Smith (of Pocahontas fame) at Jamestown but was in that colony for about six years. As a result, he brought hunting skills and a knowledge of Native Americans to the *Mayflower* expedition. His life gives us an opportunity to explore how the New England adventure was different from the earlier settlement at Jamestown and what experience of that settlement brought to the life of the new colony. Given his background, it is not surprising that he took part in the early exploration of the Cape Cod area, including the famous First Encounter with Native Americans, and the selection of the site of Plymouth, followed by the early building of the first settlement in the winter of 1620–21. We cannot explore his life and experiences without also taking a look at that Bermuda shipwreck and its impact on the exploration of North America, as well as, most surprisingly, literature, in William Shakespeare's *The Tempest*.

Stephen Hopkins married Elizabeth Fisher (his second wife) in February 1618, at the church of St. Mary Matfellon, in Whitechapel, in the East End of London. Centuries later, during The Blitz in December 1940, a Luftwaffe incendiary raid destroyed the church, and it was left in disrepair until finally being demolished after the war. Today their marriage site is a public park. It is also the burial place of a famous English mutineer—Richard Parker—who led the so-called Floating Republic, a serious naval mutiny that shook the Royal Navy in 1797 at the height of the Napoleonic Wars. This tangle of a later history of warfare, mutiny, and execution at the place of Stephen and Elizabeth's marriage is rather appropriate, since Stephen's life was itself highly colorful and involved a tangling together of all these three dramatic themes. . . .

Stephen was thirty-nine when he embarked on the *Mayflower*, having been born at Upper Clatford, Hampshire, England, in April 1581. By the year 1604 he had moved just a short distance, to Hursley, again in Hampshire. The early part of his life gave little indication of the adventures that were to come. Sometime before 1604 he married a woman named Mary (his first wife), and they lived together in Hampshire, where they had three children: Elizabeth, Constance or Constanta, and Giles. Then, in the year 1609, everything changed!

For in that year Stephen took part in an adventure that nearly cost him his life on at least two dramatic occasions and which changed the entire course of his life. At the age of twenty-eight he embarked on the ship *Sea Venture*, which was the flagship of a small fleet led by Sir George Somers, the admiral of the Virginia Company. The little fleet was tasked with resupplying the newly founded colony of Jamestown in Virginia. Founded just two years earlier, in 1607, the colony was struggling to survive. Now, on June 2, 1609, fresh assistance (supplies and new colonists) was finally on its way. Stephen found himself part of what was, in effect, a rescue mission.

Adventures in the Americas

The *Sea Venture* was also carrying the new governor of Jamestown, Sir Thomas Gates, to take up his appointment. Stephen traveled there as clerk to a minister, which indicates he possessed a fairly high level of education and some ambition. It was his job to read edifying religious works to the community, including members of the Virginia Company. It was this very group who would later provide financial support for the *Mayflower* expedition. Hopkins traveled as what was called an indentured servant. Having signed a contract (an indenture, or covenant), he had committed himself to working for the Virginia Company for a specified number of years (usually between four and seven) in exchange for the passage to Virginia and then the provision of food, clothing, and shelter while he was working there.[2] It was a curious decision, since it meant separation from his wife and children for at least four years. Perhaps he intended to send for them once he was settled in a new home. Stephen's excitement at joining the Jamestown venture must have been high, for as far as we know it was his first time out of England, and it offered a real adventure on the high seas and in a strange land. Just how much an adventure was about to be revealed, and Stephen, like his fellow passengers, could not have imagined just what drama lay ahead.[3]

For, in late July 1609, disaster struck! First the fleet was battered by a hurricane that tore down on the ships. It shredded sails and rigging, buried the decks under mounds of churning water, and scattered the ships. The storm lasted for five long days (from Monday to Friday), and all the time it smashed the ships with ferocious winds and high seas. Stephen had no previous experience of seafaring as far as we know, and the initiation must have been terrifying. Such physical violence done by the sea was beyond seasickness. The immediate danger was injury or drowning, not the nausea that was brought on by the motion of a vessel.

Some of the ships escaped the hurricane and finally limped away, battered and under torn sails. The *Sea Venture*, however, was not one of them. Driven by the storm, it faced being wrecked, and Stephen and his companions looked at approaching death in the surging waves. But disaster was averted when, on the Friday of that storm-lashed week, the crew allowed the battered ship to be driven onto a reef just a mile from land. And so, the 150 on board—crew and passengers—launched the ship's boats, which navigated the calmer waters beyond the boiling surf of the reef and made it safely to shore. The ship was wrecked on what they called the Isle of Devils, one of the islands of what was also becoming known as the Bermudas. It is easy to understand their naming of the place, for it was a truly horrendous force that had thrown them ashore there. As they waded from the water onto the white sand, they had few thoughts of tropical paradise in their minds. It was enough just to be alive and in one piece.

By a strange quirk of fate, Stephen Hopkins shared his place on the boats carrying the survivors to shore with tobacco planter John Rolfe, who would go on to marry Pocahontas in Virginia.[4] To the relief of Stephen Hopkins, John Rolfe, and the others, Bermuda was actually a tropical haven. It was no Isle of Devils. Instead, there was fruit, turtles, oysters, crayfish, crabs, seabirds, and tortoises to eat; freshwater pools provided drinking water for men and women whose throats were raw with the salt of seawater. But they had no intention of staying there, for they were men and women on a mission. Though stranded on the island for ten months, the survivors began the task of building two boats that would, they hoped, carry them to Virginia. Appropriately named *Patience* and *Deliverance*, the escape boats were ready by May 1610. By that time, though, John Rolfe's (first) wife had given birth to a daughter—named Bermuda—who had sadly died and been buried on the island. She did not live to see the dramatic escape from the island that had given her a name. However, before that occurred, Stephen Hopkins became involved in a questionable enterprise that almost cost him his life. His body, too, nearly remained behind, interred in the white sand of Bermuda when the two boats finally left the island.

Thrown ashore and with old certainties shaken as they carved out a temporary home on the island, Stephen chafed under the authority of those set over him. It was one thing to accept that rule on the ship, but in a leveling experience such as the one they now found themselves in, some men were emboldened to speak their minds over decisions and less inclined to accept authority as a given. After about six months as castaways on Bermuda—in January 1610—Stephen and a number of others began to challenge the authority of Governor Gates. The challenge centered on Gates's intention to sail on to Virginia. Surely, Stephen and a group of companions argued, it made more sense to get back to England and give up on the failed venture to Jamestown? They challenged the governor on the grounds that his authority over them had ended when the *Sea Venture* was wrecked. If this seemed a way to achieve a greater influence in decision making, then Stephen was rapidly disabused of this illusion. As a result of his impertinence, he and his fellow conspirators were arrested as mutineers and brought to trial in chains. Clearly, Governor Gates had managed to preserve his authority among a sufficient number of survivors to quell the mutiny. The punishment for mutiny was clear and harsh. Stephen was sentenced to death: his life was on a knife edge. However, others pleaded for him and he was finally pardoned. This was assisted by the appearance of such remorse on Stephen's part that one contemporary report recorded,

> *So penitent he was, and made so much moan, alleging the ruin of his wife and children in this his trespass, as it wrought in the hearts of all the better sorts of the company.*[5]

They finally persuaded the governor to pardon the mutineer, so Stephen Hopkins escaped the rope. It would not be his first brush with colonial authority, as would be revealed in New England, but it was his most serious one. And it had nearly cost the minister's clerk his life.

Eventually the castaways (including the reprieved Stephen) sailed from Bermuda on their makeshift vessels. It was May 10, 1610. They had been stranded on the island for almost a year. Now they were on their way once more. After eight days, they noticed that the color of the water was changing. Furthermore, they passed rubbish floating on the sea. They realized from the floating detritus that land must be close, though what form the rubbish took we can only guess. One wonders at how swiftly the colonists in Virginia were managing to pollute their environment. After eleven days at sea the castaways reached Jamestown. It was an impressive piece of navigation. Here Stephen, John Rolfe, and the others joined a colony that was on its knees. . . .

In many ways the colony at Jamestown offered a dramatic contrast to the one that Stephen would later help found at Plymouth in New England. The contemporary report notes the state of the fort and settlement when the relief force from Bermuda arrived. Stephen must have been aghast at the state of the place:

> *We found the palisades torn down, the ports open, the gates off the hinges, and empty houses . . . burned, rather than the dwellers would step into the woods a stone's cast off from them, to fetch other firewood: and it is true the Indian killed as fast without, if our men stirred but beyond the bounds of their blockhouse, as famine and pestilence did within . . .*[6]

What a state of affairs. The colonists called it "The Starving Time." In the winter of 1609–1610, the poor weather, deteriorating relationships with Native Americans, and the departure of the controversial but brutally efficient Captain John Smith (who had extorted quantities of corn from the neighboring indigenous tribe, the Powhatans) had brought the colony to the brink of collapse.[7] Of the 240 colonists alive in November 1609 (Smith left Jamestown in October 1609), only about 60 were still alive to see the boats arrive from Bermuda in the spring of 1610. There is even new archaeological evidence suggesting that the starving colonists turned to cannibalism in order to survive.[8] It was eat the dead or join them.

There was even a report of one of the Jamestown settlers being captured by the native inhabitants, who were enraged at their mistreatment at the hands of the colonists, and sacrificed to one of the gods of the Powhatans.[9]

The colony was in chaos, and its troubles arose from its very particular cultural DNA, a DNA very different from that which later created the colony at New Plymouth. At Jamestown, the community was largely made up of well-to-do leaders in charge of some very inexperienced settlers, stiffened by tough soldiers who were veterans of brutal European wars. One of the latter was Captain John Smith. The name of the game in Virginia was making money fast from the New World. Indeed, the overriding aim at Jamestown was to return a quick profit for the London investors who had backed the venture. And those colonists who had committed to the project hoped to gain personally from the wealth accrued. There was no talk of a New Jerusalem in the New World, such as would later bind together the little community that disembarked from the *Mayflower* farther north and sustain that community through times of harsh adversity. Instead, Jamestown was a wealth-creating scheme—and not a successful one.[10] Where was the gold? Where were other minerals? Indeed, where was anything of much value to return a quick profit? Jamestown offered no prospect of providing the fabulous wealth that the Spanish had brutally gathered from their plundering ventures in Central America.

Then there was a problem with work ethic.[11] And this too marked Jamestown out as very different from what would later emerge in New England. The colonists at Jamestown had little interest in farming, and the more socially elevated clearly felt that planting crops and tilling the soil was beneath them. Nor did they embark on exploiting the abundant fish stocks. There was something of a dearth of work ethic among many of them. Instead, they tried to barter for food with the native Powhatans. When that failed to produce enough supplies, they stole food from them. A sense of ethnic superiority drove mistreatment of the indigenous people. Not surprisingly, this was a policy that led to a lot of violence, which vividly marked the early years of the Virginia colony. Alongside this, there was dissension and arguing within the colony as things steadily deteriorated. A dysfunctional relationship with the locals was matched by dysfunctional relationships within the struggling little community. During the time that Captain Smith was the colony's president (from the summer of 1608 to the autumn of 1609), things stabilized in the fractious colony itself; not that those who were quashed by Smith thanked him for his application of tough government, which brought some order out of the preexisting chaos. His firm—but generally fair—rule within the colony sadly contrasted with his threats and use of force against the natives outside it, in order to extort corn from them. It was a policy that angered both the Powhatan people and the authorities of the Virginia Company. Eventually this brutal and shortsighted policy was to lead to terrible inter-ethnic violence. It is little wonder that the years of abuse and land seizures led to a Native American uprising in 1622, which wiped out about one third of the entire Jamestown colony. While, in the winter of 1609–1610, that all lay ahead, the seeds of massacre had already been sown, and later colonists would reap its bloody harvest.

Stephen must have wondered just how much of a refuge this place really was, compared to Bermuda. The new governor certainly thought little of the place or its long-term prospects. When the escapees from Bermuda arrived, Governor Gates calculated that there remained just a few days' worth of food in Jamestown. In a quick decision he decided to abandon the colony, sail north to Newfoundland (where English fishing fleets frequently sailed), and find a ship or ships willing to transport the Jamestown settlers back to England. The relief to Stephen and the rest must have been enormous. They would not have to stay in this failing colony. Escape beckoned yet again. But it was not to be. No sooner were they setting off than an incoming ship was spotted coming into harbor. It was yet another supply attempt and one also carrying more settlers, in the company of yet another new governor, Lord de la Warr. The escaping colonists were, therefore, forced to return to Jamestown. One can only imagine the mood of those such as Stephen who had thought they had finally quit the place! This time, though, there was no mutiny, but the mood was sour. For Stephen and the others, Jamestown was going to be home for some time to come.

Exactly how long Stephen Hopkins remained in Jamestown is not entirely certain. He was back in England by 1617, for there he married a second time (his first wife, Mary, having died in May 1613 while he was in the New World) to Elizabeth Fisher in February 1618. It is very likely that he returned to England in 1616 on the same ship that carried John Rolfe and his new wife, Rebecca (aka Pocahontas) to London. Even if Stephen returned a little earlier, it is almost certain that he would have witnessed the marriage of the newly widowed John Rolfe to Pocahontas in the spring of 1614. By then she was known as Rebecca and had converted to Christianity. Though the union was made possible by her earlier kidnapping at the hands of the English, it eventually helped stabilize relationships between Jamestown and the local Native Americans for a short time. Returning when he did, Stephen avoided the terrible massacres of 1622, which devastated Jamestown and might have claimed the life of John Rolfe, who was among those who died that year (Pocahontas/Rebecca herself had died in London in 1617). What is certain is that he would not have served under the legendary John Smith; in October 1609, Captain Smith—opposed by his enemies at Jamestown and wounded in an accidental explosion of gunpowder—resigned the presidency of the colony and returned to England.

The years in Jamestown were a useful apprenticeship for Stephen and meant that when he later returned to North America, he had experience of its plants and animals and also of working with the Native Americans; his arrival in Jamestown took place just as things markedly improved for a few years in this respect. Furthermore, he knew how to set up a settlement after a shipwreck and how to survive in an alien environment, skills honed in Bermuda. As such, it meant that valuable skills were later at the disposal of the more godly settlers in Massachusetts.

We may even have echoes of some of these formative years as seen through the lens of no less a writer than William Shakespeare! Two years after the wreck of the *Sea Venture* on that Bermudan reef, a new play was the talk of London. In November 1611 *The Tempest* was first performed. It was clearly based on reports of the shipwreck and of the adventures and misadventures of the castaways. In a subplot within the play we see a character—a drunken and ambitious butler named Stephano—attempting to depose the island's ruler, named Prospero. It is hardly surprising that a number of historians have detected in this subplot echoes of Stephen Hopkins's failed mutiny against Governor Gates.[12] It is a curious literary survival from Hopkins's life.

About five years after *The Tempest* was first performed, Stephen was back in England and married to his second wife, Elizabeth. Together Stephen and Elizabeth had a daughter, named Damaris, who was born around the year 1618. Clearly, she was either conceived soon after the marriage or Elizabeth was pregnant at the altar. This was not at all unusual in the early 17th century, as sexual relations often started following engagement and prior to marriage despite official condemnation of the practice.

When Stephen married Elizabeth Fisher, he clearly intended to transport his whole family back to Virginia (albeit to its most northern territories). In 1620, as a result of this determination, Stephen Hopkins took her and the children, Constance and Giles from his first marriage, and little Damaris from his current marriage, onto the *Mayflower* (it seems that his daughter, Elizabeth, had already died). And, of course, we know that Elizabeth Hopkins, née Fisher, was heavily pregnant with her second child: the future Oceanus.

After an eventful crossing and a failed attempt to sail south to the Hudson River, Stephen and his family found themselves looking out on the winter shore of Cape Cod on the morning of Saturday, November 11, 1620. Two days earlier he had witnessed the turbulent sea boiling above the sandbars and shoals between Nantucket Island and Cape Cod and had feared once more to feel a ship begin to break up beneath him as it was driven aground. But this time the ship had turned back in time and Master Jones had abandoned the plan to sail farther south. As a result, Stephen must have experienced relief mixed with trepidation as the ship returned to the cape. He had been spared a second shipwreck but now looked out on an alien shore. Somewhere, beyond the sand

and trees, was to be their new home. But where? The bay was known from earlier charts but not in detail. And only an expedition ashore and along the curving arc of the sheltered inside of the spit would identify a place where the ship might be safely moored and a suitable site located for settlement. Both were needed, and until the latter was found, the already cold, damp—and increasingly foul-smelling—confines of the battered *Mayflower* would be the enforced home not only of Stephen's family, including a tiny new baby, but also the rest of the weary and rather fractious company of Saints and Strangers. Until then the sheltered waters of what is now Provincetown Harbor would have to be home. Stephen had signed what we now know as the Mayflower Compact before dawn that morning. For better or for worse, he was in when it came to the unexpected settlement of the bay and the establishment of a colony far to the north of the place intended.

Putting experience into use . . . exploration of a new land

As the only member of the expedition with real experience of exploring the New World, Stephen joined the exploration of the shore of the cape. But it took time to prepare. There was a day of rest—a Sabbath of worship, both communal and private, and quiet reflection—between their weary returning to the cape on Saturday morning and the chance to start exploring on the first Monday in the New World. While Elizabeth Hopkins and the other women washed the caked salt out of clothing in a freshwater pond they had located near what is today Provincetown, the men manhandled ashore the pieces of the ship's boat—the shallop—which had been disassembled for the voyage but now needed reassembly. While the ship's carpenter and his assistants began to reconstruct the shallow-drafted sailing boat, which would be crucial for coastal exploration, the rest of the crew and passengers gathered and gorged on large blue mussels they found in huge numbers on the shore. It was the first fresh food for two months, but in their desire to consume them they threw caution to the wind and were soon throwing up as a result of seafood poisoning. Vomit *and* diarrhea . . .

a miserable start to their first exploration of North America. Stephen must have looked back with something approaching nostalgia to the tropical fruits of Bermuda in July 1609. At least then, first landfall on a strange shore had been in a Caribbean summer accompanied by the easily gathered produce of a tropical island. Now the sea they waded through was bitterly cold, and even the apparent abundance of the seashore had savagely bitten back at them. It was a hard arrival and diminished their relief at finally reaching dry land.

Something else that was proving to be a disappointment was the time it was taking to reassemble the shallop. What had been considered the work of a few days was proving to be a much larger job than expected. This was frustrating, to put it mildly. No one wanted to spend the whole winter on board ship—especially as all around them was evidence that if they could but establish themselves, this new land might indeed prove bountiful. Waterfowl were present in huge numbers and whales were seen every day. Slow swimming and coming close to shore, they were easily seen from the *Mayflower*. [13] They represented a vast, floating, money-making opportunity, and Master Christopher Jones (who had, perhaps, some experience in the Greenland whaling industry) bemoaned the lack of harpoons; if they only had them, they might have gained for them "three or four thousand pounds" from the whale oil. [14] But it was not to be. It all added to the frustration.

On Wednesday, November 15, the hardier among the men finally decided that enough was enough. It was time to get ashore and do some serious exploring down Cape Cod. If a coastal foray was delayed due to the lack of the shallop, then they would go along the shoreline and a little inland to see what kind of country lay before them. They would also establish whether or not there were native communities nearby. It was crucial to discover whether these might offer assistance or pose a threat. Given his strong will, as seen on Bermuda, it is no surprise that Stephen was among the explorers. He went ashore in a party of sixteen men led by their military expert, Myles Standish. William Bradford was included as a leading member of the Leiden congregation. The details of these explorations around the bay were published back in England as early as 1622, in the document now known as *Mourt's*

Relation (probably largely written by Edward Winslow)[15] and later also recorded in William Bradford's manuscript, *Of Plymouth Plantation*.

Now, at last, Stephen's previous North American experience was about to be deployed. Like the other men, he put on light body armor (breast and backplate, tasset plates to protect the upper thighs), gathered powder and shot for his musket, and sharpened a sword. Down from the *Mayflower* they scrambled and were rowed to the edge of the tidal mudflats, from where they waded ashore through the bitingly cold water. Once again, Stephen must have recalled the summer temperature of the shallows of Bermuda!

Now it was time to find out what was really on offer on Cape Cod. Most of all they longed to find a good-sized river that would provide a safe anchorage for the *Mayflower* close to shore (at present she was forced to anchor a good distance from dry land) and around which a settlement might be constructed that might even develop into a profitable port. They were to be disappointed, for there was nothing like that on the bay side of the cape, and the best option was well to the north in the form of the Charles River, where Boston was later to be located. Their ignorance of the coast was going to cost them a lot of time and effort.

However, they did discover that they were not alone. Led by Standish, Stephen and the others had barely walked a mile down the sandy beach when they saw people ahead. At first they mistook the men and a dog for Master Jones and some of the crew who had already gone ashore. But they were wrong. When the group turned and ran away from the shoreline and into the woods, stopping only to call their dog, it became clear that these were Native Americans. Standish led his party in pursuit, but they were weighed down by their armor, and their muscles were slack from the enforced idleness of two months cooped up on the *Mayflower*. Try as they might, Stephen and his companions could not catch up with the natives, who had moved quickly to the south, down the cape. Darkness was coming on, so they made a fire and settled into an uneasy sleep, with three of their number on guard at any one time through the long, cold November night. Their sleep in the cold might have been eased a little by sips of the aqua vitae liquor they carried, but it did little to quench their thirst. All they had to eat were ships' biscuits and some Dutch cheese.

Waking stiff and cold on Thursday morning, they skirted a tidal creek and struggled through dense woodland that snagged on their armor and muskets and made it heavy going. By midmorning they had spotted their first deer, but, more importantly, they found a spring of clear, fresh water, which they gulped down with gratitude. They also noted the abundance of sassafras trees, whose wood, roots, stems, bark, flowers, and fruit were highly prized for their perceived medicinal properties and the wood for furniture manufacturing. Returning to the shore and the sight of the *Mayflower* across the bay, they once again set up camp and lit a large fire, which both warmed their stiff limbs and signalled their safety to those on the *Mayflower* as a prearranged signal. And so Stephen and his companions passed their second night ashore.

On Friday, November 17, they made a significant discovery. This was in the form of winter fields that had once carried a crop of corn. They also found burial mounds. Digging into these, they unearthed something that Stephen immediately recognized from his years at Jamestown: a bow and decayed arrows. In order to avoid offending the native peoples, they reburied them and moved on. But these were not their only discoveries. Farther south, they came across ships' planks and the rusted remains of a kettle. Clearly, they were not the first Europeans to explore the bay side of Cape Cod. This was not all. Beside a creek running into the bay they discovered the remains of a fort. There is no hint in any of their records that they knew the history of this place, but we can guess that it was almost certainly built by an explorer from Bristol, in the west of England, named Martin Pring, who explored the area around Cape Code in 1603. Coincidentally, he sailed on a ship called the *Speedwell*, though not the one that failed the Leiden Pilgrims in 1620. He spent about two months ashore, near what is today Truro, Massachusetts, building a fort and harvesting fragrant sassafras. More alarmingly, he was attacked by a large group of Native American warriors from the tribal group later known as the Wampanoag.

Had Stephen and his companions known this, they might have reconsidered what they did next. Or their hunger might have driven them to it anyway. Noting recently disturbed ground, they dug down to discover a large cache of Native American corn buried in baskets made from woven reeds. They took as much as they could carry and consoled themselves with the thought that they would compensate the owners in due course. They named the place of their discovery Cornhill. They had gained local seed for the next year's planting. As William Bradford later concluded, it was "a special providence of God and a great mercy."[16]

Night was drawing in and a thin, cold rain was falling, driven by the wind from the sea. Aware now that they were not alone on Cape Cod and having taken the property of others, they barricaded themselves with branches. The next day they turned north and got lost in the tangled woodland. It was here that Stephen revealed something of the woodland experience that he had gained from his time in Virginia. He at once recognized the tense, bent sapling attached to a rope that formed a noose around a pile of acorns. It was a deer trap. As he explained its workings to his companions, William Bradford joined them and unintentionally demonstrated just how the trap was supposed to work! Accidentally stepping into the noose and springing the trap, he was hoisted into the air in place of the intended deer.

Then they returned to the *Mayflower*. They had seen the locals, had explored the area, found and returned with corn and the news that other Europeans had been there before them. But they had not found the good, safe, inshore anchorage for their ship or the place for a settlement. The saltwater creek at what is today Pamet Harbor, Truro, was just not suitable. As Stephen rejoined Elizabeth and his family, he must have had mixed feelings about the success of the expedition. The rather limited achievement of the venture temporarily weakened the authority of Myles Standish in the eyes of those who had argued for waiting until the shallop was ready *before* attempting a reconnaissance. But at least Stephen had the amusing memory of William Bradford dangling from a tree like a startled deer!

The demotion of Standish was seen in the fact that when the next expedition set off, it was commanded by Master Christopher Jones of the *Mayflower*. This set off in the newly reconditioned shallop on Monday, November 27. We do not know if Stephen Hopkins was with them this time, but we do know, from William Bradford's later account, that wading through the water to the shore and freezing by night almost certainly led to death (from exposure) of some of those who did this. The next day it was snowing. No wonder they named the harbor they sailed south to Cold Harbor. Disappointingly, it was not suitable as an anchorage for the *Mayflower*, but they did find more Native American corn at Cornhill. While Jones returned with it to the *Mayflower*, Standish and the others discovered another grave, which seemed to be that of a blonde European, and, nearby, a deserted Native American settlement. They took from the village what appealed to them most. They intended to leave some trade goods in return, but night was coming on and they forgot.

Winter was advancing, and they still had not located a settlement site that possessed good anchorage for the *Mayflower*. Things were getting desperate. People on board the ship were suffering terribly, and some were dying. So it was that on Wednesday, December 6, yet another expedition set off, and this time we know that Stephen Hopkins was a member. He went in the company of leading Pilgrims, including William Bradford, John Carver (chosen as the colony's governor for the first year), Myles Standish, and Edward Winslow; they were accompanied by the two pilots of the *Mayflower*. One of these, named Robert Coppin, had sailed to New England before and had a vague memory of a good harbor on a navigable river across the bay. It was, he recounted, called Thievish Harbor by those who had discovered it, due to thefts committed by "one of the wild men" there.[17] This was a reference to a Native American. He was likely thinking of the site that would one day become Boston.

Stephen and his companions sailed south down the bay side of Cape Cod once more. The sea spray froze on their jackets and glazed them with a sheen of thin ice, "like coats of iron."[18] This time they passed Native Americans butchering a stranded pilot whale, but the locals fled when the shallop put in to shore. They built a strong barricade and huddled around a large fire, noticing another fire burning some distance away. They stood guard, for the local people were close. Yet the next day they once again found only abandoned dwellings and graves. Those exploring ashore rejoined those cruising in the shallop at a tidal creek, which today is known as Herring River. It was the evening of December 7. Perhaps Stephen remembered the report he had heard at Jamestown of a settler seized and sacrificed to a god of the native inhabitants. If so, he gripped his musket tightly and kept his powder dry.

That night Stephen and his companions were woken by a howling cry. They fumbled for muskets, and some fired them into the thick, cold darkness. But no attack came, and they consoled themselves with the possibility that the noise might have been made by wolves. They were wrong!

Before dawn on Friday, December 8, they rose from their cold slumbers, tested their matchlock muskets (never very reliable in the damp), were led in prayer, and then ate some of their dried or salted provisions. Then it happened! A sentry shouted and ran back to the barricade. Arrows hissed through the air. Standish fired. The others fumbled as they dipped their matchlock wicks into the embers of the fire, lifted them, pulled triggers, and snapped the glowing "match" into the pan of powder. The air was suddenly torn by the flash and detonation from the raised matchlocks. Acrid smoke swirled about them as war cries were screamed out at them from among the trees. Those who had run to the shallop in order to grab guns were soon trapped there by showers of arrows. This was the kind of situation that men such as Standish and Hopkins had been engaged for. They discharged their muskets at a native leader within easy range but seemingly unafraid as he sent arrows singing towards those sheltering behind their barricade on the beach. Only when a shot tore wood from the tree beside him in a splintering shower did he cry out once more in defiance and vanish back into the darkness of the woods. Some of the Pilgrims pursued for a short distance but then returned to the shoreline. Edward Winslow was later to write, "Thus it pleased God to vanquish our enemies and give us deliverance."[19] It was a small victory. It seems there were no casualties on either side.

In the 21st century, the site of this "First Encounter," as the Pilgrims called it,[20] is still remembered as the name of the beach in Eastham. The contrasting ways in which it is remembered can be seen in two memorials raised there. One of them, put up to commemorate the Provincetown tercentenary of 1920, read:

ON THIS SPOT

HOSTILE INDIANS

HAD THEIR

FIRST ENCOUNTER

DECEMBER 8, 1620

OLD STYLE

WITH

MYLES STANDISH JOHN CARVER

WILLIAM BRADFORD JOHN TILLEY

EDWARD WINSLOW JOHN HOWLAND

EDWARD TILLEY RICHARD WARREN

STEPHEN HOPKINS EDWARD DOTEY

JOHN ALLERTON THOMAS ENGLISH

MASTER MATE CLARK MASTER

GUNNER COPIN AND THREE SAILORS

OF THE MAYFLOWER COMPANY

Another perspective on what happened in the gray light of a cold dawn on that December morning is apparent in a contrasting memorial set up in 2001. Its opening wording reads:

NEAR THIS SITE

THE NAUSET TRIBE

OF THE

WAMPANOAG NATION

SEEKING TO PROTECT THEMSELVES

AND THEIR CULTURE

HAD THEIR
FIRST ENCOUNTER
8 DECEMBER 1620[21]

Sited by the beach parking lot, it is the second and latest of the two monuments that became the most visited and the one from 1920 has since been removed. One suspects that the Pilgrims would have been most in tune with the sentiments of the earlier memorial. But we, knowing the eventual destruction of Native American life and culture, will be more divided on which one most resonates with us today. The legacy of Friday, December 8, 1620, continues to echo down the centuries, and to divide opinion.

Leaving behind the scene of conflict, the shallop was pushed out into the bay, and the exploration around the southern shore continued. They had a tough time of it. Freezing sleet and spray, driven by a strong, hard-edged wind, drenched them. So strong was the wind and so wild the sea that the rudder shattered and the mast splintered. It was only by a supreme effort with the oars that they avoided being smashed onto the shore. It was a close run. They had almost been thrown headlong into disaster.

Pulling away from the shore a little, they found themselves in the more sheltered waters off an island. It lay behind a sheltering L-shaped spit of land, now called The Gurnet and home to Plymouth Lighthouse. Despite fear of attack, they eventually decided to put ashore and build a fire against the plummeting temperature. The island is still remembered today as Clark's Island after John Clarke, one of the pilots of the *Mayflower*, who was the first to go ashore (over the centuries it has lost its final *e*). It is located in what we might broadly call Plymouth Bay, though facing that patch of water now called Duxbury Bay. The island's other claim to fame is that it reputedly was on the island that Truman Capote later wrote the novella *Breakfast at Tiffany's*.

At first light, feeling safe on the island, they started repairing the shallop. The sun was finally shining. The next day, being the Sabbath, they rested, as was the tradition of all English Puritans.

Little did they realize that as they prayed and sought God, they were about to make history and establish the location of the godly colony that had been the dream of many of them since the days of exile in Leiden.

On Monday, December 11, they explored the curving sweep of the bay that lay between the island and the shore. From taking soundings of the water's depth they were assured that the *Mayflower* could anchor here. Then they went ashore. The sandy beach was receiving footprints that would be stamped on the mythology of the United States, and it was fitting that Stephen Hopkins—who had survived shipwreck at Bermuda and the struggles of settlement at Jamestown—was alongside the more famous leaders of the colonists when this momentous event occurred. For this was to be the location of New Plymouth. After weeks of wintry wandering, they had finally crossed the "Jordan River" and reached their Promised Land. Well, that was how William Bradford later remembered and memorialized it. And Stephen Hopkins, though a Stranger, now had his life intimately intertwined with those of his godly companions.

It will be noticed that at no point has there been any mention of Plymouth Rock or of "stepping ashore" onto it. The explanation for the omission of this almost mythic piece of real estate will have to wait until another of our Mayflower Lives, that of Mary Chilton. Then all will be revealed!

The site of New Plymouth was not perfect. It lacked the major river and close-in anchorage that would later be the foundation for Boston's success and the development of the Massachusetts Bay Colony a little to the north. They had not made it to that navigable river remembered by Robert Coppin. Plymouth Bay lacked a large river that would provide a water highway into the country beyond, and ships of the draft of *Mayflower* would still have to sit some way off shore and rely on boats to ferry to and fro. However, it had its advantages. It was sheltered. It had numerous streams of fresh water running down to the sea. The land had been broken in by former inhabitants and had the remains of corn crops, which would reduce the labor needed to farm there. And there was no sign of recent native activity. Whoever it was who had cleared the land, they had since vanished. It seemed, to the newcomers, that God had cleared the Pilgrim's title to the place.

On Tuesday, December 12, they returned to the *Mayflower* with the good news. It was then that William Bradford discovered that Dorothy, his wife, had fallen from the *Mayflower* and drowned. The sweetness of finding a home had turned to the bitter gall of tragic loss. But for Stephen Hopkins, his family was safe and well, though others were dying around them, for the killing time of that winter of 1620–21 was about to descend upon the exhausted Pilgrims.

On Friday, December 15, the *Mayflower* upped anchor and headed for the chosen settlement place. Contrary winds meant that it did not enter Plymouth Harbor until Saturday, December 16. Here it anchored at the end of another sandy spit, now called Long Beach. It had finally found an anchorage at a place where its passengers could call home.

Stephen Hopkins in New Plymouth

Stephen Hopkins's adventures were not over, and he will feature again in the Mayflower Lives of others we have yet to meet. After the sea birth of Oceanus, Stephen and Elizabeth had a further five children while living at New Plymouth. Elizabeth died sometime around 1639 and was buried in her new hometown in the New World.

In Plymouth, Stephen Hopkins proved very useful to the other colonists as a direct result of his knowledge of the hunting skills, culture, and lifestyles of Native Americans, which he had gained through his time spent in Jamestown. As we shall very shortly see, when an English-speaking Native American, named Samoset, first came into Plymouth, he spent the night in the home of Stephen Hopkins. The others felt that Stephen understood and could relate to such a man, who was an exotic alien to all the other colonists. Stephen might also have had some basic grasp of the Algonquian language. For the same reason, the first formal meeting with the local peoples took place in Stephen's home; he accompanied other senior Pilgrims when they visited Massasoit, the *sachem*, or overall leader, of the Wampanoag confederacy. [22]

All of this meant he became something of a senior figure at Plymouth. He served as an assistant to the colony's governor in 1636, and he volunteered for action in the Pequot War of 1636–38, although he did not actually fight.

However, Stephen remained something of a Stranger among the Saints. He established a tavern (an establishment described at the time as "an ordinary")[23] and ran into trouble with the authorities on several occasions as a consequence. In 1636 he seriously wounded a man named John Tisdale in a fight. Then, in 1637, he was fined for permitting drinking and also shuffleboard playing in his tavern on the Sabbath. Within a year of this he was fined for allowing excessive alcohol consumption in his house. That same year (1638) he was fined for selling beer at twice the established price, and then later fined again for the same offense! In 1639 he was fined again for overcharging (this time for a mirror). Clearly, he was a man not above a bit of sharp practice. And he could be a tough employer too. In 1638, his maidservant became pregnant by a man named Arthur Peach (a man who was later executed for the premeditated murder of a Native American). As the maid was the indentured servant of Hopkins, the Plymouth court ruled he was financially liable for the child for the remainder of the maid's indenture (two years). Stephen was having none of it and threw her out. For this he was arrested, but the matter was resolved when another colonist purchased the remaining two years of the indenture and agreed to support the child. It did not reflect well on Stephen. It may be no coincidence that it was two of his servants who fought the first duel in New England in 1621![24] Maybe something of a rough-and-ready man had rubbed off on them.

Stephen died in 1644 and made out a will, asking to be buried near his wife, and naming his surviving children.

The sixt of June 1644 I Stephen Hopkins of Plymouth in New England being weake yet in good and prfect memory blessed be God yet considering the fraile estate of all men I do ordaine and make this to be my last will and testament in manner and forme following and first I do committ my body to the earth from whence it was taken, and my soule to the Lord who gave it, my body to be buryed as neare as convenyently may be to my wyfe Deceased.[25]

From the wreck of the *Sea Venture*, to a negotiator with Native Americans, and then a Plymouth tavern keeper, Stephen Hopkins had certainly lived an eventful life.

5

The Outsider's Story:
Tisquantum (Squanto),
Native American

The Pilgrims lived on the *Mayflower* over the harsh winter of 1620–21 in Plymouth Harbor. During that time they ferried people, tools, and materials to the shore in order to build their first storehouses and accommodations. This took them from December to the end of February, and it was not until March 1621 that they finally completed the movement from ship to shore. In those three months they saw almost no signs of any Native Americans, with the exception of the light from fires they saw burning in the distance. Whoever had once tended the overgrown fields of what they were now calling New Plymouth seemed in no hurry to return. Given the hot reception that their exploratory party had met at First Encounter Beach back in December, this absence was a puzzle. But the apparent absence of local peoples was an illusion, because the Pilgrims were actually being watched closely.

The reality that they did have neighbors was revealed in the middle of February when one of their number was out duck shooting and a party of Native Americans passed close to where he was in hiding. We can only imagine his fear as he lay silent among the tall rushes, holding his musket close while shielding the glowing match that would fire it if required. When they passed, he hurried back to raise the alarm. Other settlers, out working in the woods, got back to the village and took up their weapons. One of these was Myles Standish and a companion; they went to get their weapons, but on returning to where they had been working in the woods, they found that their tools had been stolen. It was unexpected payback for the corn they had looted on first exploring Cape Cod.

Now they knew they were not alone. The tension and fear were palpable. Muskets were cleaned and made ready. The next day two Native Americans appeared on a nearby hill, but they vanished into the trees when Standish and Hopkins (the two with experience of Native Americans) approached them. Everyone in Plymouth was now in a state of high alert, and cannons were prepared to meet any attack.

Then, on Friday, March 16, they received a surprise visit. A Native American walked into their settlement and spoke to them in faltering English. "Welcome Englishmen," he said! The shock could not have been better delivered; not only did they have neighbors but the neighbors also spoke their language. Well, one of them did anyway.

His arrival had a huge impact on the settlers living at Plymouth. A year later, news of it was published in England in a pamphlet penned by Edward Winslow, today called *Mourt's Relation*, which we have come across already. Winslow remembered that Friday as being a warm day. People would have been out and about, grateful for the warming sun after the cold winter that had killed so many of them. Chickens and pigs needed feeding, there was building going on, and there was the ongoing task of clearing the overgrown fields that they had inherited from the former inhabitants of the land overlooking the bay. Then, bold as brass, this stranger appeared. Winslow remembered how he "very boldly came all alone" as he walked straight into the middle of the settlement.[1]

He was named Samoset, although some accounts called him Somerset because his name sounded a little like the name of an English county. He was a *sachem* or *sagamore* (a chieftain) of the Abenaki tribe, and he originally hailed from Maine, where he had picked up some English from the fishermen who came ashore at Monhegan Island (now in Lincoln County, Maine) for water and trade. His appearance reminds us that English-speaking visitors had been occasionally landing on the coast of what would soon be called New England for about a century. And it was not just their language that they left behind, as we shall soon see.

As he casually chatted to the colonists, he explained that he had lived for about eight months in their area, and he told them the names of the local leaders of the nearby tribes and the numbers of their warriors.

While he was talking, the wind picked up. It got a bit cold, but this seemed to not even be noticed by their new friend, although the Pilgrims felt it enough to offer the man a coat. Winslow noted how he wore hardly any clothes. The details in Winslow's recollections transport us back to that mid-March day, with the sun shining, but inclined to be a little cool when the sea breeze picked up. And to a conversation between the newcomers and a Native American that was conducted in English, making the whole thing seem rather surreal.

Looking back, Edward recalled how the newcomer was tall and upright, with long black hair but clean shaven. He carried a bow and just a couple of arrows. Winslow goes on to say that, furthermore,

> He asked for some beer, but we gave him strong water [liquor] and biscuit, and butter, and cheese, and pudding, and a piece of mallard [duck], *all which he liked well, and had been acquainted with such amongst the English.*[2]

It was then that they discovered that language and a taste for alcohol were not the only legacies of the visiting English fishermen. It transpired that the place they had named New Plymouth had already had a name: Patuxet. And it had once had inhabitants, which explained the cleared land and the overgrown fields. But an epidemic had killed them all four years earlier. This explained the total absence of native people in the area. It also meant, said Samoset, that there was nobody left who could contest the Pilgrims' title to the land on which they had settled.

They talked all afternoon. Since the man seemed in no hurry to leave, they lodged him with Stephen Hopkins and his family. Stephen, as we have seen, had experience of meetings with Native Americans from his days at Jamestown and was clearly the right man to host the newcomer. But Elizabeth Hopkins and the children had no such experience and must have been intrigued by their strange guest. One can imagine the older children hiding behind their mother's skirt and peering around her at the half-naked man with bow and arrows who was lodging with them. Winslow tellingly says that there they "watched him," which suggests that, for all the shared liquor, duck meat, and friendly conversation, they were wary of the man.

On Saturday morning he left them, but not before he had explained that their closest neighbors were the people of a tribe he named as the Massasoits. There only seemed to be about sixty members of this tribe, although a larger tribe—the Nauset—lived on Cape Cod. This was the tribe that they had met on First Encounter Beach back in December. Samoset then shared information that explained the showers of arrows that had greeted the explorers on that cold December morning. The Nauset hated Europeans; less than a year earlier (eight months, according to Samoset) they had killed three who had landed on the coast. Clearly, the Pilgrims had gotten off lightly. The reason for this animosity lay in the bitter experiences they had of Europeans enticing members of the tribe on board ship for trade and then kidnapping them, to sell them as slaves. In this way the Nauset had lost twenty of their people to treacherous Europeans in the past. That clearly explained the hot reception on the cold winter morning at First Encounter Beach.

Before he left, Samoset expressed admiration for the tools used by the colonists, and then he was gone. But not before his new friends impressed on him that they were cut from different cloth to the slavers who had earlier poisoned relationships with their cruelty:

We dismissed the savage, and gave him a knife, a bracelet, and a ring; he promised within a night or two to come again, and to bring with him some of the Massasoits, our neighbors, with such beavers' skins as they had to truck [trade] *with them.* [3]

Things had taken a remarkable turn. The Pilgrims had hoped to make contact with local people in order to trade but had failed. Now, however, the locals had made contact with them, and in a friendly fashion too. In addition, Samoset offered to bring in beaver skins. To the settlers, conscious of their debts to the Adventurers in London and their need to turn a profit, this was very welcome news indeed. Things were looking up.

Enter: Tisquantum

A couple of days later he returned, but with just a few beaver skins and five companions. They ate a lot of the Pilgrims' food, which was a bit alarming, as they did not have much to spare. Three days later he appeared again, but they turned him away. If they were going to give up their limited supplies, it was going to have to be in return for a quantity of trade goods, not just whenever Samoset was hungry.

This seems to have worked, as on Thursday, March 22, at about 1:00 P.M., Samoset returned in the company of another Native American, who was destined to play an important part in the developing relationship between the Pilgrims and the local tribes. This was Tisquantum, whose name is often abbreviated to Squanto. He could speak better English than Samoset. The two were carrying furs and dried herrings for trade.

More significantly they had brought a leading local figure known as Ousamequin, who was the *sachem* of the Algonquian-speaking people called the Pokanoket, and the *massasoit* (great sachem) of the Wampanoag confederacy. His ascendancy was based on his overlordship over seven lesser Wampanoag *sachems*. Today we usually refer to him as Massasoit, in the same conflation of tribal name/title and personal name that causes us to refer to the father of Pocahontas as Powhatan (another tribal name). This is not totally unjustified, since Edward Winslow tells us that Samoset referred to the local people as if Massasoit was their group name, although it was more the title of their leader. Perhaps this crossover identification was part of a fluid terminology at the time, or maybe Winslow just misunderstood something. Either way, we now know him as Massasoit, so that is the "name" we shall now use, to avoid any confusion.

The *sachem* Massasoit, his brother, who was named Quadequina, and a group of their warriors were close behind Samoset and Tisquantum. About an hour later the *sachem* and some sixty of his warriors appeared on a nearby hill. But who should make the first move beyond that? The Pilgrims were reluctant to send their governor, John Carver, out to them, and Massasoit was unwilling to come among the strangers. After all, the Europeans did not have a great track record when it came to trust. Finally, Edward Winslow went, and it was an historic meeting. Negotiations were possible because the Pilgrims now had two English-speaking Native Americans to work through.

In order to get discussions off to a good start, Winslow took over knives and jewelry for Massasoit and his brother, along with liquor, biscuits, and butter. He delivered a speech offering Massasoit the love and friendship of King James of England (which would have come as a surprise to the monarch back in London) and expressing desire for a peace treaty. That seemed to go down well, even if Winslow was not tremendously impressed by the interpreters' work. Massasoit was keen to trade for Winslow's armor and sword, but Winslow was not prepared to do so. Despite this, sufficient progress was made for Massasoit to agree to come down into the settlement while Winslow remained behind as a hostage. Captain Myles Standish and William Brewster met the *sachem* at the stream that flowed between the two parties, accompanied by six men armed with muskets. It was an historic meeting, and we have a vivid depiction of the man who was then escorted to the negotiations that took place in a part-built house:

a very lusty [strong] *man, in his best years, an able body, grave
of countenance, and spare of speech. In his attire little or nothing
differing from the rest of his followers, only in a great chain of
white bone beads about his neck, and at it behind his neck hangs a
little bag of tobacco, which he drank and gave us to drink; his face
was painted with a sad* [deep] *red like murray* [mulberry], *and
oiled both head and face, that he looked greasily. All his followers
likewise, were in their faces, in part or in whole painted, some
black, some red, some yellow, and some white, some with crosses
and other antick* [antique] *works; some had skins on them, and
some naked, all strong, tall . . .*[4]

It was impressive, to put it mildly, and Governor Carver made his
own addition to the drama of the occasion by advancing to the meeting
accompanied by the sound of drum and trumpet and with an honor
guard of musketeers.

Then they got down to business. Alcohol was shared and toasts
drunk. That Massasoit was unused to strong liquor is revealed by the
telling little detail that it made him sweat. His companions were also
impressed by the trumpet, which they took turns in blowing. The Pilgrims used the opportunity of the visit to negotiate a peace treaty and
also to establish a trading relationship with the local people.

This treaty would influence relations with the Wampanoag confederacy for a generation and would not be broken until 1675, at the start
of King Philip's War. By the treaty, Massasoit promised to do no harm
to the Pilgrims and agreed to hand over any who did; they promised
that if either side took the tools of the other, they were to return them;
they would aid each other if attacked by others; other tribes would be
warned off from harming the Pilgrims; weapons would be left behind
when meetings were arranged. We can see why the Pilgrims needed the
treaty. But why was Massasoit so keen to establish friendly relations?
Clearly, the acquisition of trade goods was appealing, but the pressing
reason was more serious. He hoped that the newcomers might protect
him against his enemies, the Narragansett tribe. There was mutual
protection as a motivation for both sides. It was an impressive start to

relationships with the Native Americans. Only time would tell if it would continue that way.

What had occurred had also transformed the original attitude of Massasoit towards the new arrivals. According to William Bradford's nephew, Nathaniel Morton, when Massasoit had first became aware of the newcomers, he had commanded his *pow-wows* (medicine men) to curse them. This they had done for three successive days in a swamp-land meeting place. It was only when this had failed to dislodge the English that Massasoit had turned to diplomacy and sent in Samoset and then Squanto.

We will meet Massasoit again in the Mayflower Life of Edward Winslow, but now we need to turn our attention back to Tisquantum. William Bradford nicknamed him Squanto, while Edward Winslow generally referred to him by what historians believe is his proper name, Tisquantum.[5] However, it is by the simpler name that we will refer to him, as it seems it was intended to be used with some affection. But there is one very obvious question that needs to be answered: How did a Native American gain such a grasp of English? For it is clear that his grasp of the language exceeded that of Samoset's. The truth of how he gained the ability to act as translator is stranger than fiction.

The strange history of Tisquantum/Squanto

Squanto was the last survivor of the tribe of the Patuxet, who had once farmed the coastal land west of Cape Cod Bay. According to a comment later made by Squanto, the Patuxet once numbered some two thousand men, women, and children. They spoke a dialect of what we now call Eastern Algonquian, which was spoken by all the peoples living between the Plymouth area and Narragansett Bay to the west. At some time in the past it seems that the Patuxet had been brought into the orbit of the Pokanokets, over whom Massasoit was the chief. This group of native peoples we now remember as the Wampanoag confederacy, although the name was not actually used until the 1680s. Like many of the peoples of the East Coast, they had split the year between winter in the forested areas of the interior and summer at the cornfields on the coast, where they also fished. Edward Winslow wrote of how Squanto was skillful at catching fat, sweet-tasting eels with his feet. Like the other tribes in the area, they would have been ruled over by a *sachem* (usually male but it could be a woman) who might have lesser *sachems* below them and higher ones acting as their overlords. Massasoit was just such an overlord. The English referred to him as a "king." It was due to his authority that Massasoit could order Squanto to go and live among the Pilgrims.

Among the Pokanokets and others in the Wampanoag confederacy, in addition to the *sachems* (who were sometimes referred to as *saga-mores*), there were warriors called *pnieses*, who collected tribute for the *sachems* and who were renowned as elite, hardened fighters. Another Native American, named Hobbomock—who was also to live among the Pilgrims—might have been a *pniese*. In addition, there were leaders known as *pau waus* (the English called them *pow-wows*) who were believed to be able to mediate between ordinary people and the native god of healing (known as Abbomocho).

It is now hard to work out exactly what the status of Squanto was, but we can piece together how he came to know English so well and also how he came to be the only survivor of his once populous tribe.

According to some historians, Squanto was first captured as a young boy way back in 1605, by an Englishman named Captain George Weymouth. Weymouth was investigating the coastal lands of Maine and Massachusetts for a wealthy patron named Sir Ferdinando Gorges, who himself never actually made it to North America but who was promoting the setting up of colonies there. However, Maine was not Squanto's home (as revealed by other evidence), and his name does not appear among those stated as taken then, in an account written by one of the Englishmen involved. In fact, it would be some fifty years, until 1658, before Gorges wrote a pamphlet, entitled *A Brief Narration of the Original Undertakings of the Advancement of Plantations into the Parts of America*, where he mentioned Captain Weymouth kidnapping a Native American named Tisquantum from the coast of Maine in 1605. By this time, the fame of Squanto seems to have caused him to be annexed to the story; a literary kidnapping to mirror the actual one. The actual event that caused Squanto to be able to speak English almost certainly occurred about ten years later.

In the year 1614 an English expedition, consisting of two ships under Captain John Smith of Jamestown fame, sailed into Massachusetts Bay and also explored as far north as Maine. They were collecting fish and furs and mapping the area around Cape Cod. Smith had an interest in eventually founding a colony in New England. Engaging local tribes in trade would facilitate that and perhaps avoid something of the conflict that was brewing at Jamestown (albeit prompted by Smith's own heavy-handed treatment of indigenous peoples). Smith eventually returned to England and left an associate named Thomas Hunt to continue the exploration in a second ship. Hunt's job was to continue fishing and then transport the catch to Málaga, in Spain, where there was a high demand for dried fish.

However, Hunt was an entrepreneur of an antisocial kind and decided to add to the value of the voyage with some human cargo. It was this that brought him to what would later be known as Plymouth Harbor in order to "trade" with the Patuxet. Having recently gotten wise to the valuable trade goods that could be had in exchange for furs, Native Americans were only too keen to trade with Hunt. This fur trade, first started by Newfoundland fishermen and then developed by French and English merchants, had destabilized the traditional trading networks of the tribes on the northeastern coast of North America. Now, instead of varied local products, one item dominated everything: animal pelts, and especially beaver fur. The Patuxet were finally plugging into the network. It was a decision they came to regret.[6] As a result of their desire to trade, Hunt was able to lure about twenty of the Patuxets, including the man we would come to know as Squanto, aboard his vessel. Once on board they were kidnapped. Then the duplicitous Hunt sailed across Cape Cod Bay and stole seven more people from among the Nauset. He then sailed to Málaga with his wretched cargo of stolen human beings. This act explains the hostility of the Nauset tribe to the Pilgrims, which is remembered today as the First Encounter.

Echoes of this human trafficking later united the three threads of the Nausets, the Pilgrims, and Squanto, since he later translated during a meeting between the Pilgrims and the Nauset on Cape Cod. There the English met an old woman, whom they thought was at least one hundred years of age, who could not look at the visitors "without breaking forth into great passion, weeping and crying excessively." Hunt had taken her three boys, and, as a consequence of his slaving, "she was deprived of the comfort of her children in her old age."[7] This meeting took place at what was then called Cummaquid, but now Barnstable, Massachusetts, on the southern shore of Cape Cod Bay. They were fed by the local *sachem*, who was less than twenty-six years old and—in the rather patronizing tones frequently used by the settlers, even of those Native Americans they liked—"very personable, gentle courteous . . . indeed not like a *savage*, save for his attire."[8] Incidentally, the Pilgrims and their translators were seeking a boy from the colony who had gotten lost in the woods. The fact that they were received in a friendly fashion and that the boy was soon returned by the Nausets, safe and sound, shows how much things had improved since the terrible damage done to relationships by the earlier actions of Hunt.

When he finally heard of Hunt's actions, John Smith disapproved and later commented that Hunt had acted

> *most dishonestly, and inhumanely, for their kind usage of me and all our men, carried them with him to Málaga, and there for a little private gain sold those silly savages for rials of eight* [Spanish coins].[9]

There is a later tradition that Spanish friars, looking to spread the Christian faith, rescued Squanto from this captivity and converted him to Roman Catholic Christianity, but the evidence for this is thin. We do not know how long Squanto lived in Spain, what he did there, or how he made it to England. However, from what he told the Pilgrims, we know that he eventually ended up living in the district of Cornhill in the City of London. He lived there with one Master John Slanie, who was one of the Merchant Adventurers hoping to make a profit from colonizing North America and who earlier had invested money in the East India Company. By the time Squanto arrived, Slanie was heavily involved in funding English settlements in Newfoundland, an area famed for its abundant sea fish stocks. So, there is a possibility that this may explain how Squanto got from Málaga to London. Slanie was, no doubt, on the lookout for natives who could provide translation assistance, and he might have been the one responsible for getting Squanto from Spain to London. So it was that a native of the Patuxet village by the sea ended up in the busy, noisy, and smelly city of London, by way of Málaga in Spain. It reads like a novel, but it really happened. What he made of the place is anyone's guess. We would like to know, but his thoughts are lost to us.

The reality of this trade in human beings can be witnessed in the same Shakespearean play we came across with regard to Stephen Hopkins. This provides evidence that by 1611, the sight of Native Americans on public display in England was sufficiently commonplace to cause Shakespeare to make a joke of it in *The Tempest* (act 2, scene 2, lines 31–33). The Londoners, he says, are so entertained by the sight of the exotic and so hardened to human suffering that

> *when they will not give a doit* [small Dutch coin] *to relieve a lame beggar, they will lay out ten to see a dead Indian.*[10]

This is not a happy insight into the attitudes to be found among many in 17th-century London, but it is all too believable. And it was among them that Squanto now found himself. There on Cornhill he lived on one of the three low hills that dominated the ancient City of London, the others being Tower Hill, where the Tower of London is sited, and Ludgate Hill, where St Paul's Cathedral stands. In Charles Dickens's story *A Christmas Carol*, Bob Cratchit, the underpaid clerk of Ebenezer Scrooge, slides down Cornhill twenty times in celebration of Christmas Eve. But all that lay far in the future when Squanto lived there. When he went out the door it was just a short walk to the bustling markets of The Poultry or the merchants parading down Lombard Street. As a member of the household of a leading Londoner he would have been expected to attend church with his master's household and so would have been an exotic sight at either St Michael, Cornhill, or St Peter upon Cornhill. It was all a long way from the lobster and eel fishing of Cape Cod Bay, the cleared fields of corn, catching migrating wildfowl in the fall, and deer hunting in the winter woods. Did Squanto dream of returning to that lost world? It is reasonable to think that he did. And he was shrewd enough to know that if that ever was to occur, then making himself useful to a London businessman who had a financial interest in North America might make the dream a reality. For if Master John Slanie was intent on using Squanto, then Squanto might also have hoped to use his master's curiosity in order to get home. In this way, the stolen Native American was not quite as powerless as his predicament indicated. When Slanie sat beside his evening fireside and quizzed his servant Squanto about the furs, woods, fisheries, and peoples of New England, the familiar landscape formed once again in Squanto's mind and memories peopled it with those he knew and loved, and once had thought lost forever. For what had seemed utterly stolen as he'd cowered in the fetid hold of Hunt's ship now appeared graspable again as he answered the questions of the London merchant. Home might yet be attainable if he was patient and if he was useful.

However, while Squanto was away in Spain and then in England, a disaster occurred among the Patuxet. A killer epidemic devastated the southern part of New England. Today nobody is entirely sure which disease or combination of diseases struck, but we may be absolutely sure that it was an unintended consequence of European explora-tion. The Native Americans were collateral damage in the European trading obsession with fur and also with whale oil and cod. English explorers observed the horrors at the time without understanding what had caused them. In Maine, one of Ferdinando Gorges's employees, named Richard Vines, spent the winters of 1616 and 1617 there among the native peoples, but he and his companions seemed immune to the crippling headaches that accompanied an illness that left the country-side "void of inhabitants." A man named Thomas Dermer—also in the employ of Gorges—sailed down the New England coast in 1619, towards the colony in Virginia, having sent a shipment of furs and fish back to London. In an account of what he found there, he recorded seeing "the sores of some that had escaped, who described the spots of such as usually die." In 1692 one who had conversations with some very old native people concluded that from their memories of the events of their distant childhood, "the bodies all over were exceedingly yellow."[11] Headaches, sores, jaundice, fever, and bleeding from the nose were all described by those who witnessed the horrors. Yellow fever, smallpox, bubonic plague have all been suggested as possible causes.[12] At present, we can only guess.

The coastal devastation stretched from the Kennebec, in the north, to southwest of Cape Cod. The tribes who lived in the vicinity of what would one day be New Plymouth—the Pennacook, Massachusett, and Pokanoket—suffered very badly indeed. That the disease did not impact on the Narragansetts, to the west of the Pokanokets, was probably because the former traded with the Dutch, whereas the latter and those to their northeast traded with the French, who were probably the ones who inadvertently introduced the contagion. No wonder, as we shall shortly see, that Massasoit of the Pokanoket was so eager to do a deal with the Pilgrims, having seen his people crushed by disease and now reduced to living in the shadow of his traditional enemies, the Narragansetts.

When Edward Winslow later made his first journey inland to the village of the Pokanoket, he saw the appalling evidence left behind by the disease:

> *Thousands of men have lived there, which died in a great plague not long since; and pity it was and is to see so many goodly fields, and so well seated, without men to dress and manure the same.*[13]

Not many years later, in 1625, Thomas Morton walked the forests around Boston Harbor and saw how

> *in a place where many inhabited, there hath been but one left a live, to tell what became of the rest, the livinge being (as it seemes) not able to bury the dead, they were left for Crowes,*

Kites, and vermin to prey upon. And the bones and skulls upon
the severall places of their habitations, made such a spectacle
after my comming into those partes, that, as I travailed in that
Forrest nere the Massachusetts, it seemed to mee a new-found
Golgotha. [14]

Later 17th-century traditions would claim that the cause was the enslavement of French traders who brought the diseases into the Native American settlements to which they were taken. The Puritans who later recounted the tradition claimed that this demonstrated the actions of God against the heathens who had seized the Frenchmen. In 1702, the Puritan preacher Cotton Mather considered the epidemic—which he reported took away nineteen out of every twenty Native Americans—to be the divine means by which "the woods were almost cleared of those pernicious creatures, to make room for a better growth." [15] It was not a kind assessment of the suffering experienced by fellow human beings, but, sadly, it was par for the course among many of the settlers in New England.

Return to North America

William Bradford's journal, *Of Plymouth Plantation*, corroborates the version now accepted by most historians, that after Spain and London, Squanto was taken to Newfoundland, in 1617. He worked there for the governor of the Newfoundland Colony, before being taken back to England, in about 1618, in order to act as an interpreter for Captain Thomas Dermer, an employee of Gorges, who was tasked with further exploration of the coast of New England in order to exploit the resources of beaver fur. The employment of Squanto offered the possibility of reestablishing constructive relations with the tribes there, which had been so badly damaged by Hunt's kidnapping exploits.

In 1619, Gorges sent Squanto with Dermer on a trip to New England to trade with local Native Americans. We have already heard Dermer's account of the impact of disease, but now Squanto was about to discover how that disease had had an impact on his own plans to get home to his people. For, as Dermer and Squanto sailed along the New England coast towards Squanto's village, Dermer recorded his findings in his journal:

> [We] *passed along the coast where* [we] *found some ancient* [Indian] *plantations, not long since populous now utterly void, in other places a remnant remains, but not free of sickness . . . When* [we] *arrived at my savage's native country* [we found] *all dead.*[16]

What a homecoming after such a terrible adventure. Looking around him at the skeletal scenes of devastation, Squanto must have wondered which was worse: to have been enslaved for all those years but to have been spared the pestilence? Or to have remained at home and so to have died with all his family and friends? It was a bitter homecoming indeed. It would soon transpire that Squanto was the last of the Patuxet.

While Squanto left Dermer in an effort to track down any survivors from his village (he failed to do so), Dermer had three run-ins with Native Americans who clearly distrusted his intentions. And he lacked his native guide to persuade them otherwise. He was finally taken prisoner by the Nauset in the vicinity of Cape Cod, only to be released as a result of Squanto's intervention. But things continued to go badly for him. On Martha's Vineyard he was again attacked by a local *sachem* named Epenow, who himself had once been kidnapped by the English and exhibited in London before being brought back to North America in the hope that he would lead his English captors to sources of gold. However, he had escaped. And it was now payback time. Most of the English crew were killed, and Dermer was seriously wounded, although he escaped and later died at Jamestown.

In the meantime, Squanto had been taken in by the tribe of the Pokanokets. It is unclear to what extent he was a free man who had been admitted to the tribe, or a man distrusted by his fellow Native Americans and a virtual captive due to his suspiciously close associations with the English. But in one capacity or the other, this is where he was in the fall of 1620 when the *Mayflower* Pilgrims arrived at Cape Cod. So it was that in March 1621, Massasoit, of the Pokanokets, and the leader of the Wampanoag confederacy, put Squanto's English language skills to the test with the newcomers who had set up home among the abandoned fields of the Patuxets, Squanto's former tribe.

Whether a free agent among the Wampanoags or a virtual prisoner up to this point, Squanto was now allowed to have free access to the Pilgrims so that he could act as a guide and interpreter for the colony. In fact, he lived in the colony for almost two years after his initial meetings with the Pilgrims. He was soon regarded as an integral member of the Plymouth Colony, engaged in both translating and negotiating between Plymouth's early governors (John Carver, then William Bradford) and local tribal leaders. All in all, things seemed better because of his involvement: peace was made with the Nausets and with other groups within the Wampanoag confederacy. As a guide, he took settler ambassadors through unfamiliar territory and helped them establish trading relations with their Native American neighbors. This played a vital role in linking them into the highly profitable fur trade. It was on such a foray in August and September 1621—to what we would now call the southern shore of Boston Harbor—that they gained considerable numbers of furs from the Massachusett people and ascertained that disease now prevented this tribe from posing any threat to the colony at Plymouth. Squanto recommended taking the pelts by force from those he considered "a bad people," but in this instance, the English were more diplomatic than their translator and traded fairly with the depleted Massachusetts. Incidentally, some of the colonists also looked enviously at the deep water anchorage and concluded they had settled in the wrong place! But that is another story.

Squanto is also recorded as giving the Pilgrims practical advice on survival in New England. This included instructions on how to plant Indian corn and other local plants and how to fertilize the seed by planting it with a dead fish. It is an image that appears in school textbooks and is now woven into the mythology of Plymouth Colony. The English clearly believed that this practice of fertilizing with fish was a local tradition, although some historians have suggested that Squanto learned it in Europe or Newfoundland. With his assistance, the Pilgrims grew enough food to survive the winter of 1621–22, and they invited Massasoit, along with ninety of his tribe, including Squanto, to the first Thanksgiving feast in the fall of 1621, following a successful harvest that saw them stocked up for the coming winter. If the tradition about the Catholic friars being responsible for Squanto's conversion is true, then it was a Roman Catholic who helped make possible the Puritans' Thanksgiving.[17] Though how far Squanto understood the rivalries between Protestants and Catholics, and the fact that he had signed up to one side or the other in the quarrel, is rather open to question.

Looking back, William Bradford referred to Squanto as "a special instrument sent of God for their good beyond their expectation."[18] They even launched a rescue mission, led by Myles Standish, to rescue him when his life was in danger because a jealous tribal rival named Corbitant (a *sachem* formerly subservient to Massasoit) held him prisoner and might even have been intent on overthrowing Massasoit, the ally of the Plymouth colonists.

However, life can be very complex, and in time, Squanto gained a reputation for being manipulative and self-serving. Rumors reached the Pilgrims, via another of Massasoit's people who lived at Plymouth, that all was not as it seemed with regard to Squanto. The informant was Hobbomock, whom we referred to a little earlier. Both Edward Winslow and William Bradford record their mounting concerns at what they heard about Squanto's secret strategies. The accusation was that over the winter of 1621–22, Squanto had been claiming that he alone could decide if the English were inclined towards peace or war and that only if he was rewarded by other Native Americans would he protect them from the newcomers. It seems that he hoped to gain power as a native leader; he might also have been motivated by a desire for revenge against Massasoit and others among the Wampanoags for holding him prisoner in the past. He was very aware that the local tribes feared both the guns of the settlers and the diseases that struck in the wake of the newcomers. Seeing how the settlers stored their gunpowder underground, he came up with the ingenious claim that this was, in fact, where they stored their stock of diseases, and unless he was rewarded, he would get the English to release the plague against his enemies.

In March 1622, Squanto went a step too far. He began spreading a rumor that Massasoit was conspiring with both the Narragansetts and the Massachusetts to wipe out Plymouth Colony. The end game for Squanto was clear: out of the ruins of Massasoit's power, he hoped to elevate himself to become the key player in the inter-ethnic politics of the bay area. But he was found out when the colonists investigated the matter. And Massasoit was, understandably, beside himself with anger. He invoked the March 1621 treaty of mutual assistance and demanded Squanto's life. He was not too concerned how this was achieved, for while he preferred it if the traitor was handed over to him, he told Bradford that it was acceptable if the colonists did the job and simply sent him the head and hands of the slippery Patuxet survivor!

William Bradford was reluctantly close to turning Squanto over for execution, when a ship appeared. In the resulting alarm over whether it was "friend" (English) or "foe" (French), the matter of Squanto was put to one side. It turned out that it was the shallop of a ship called the *Sparrow* that was bringing the advance party of a new (and it transpired, poorly equipped) group of settlers to start a second colony at nearby Wessagusset (in present-day Weymouth, Massachusetts). That venture turned out very badly indeed, and we will hear more of them under the Mayflower Life of Myles Standish. What is relevant here is that the disturbance caused by its unexpected arrival got Squanto off the hook—or in this case, the "knife" sent by Massasoit. Besides which, Squanto was needed more than ever as a translator in order to settle the new arrivals through negotiations with nearby *sachems*. Massasoit was angry, but he accepted the inevitable and was reconciled with Plymouth when—in March 1623—Edward Winslow visited him and tended him during a serious illness.

Despite Squanto's duplicity, the alliance with the Wampanoag confederacy had survived this rocky patch. The Wampanoags and the English of Plymouth Colony maintained a friendship until Massasoit's death in about 1660. It was an alliance that Squanto had helped establish, even if later he almost ruined it. Only in the next generation would it fall apart in bloody warfare.

As for Squanto, as Edward Winslow later recollected, there was now no future for him (or assurance of safety) outside the boundaries of Plymouth. He was shunned by all of the Wampanoags and totally dependent on the Pilgrims, to whom he continued to offer service as a translator, if a chastened one.

In November 1622, with the arrival of yet more English settlers who were badly prepared for the oncoming New England winter, food was again an issue in the colony. So, Squanto guided an expedition led by William Bradford, to trade with Cape Cod communities for additional supplies of corn and beans. They traveled south on the ocean side of Cape Cod and sailed into Manamoyick Bay (now Pleasant Bay, Cape Cod) because bad weather was approaching. It was to be his last mission for the Pilgrims, for he soon fell ill, with what William Bradford described as an "Indian fever," suffering from bleeding from the nose. He informed Bradford that this was a sure sign of death among his people. He asked Bradford to pray for him so that he could go to the Englishman's God in Heaven, so it seems that his days among the Christian godly (perhaps also the Spanish friars too?) had impacted on his outlook and beliefs. Then he asked Bradford to distribute various items as gifts to his English friends back home in Plymouth. He died within just a few days. Tisquantum, known affectionately to the Pilgrims as Squanto, was buried in an unmarked grave, in an unknown location. He passed from history into legend.

What was his legacy? In the mythology of Plymouth Colony he is remembered as the one who brokered peace with the Wampanoags and helped the colonists grow crops in an alien land. As such, he plays a key part in explaining how the Pilgrims survived their first, critical year. On the other hand, his attempts to manipulate the relationship between the Pilgrims and the Wampanoags came close to undermining the peace between them.[19] This leaves a rather sour taste in the mouth and means that his legacy is mixed. But what might Squanto have said if he had been given free voice instead of forever having his words "spoken" by others? Perhaps it might have been something like this:

> *I was stolen from my people and my land. The same people that stole me then stole my people from me by pestilence. They made me utterly powerless and, even when I was finally back among those who spoke the language of my birth, I was regarded as an outsider, an alien, one without a people. This was because all that would have challenged that status had been stolen from me. But I survived. With only myself to rely on, I survived. By my wits I survived. Others I assisted, but knew that there was no one to look out for me. For always I was the last of the Patuxet and alone. And only if you have traveled the road I traveled, could you judge me. . . .*

One of the striking ironies of the life of the interpreter we know as Tisquantum is that all his thoughts have been communicated to us by others. They have become *his* interpreters, and we always have that nagging doubt that something essential about the man has been lost in translation.

6

The Teenager's Story:
Mary Chilton, Reputedly the
First to Step onto Plymouth Rock

One of the most visually striking and enduring images of the arrival of the *Mayflower* Pilgrims in the New World is that of their arrival at Plymouth Rock. After two months at sea and another month anchored just within the curving arc of Cape Cod, in Provincetown Harbor, they finally trod on ground that would become home. The seemingly endless months on the dark, dank, cold ship were finally over. The searching for a settlement site was in the past. And the stepping ashore at Plymouth signalled that event in a simple but profound fashion. It was "one small step for man . . ."—three centuries before those words dramatically summed up the huge adventure that led to the first human footsteps on the moon. Or rather, it was "one small step for woman," because the honor of that achievement was later accorded to a thirteen-year-old girl. This Mayflower Life is Mary Chilton's story.

The event has been artistically represented many times but perhaps most evocatively by Henry Bacon in 1877. His painting entitled *The Landing of the Pilgrims* now hangs in the Pilgrim Hall Museum, in Plymouth, Massachusetts.[1] Standing in front of that painting, one is suddenly in touch with so much that resonates in the *Mayflower* story. The scene is dominated by a party of people on board one of the ship's boats. This has pushed up against a large chunk of sea-weathered gray rock that juts out from the shore. To one side the land rises up to a low cliff covered with snow and crested by stunted trees whose branches are pushed back by the prevailing winds. This frames the picture on its right. A small, pebble-strewn beach below the rock is bounded by a little low shelf of stone to the left, but the open left-hand side of the painting offers no natural frame to mirror that on the right. It leads one's eye up and into the expanse of the blue-green sea and the *Mayflower* moored out in the bay. Another small craft can be spotted making its way to shore. But what seizes the attention is the group in the first boat. While a man, wearing helmet and neck-protecting armor, steadies the boat with an oar pushed back into the waves, a young woman steps ashore. Another man, armed with a musket, offers his right hand to steady her. The girl steps forward, and one small foot is already lightly placed on the great, gray rock. The eyes of most of those aboard are on her. Her hair is demurely covered by a white-trimmed black coif, and she is dressed simply in brown and off-white. Her Puritan credentials are there for all to see. From her right arm hangs a bundle of possessions; we assume this is all she owns. In the boat, others prepare to follow her ashore. We note two other helmeted men, one armed with another musket. A woman, similarly demurely dressed, holds a bundled-up, wide-eyed child. A young man reaches out to hold the rock in preparation for following the young girl ashore. Soon, we think, all will be ashore on that pebble-strewn beach.

On reflection, Mary looks a bit big for a thirteen-year-old. And is the baby meant to be little Oceanus Hopkins? If so, he also looks a little older than we might expect for a baby born just a couple of months previous to this event. But these are small criticisms. What matters is the drama of the painting, and this it delivers with arresting simplicity.

This is exactly what we expect from the legend of the landing on Plymouth Rock in December 1620.

This was not the end of Mary's importance, for she survived the "general sickness," or the "common infection" as the Pilgrims later recalled it, of that first winter.[2] She was there as the first buildings at Plymouth were erected and the first crops planted and then harvested; and she was present at the first Thanksgiving meal in the fall of 1621. Through her we can explore the reality behind these iconic— and almost mythical—events and also reflect on what life was like for a young, unmarried woman in such a frontier environment. As if this was not enough to mark her out as worth getting to know, she also made a will in 1676, one of only two female Pilgrims from the *Mayflower* who did so, which gives us an insight into her later life.

However, before we explore more about the famous events so closely associated with Mary Chilton at Plymouth, it would be helpful to learn a little more about the backstory of the girl who is so central to this Mayflower Life.

Mary Chilton before Plymouth Rock

The surviving evidence reveals the origins of Mary Chilton.[3] She was baptized on May 31, 1607, in the coastal town of Sandwich, Kent, in England. This was the town which later, through its eponymous earl, was to give us a name for food squashed between two slices of bread. The records from Sandwich tell us that she was the daughter of James Chilton, who would later be a *Mayflower* passenger. As to her mother, she is often listed as one "Susannah, possibly Furner" in many modern books and studies, but there is no surviving documentation that allows us to confidently state this. With rather less information attached to her, we find her listed by William Bradford in his journal *Of Plymouth Plantation* as "Mrs. Chilton" or as "James Chilton's wife." It is possible that Bradford, for all his eyewitness credentials, did not actually know her first name.

What is clear, though, is that Mary should certainly be numbered among the Saints on the *Mayflower* and in the colony. For, when she was no more than two years old, charges were laid against her mother before the Archdeaconry Court in Kent as being guilty of having attended the secret burial of a child. This dead child had been buried in secret because the child's family opposed the official burial ceremonies required by the Church of England.[4] In keeping with strict Puritan ideas of what should and should not be done, prayed, and declared, they regarded these as "popish superstitions" and renounced them as having no relevance to their own personal tragedy. This had led to the secret burial, conducted in a way acceptable to the sensibilities of the godly. As a result, there were moves by the Church authorities in England to excommunicate her as a heretical deviant from the established norms of behavior (let alone the law of the land).

As a result, Mary and family joined the movement of religious asylum seekers leaving England in the reign of King James. As with so many of those who would later sail on the *Mayflower,* they ended up in the Netherlands and eventually settled in Leiden. There they joined the Pilgrims' church that had been established under the leadership of the Rev. John Robinson after a move from Amsterdam. However, if Leiden offered some protection from the agents of the English bishops and the English crown, it could not shelter the family from other, and unexpected, local dangers. In 1619, Leiden witnessed religious riots connected with disputes within Dutch Protestant churches over the rival doctrines of Calvinism and Arminianism. Centered on heated disagreements over beliefs connected to predestination and Church government, they did not directly affect the community of Leiden Pilgrims, since they shared the Calvinism of most of their Dutch neighbors. But the unrest did cause trouble for the Chilton family by way of collateral damage. This was because Mary's father and oldest sister got caught up in an anti-Arminian riot, which led to her father being struck on the head with a stone. It was an injury bad enough to force him to get the attention of a surgeon to check out the wound. Mary was just twelve years old when this occurred, and the alarm of seeing her father's head streaming with blood and the white face of her frightened sister must have made a lasting impression on her. It was clear that Leiden was not as safe a place as it had once appeared. More distant horizons beckoned.

So it was that, aged just thirteen, Mary Chilton accompanied her father and mother as they threw in their lot with those from the Leiden congregation of English exiles who had decided to sail for America. For all the problems they faced in the Netherlands, it was not an easy decision, as it meant leaving Mary's older siblings behind. We may assume that the family prayed together and searched the scriptures, with its accounts of God's chosen pilgrim people who had left Egypt for the Promised Land. Together they sought the Lord and, finally, her father and mother reached their momentous decision: they would go. Her father, James Chilton, was sixty-four when the *Mayflower* sailed. As such he was the oldest passenger on the ship.

Given the small world of the exiled community, the decision was perhaps less daunting for Mary. Leiden was not really home; that was provided by the closely bonded little English community. With so many of the Leiden exiles determined to sail in 1620 or to follow on at a later date, the voyage took place in the company of neighbors and friends who were well known as fellow Saints. With such a total transplanting in mind, the change was less traumatic for the teenage girl. Instead, it was an adventure; an exciting mission conducted in the company of those she knew and trusted. Time, though, would soon strip the venture of its romance. First, there was the terrible extended voyage; the boredom, cold, and seasickness would have taken their toll on a young girl's morale. Then, when the longed-for North American coast was finally reached, the relief was made sour by bitter tragedy: Mary's father was one of the first to die in the New World. It happened while the ship was anchored in the cold shelter of Provincetown Harbor. James Chilton died on Friday, December 8.[5] It was the same day, unbeknown to Mary and her mother as they prayed beside the dying man, that the exploratory party was clashing with the Nauset tribe on First Encounter Beach, farther down Cape Cod. James's death was a devastating opening of their life in the New World.

Seven days later, the *Mayflower* left Provincetown Harbor and sailed across the bay towards what would soon become Plymouth. On Saturday, December 16, it anchored in Plymouth Harbor. It was a full week later, to the day, before a working party went ashore to start construction work on the first building. Time spent deciding on the exact settlement spot, followed by two days of storms, had eaten away at the week. But at last they arrived at a place they could call home. Which brings us back to the little matter of Plymouth Rock.

Plymouth Rock revisited

As we have seen, Mary Chilton is traditionally honored as the first woman, indeed the first Pilgrim of either gender, to step ashore at Plymouth Rock. The matter has been well known for generations as a quintessential part of the American national story. Samuel Adams Drake, a 19th-century collector of New England folklore, even memorably remarked that, "No good American would willingly die without having seen Plymouth Rock."[6] He went on to date the event as most likely having occurred on December 22. While conflicting family traditions made the claim variously for John Alden and Mary Chilton, it is clear that Drake rather preferred the case for May Chilton, as it was a picture of her leaping from the boat onto the rock that he chose as an illustration of the event. He then, in typical 19th-century prose, summed up its significance:

> *A young girl in the first bloom of womanhood, the type of a coming maternity, boldly crosses the threshold of a wilderness which her children's children shall possess and inhabit, and transform it into an Eden.*[7]

It is dramatic stuff, and based on a Chilton family tradition, apparently first recorded in the mid-18th century, which claims that the teenager Mary Chilton was the first woman to get ashore at Plymouth. The problem is that there is no historical documentation whatsoever to support this grand and famous tradition. None at all. Furthermore, it is rather odd that the later landing at Boston (in 1630) comes with an identical tradition of a young girl (in that case, Anne Pollard) leaping to be the first ashore.[8] One wonders if both have drawn on some common desire to portray the first arrival as an innocent girl, or whether that at Plymouth was a localized version of the legend from nearby Boston. What is absolutely certain is that nobody at the time reported anything remotely like the claim later made for Mary.

The actual first arrivals at Plymouth were the explorers in the shallop that had set off from the *Mayflower* earlier in December. They landed in Plymouth Harbor on December 11. The group was made up entirely of men, and there is no mention of a rock of any kind. The two earliest sources of evidence regarding the founding of Plymouth Colony are *Mourt's Relation*, probably written principally by Edward Winslow, and *Of Plymouth Plantation*, written by William Bradford. Neither refers to Plymouth Rock or Mary Chilton. The silence is deafening.

In fact, the earliest written reference to any rock at Plymouth dates to the year 1715, when a description of "a great rock" first appears in the records relating to the boundaries of the town.[9] After this, the fame of the rock grew and (consequently) so did that of Mary Chilton, as its myth and hers were intertwined. The first great breakthrough for "the rock" took place in 1741. It was then that its claim to fame as the landing place of the Pilgrims was first made. In that year a plan to build a wharf out from Plymouth beach sparked something that the promoters of the project could never have dreamed of. The problem was that the building would bury a large stone projecting from the beach. The rock was just at the foot of Cole's Hill. This came to the attention of a 95-year-old named Thomas Faunce. He was an elder of the church at Plymouth and lived three miles from the center of town. It was, he declared, that very boulder which had been the landing place of the first Pilgrims. Mindful of the old man's wishes, neighbors carried him the three miles to the beach so that he could bid farewell to the venerable rock.

The story was taken up by a later historian, named James Thacher, in 1835, in his book *History of the Town of Plymouth*. He was told the story by a man who was there as a fifteen-year-old boy and witnessed old Elder Faunce bidding a tearful good-bye to the beloved rock. According to Thacher, "He bedewed it with his tears and bid to it an everlasting adieu." Now, Elder Faunce would have been born in about 1646 or 1647, but he recounted how he had heard of the rock's history from his father. Thacher begins his record of these strange events with the assurance that the rock "has never been a subject of doubtful designation,"[10] which prompts exactly the kind of doubt that Thacher was trying strongly to dispel!

Elder Faunce's father had first arrived in Plymouth Colony on board the ship *Anne* in 1623. This meant that he arrived within three years of the original *Mayflower* landing. He was, therefore, close to being an eyewitness—but not quite. And it had taken a very long time for the great event to be linked to the rock—no less than 121 years, and then via a man who was almost one hundred years old. Plus no reference to it whatsoever was made by Bradford and Winslow, who *were* eyewitnesses, and that is definitely something of a problem. It is little wonder that not everyone today has confidence in Elder Faunce's declaration. Bill Bryson has gone as far as commenting, "The one thing the Pilgrims certainly did not do was step ashore on Plymouth Rock."[11] The jury is out and will remain out on the matter of the rock.

Back in 1741, the wharf that had triggered all the attention was eventually built, but the rock survived. The top of it was left protruding from the ground and became the center of attention for visitors. Shortly afterwards, Mary Chilton's name became associated with it. A rolling stone gathers no myths, but Plymouth Rock was, to start with at least, sitting tight and gathering myths. From that time to this it has grown in fame while reducing in stature, and, as importantly, it has moved a bit.[12] In 1774 some local patriots decided to promote Plymouth Rock as a symbol of liberty, as relations deteriorated with Britain. Oxen were assembled in order to move the boulder from the harbor side to what was called a liberty pole, which had been raised in front of the town's meeting house. However, the move went embarrassingly wrong as the rock was accidentally broken in two during the effort to load it onto the ox cart. The bottom part was left behind on the shore, while the top part was duly shifted to the town square. There the top part stayed until 1834, when it was moved again. This time it went to the front lawn of the Pilgrim Hall Museum. Once again things did not go as planned. The rock fell from the cart, hit the ground, and broke in half. When finally reassembled and put on display, it then fell victim to souvenir hunters, who chipped away at it with hammers.

Down by the sea there still remained the bottom section. In the 1860s a canopy was constructed to go over it. But reduction of the stone accompanied even this attempt to protect it, as it was reduced in size in order to better fit within the monument. A 400-pound (181 kg) piece that was removed at this time was later discovered being used as a doorstep elsewhere in the town. In the 1980s, the Plymouth Antiquarian Society broke the doorstep into three pieces and donated one of them to the Pilgrim Hall Museum. In 1984, they offered another piece to the Smithsonian, who accepted it in 1985. For a piece of highly esteemed Americana, it has been roughly treated over the years, to put it mildly. In the 1880s the top of the rock was removed from the front lawn of Pilgrim Hall and returned to the harborside. There it was reunited with its base. It was then that the date 1620 was carved on the surface. This replaced a painted date that had previously occupied the same space.[13] Finally, in the 1920s, a granite canopy was constructed over the remaining seaside pieces. Visitors to it can read a sign that has been placed there by the Commonwealth of Massachusetts, which resolutely declares that this is "Plymouth Rock: Landing Place of the Pilgrims." Elder Faunce would have been very pleased indeed.

Today the top (the visible) section of Plymouth Rock weighs approximately four tons (3,628 kg). The lower section remains beneath the sand and weighs somewhere in the region of six tons (5,443 kg). Perhaps as little as one third of the original rock now survives in place, with the greatest damage having being done to the top part, which has been so often moved. Over the years this has been hugely reduced, with lots of small pieces vanishing into private ownership; in the 1920s, the local antiquarian society even sold pieces off as paperweights. Today, alongside the piece(s) by the shore, there are larger pieces in the Pilgrim Hall Museum and the political history collection at the Smithsonian's

National Museum of American History, in Washington, D.C. As the French writer Alexis de Tocqueville wrote in 1835,

> *Here is a stone which the feet of a few outcasts pressed for an instant; and the stone becomes famous; it is treasured by a great nation; its very dust is shared as a relic.* [14]

Mary Chilton and life in early Plymouth

Whether or not she stepped onto the famous rock now so revered across the United States, she was certainly in Plymouth that December 1620 and January 1621 as the first rough houses were put up to shelter the passengers from the snow, rain, and wind of a Massachusetts winter.

She watched the men go ashore on the Wednesday of their first week at the new anchorage and must have felt relief that the period of being cooped up on the *Mayflower* was at last coming to an end. The men so chosen stayed ashore that night, ready to commence work the next morning, while Mary, the other women and children, and those men too sick to work remained on the *Mayflower*. Then, on the Thursday morning, the ship began to shift uneasily at its moorings. The wind from the mouth of the bay picked up and lifted the waves against the timbers until the salty spray soaked those on deck. The sailors set an additional anchor, so great was the danger of the ship being driven from its mooring by the rising water. Despite the gale and dangerous seas, the crew braved the storm in the shallop in order to get provisions to those men ashore. As darkness fell the storm continued. Before the day was out another passenger had died. This was a man named Richard Britteridge, and he carried the doubtful honor of being the first to die since the ship had crossed the bay to Plymouth. His death cast a bitter shadow across the relief of finally arriving at the settlement. Although Mary and the others did not yet know it, he would be the first of six who would die before the month was out. It did not bode well.

On Friday, December 22, the storm continued, and so did the dying. It was on this day that Mary Allerton gave birth to a stillborn son. What might have offered a glimpse of hope for the future had been snatched away. However, the next morning dawned cold and calm. Calm enough to allow the work party ashore to cut down trees and haul them to the building site atop what would become known as Cole's Hill, overlooking the salt marsh beside the sea. But still death had not finished with the Pilgrims, as on that day yet another passenger died. This was 24-year-old Solomon Prower, one of the Saints but not of the Leiden congregation, so not known personally to Mary and her family.

That Sabbath they rested, and those on board ship and those sheltering ashore gathered around the familiar words of the psalms and prayed for God's deliverance. Then on Monday, December 25, the building started. Considering the celebration of Christmas Day a piece of unscriptural popish invention, nobody rested that day and there was no celebration. However, what was achieved was the raising of the frame of the first house. And this despite the cries of native peoples from the darkening forest inland, which caused great alarm. That night it rained again, a cold winter rainfall.

By early January the great square "common house" was completed. Roughly thatched and with walls of raw cut timber and wattle, daubed with mud, it offered both a temporary resting place while other houses were constructed and a meeting place for the future. In its smoky interior, with a fire burning on the earth floor, it gave shelter, even if the smoke—reluctant to leave without a proper fireplace and chimney—caused the eyes to smart and water.

On nearby Fort Hill, a higher place with more commanding views, the men also labored to construct a platform for cannon and a fortified refuge place in case of attack from Native American tribes. Below it, work continued on a house for each family. There were to be nineteen in all, but death soon reduced the necessary number of dwellings to seven, plus another four common buildings in which to store goods and animals. These ran in a single line from Fort Hill down to the sea. Soon known as Leyden (Leiden) Street, in memory of their former home in the Netherlands, it was crossed by another track, which was ambitiously described as a "highway." This ran down to the Town Brook, with its precious supply of fresh water. Here, within the protection provided by the houses, Plymouth was forming. Now at last passengers could begin to spend more time ashore as the homes went up.

However, the shelter these provided was not enough to protect the Chiltons; death had not finished with Mary. Her mother died within two months of her father; this occurred on January 21, 1621. William Bradford later recorded, in 1650, that "James Chilton, and his wife also, died in the first infection," which was to wipe out 50 percent of the colony before the summer of 1621. Bradford himself fell dangerously ill on the morning of Thursday, January 11. He survived, but many others did not. Soon the great common house was full of the sick, laid beside each other in the smoke and gloom like drying fish. Those who had escaped the sickness gripping the colony tended the ill and dying. Work on construction ground to a halt. That same month one of the common storehouses caught fire and burned down. With it, precious supplies were reduced to ashes. It would not be until the summer that the last of the planned houses would go up, as the dying-time passed into memory.

Following the death of her mother, Mary was alone in a strange world. There is some debate as to exactly what happened to her next. It seems that she became the ward of either Myles Standish or John Alden. She had been one of eleven girls who had sailed on the *Mayflower*. Of these, nine survived the first year at Plymouth. In contrast, only four of the fourteen adult women survived that first year. If it was hard for the young girls, then it was worse for the women.

What to do with the young people left alone posed a problem. Not only did Mary and the others need care and comfort but there was also a concern about the life and morality of any single person, male or female, who was not under the guiding authority of a family. It was this, alongside the need to focus energy on raising only as many houses as was absolutely necessary, that caused the able young men to be allocated to one of the surviving family units. Everybody needed to be under authority, under God. Each family was regarded as a "little commonwealth." An English Puritan named Robert Cleaver summed it up nicely. Such a family provided

good government whereof, God's glory may be advanced, the
commonwealth which standeth of several families, benefitted,
and all that live in that family may receive much comfort and
commodity.[15]

And if that was true of the young men, then it was even more pressing with regard to a single young woman such as the recently orphaned Mary Chilton. To those around her, both her physical protection and the guarding of her morals could only be confidently assured within the protective and watchful context of a family. Disciplining young people like Mary, in order to produce godly behavior and an attitude of responsible living in keeping with a member of the elect, played a major part in family life. Only in this way could the weak nature of fallen humanity be brought into line with God's will.

Brought under the authority of another family, Mary assisted in the work of the household. With the women focusing on cooking, mending clothes, attending to the small number of domestic animals, tending to little children and the sick, the men were free to do the heavy work of cutting timber and raising buildings. It also freed the men up to explore the local environment and to be ready to defend the colony from attack.

The ever-present danger of fire, as seen in the storehouse that burned down in January, meant that Mary and the other young girls and women had to attend with great care to the ever-burning fire, which was the only form of heat. Keeping it going, banking it down safely at night, and encouraging it to revive but not blaze (with the attendant danger of sparks) in the cold morning was a serious business. As was raking out the ashes and scattering them on the plots of land beside each simple dwelling place.

In these ways Mary continued to learn, as she had done earlier under the tutelage of her mother, the role of a woman within that "little commonwealth" of the family. As she cooked, baked, knitted, sewed, and made simple fattened strings of tallow candles, she both contributed to the welfare of her new family and also prepared herself for when she would be a "goodwife" within her own home, under the authority of her own husband.

The reality of the first Thanksgiving

Cooking and feeding the household was one of the major tasks of any woman—young or old—in the colony at Plymouth, but no meal, communal or otherwise, has entered into the very heart of the modern United States to compete with that which occurred in the fall of 1621 and in which Mary Chilton and the other surviving women played a crucial role. That, of course, was the first Thanksgiving, now a central part of art, drama, song, and story.[16] However, as with so much of the life of Mary Chilton, even that great myth cannot be accepted as it stands. In order to get to the heart of the real Thanksgiving, as Mary Chilton experienced it, we must put aside our images of great wide Puritan collars and large buckles (never worn by the godly of early Plymouth, who rejected all jewelry), roast turkey (absent from the earliest record of the event), and cranberry sauce (quite unknown in the early colony). By doing this we are not denigrating the event. Rather we are getting to grips with what really occurred and, in so doing, will become more familiar with the real world that was inhabited by Mary Chilton in that crucial first year in the life of Plymouth Colony.

After a desperate twelve months, the assistance of Native Americans and the use of North American seed finally brought in a harvest that would see the colony through its second winter. We should recall that it was Squanto who had taught them how to fertilize the cornfields with dead fish, and to plant both beans and squash once the corn had started growing, which could then grow up the corn stalks.

To mark this bringing in of the ripened crops, they held a harvest festival. It was technically not a Thanksgiving. Mary and the others were very familiar with those *occasional* events. They were solemn observances, with long services, preaching, prayer, and praise. They did not officially have one of these until July 1623.

What occurred in 1621 was a Harvest Home celebration. We do not know exactly when the event happened, but it probably took place in late October or early November of that fall season. The Wampanoag leader, Massasoit, and his entourage were there too (numbering some ninety men). However, whether they were invited in gratitude for their assistance or simply turned up because food was available (that had been a feature of their behavior towards the colonists since the previous March) we cannot now tell.

What is strange is that when William Bradford later compiled *Of Plymouth Plantation*, he failed to mention the event at all. He just said the Pilgrims enjoyed "good plenty" after the harvest of 1621. He had clearly forgotten the event! If it was not for the 115 words preserved in *Mourt's Relation*, we would know nothing about it. This account, probably written by Edward Winslow, was penned in order to persuade the London Adventurers that the colony was worth further investment. It says that after the harvest was safely brought in, four men were sent off on a day of duck hunting to provision a special celebration. This celebration included marching and the firing off of muskets, viewed by both the Pilgrims and Massasoit and his companions. This was then followed by a feast that lasted three days. To this feast the Native Americans added a contribution of five deer. We can imagine Mary and the other women making corn bread and corn porridge and cooking the butchered wildfowl and venison. Not a plate of turkey or a bowl of cranberry sauce was in sight.

Furthermore, most of the preparations were carried out by young people like Mary. By the fall of 1621, children and teenagers made up about half of the colony after death had carried away so many older people. The adult women who supervised the preparations were outnumbered by adult men by a ratio of five men to every one woman. Present were only four married couples, since death had bereaved so many others. That harvest celebration was a very strange event: so lopsided with regard to age, with so few women, and heavily outnumbered by Wampanoags. No wonder the men demonstrated the power of their muskets. It was a very strange gathering indeed and not as we often imagine it today.

What followed that first feast and celebration in 1621 was an event that certainly rained on the parade. Within a couple of weeks, a ship, the *Fortune*, arrived at Plymouth. However, Thomas Weston and the London Adventurers had continued to be as penny pinching in 1621 as they had been in 1620. The thirty-five new settlers on board were poorly supplied and, as William Bradford bitterly recorded, brought "not so much as biscuit cake or any other victuals." Not that Mary knew it at the time, but the newcomers included the man who would eventually become her husband. With the newcomers, the Plymouth Colony population rose to a total of eighty-five. There was not even enough food on board the *Fortune* to feed the crew on the return trip to England. Right after celebrating the abundance of the first harvest, there were now more mouths to feed and a ship to provision for its home run. A bitter blow indeed.

As a result of this unexpected arrival, Mary and the other women faced a winter in which their culinary skills had to be practiced using half the rations that they had been given for cooking before the *Fortune* arrived. Hunger was back on the menu. It was a miracle that the death rate did not soar again—but it did not. Clearly the toughest were the ones who were left, and the fact that they had homes now and were not wading through a mile of cold water every time they went to and from the *Mayflower* (a regular event the previous winter) cut the death rate from exposure. Nevertheless, by May 1622, Mary's pot on the fire relied on shellfish from the bay and a little grain purchased from passing fishermen. This had to suffice until the wildfowl returned and meat was again on the table. That same month more settlers arrived on the shallop of the ship *Sparrow*—the small advance party of a new set of colonists sent out by the London Adventurer Thomas Weston. The main party sent out by Weston finally arrived on board the *Charity* and the *Swan*, at the end of July or in early August. The poorly prepared and poorly equipped new settlers were destined for a new colony, to be located farther up the Massachusetts coast at Wessagusset (now Weymouth). That new colony would end in tears in late March 1623, but we will hear more about that in the Mayflower Life of Myles Standish.

The winter of 1622–23 proved to be another tough one, despite a fairly successful harvest at the end of the summer in 1622. Grain stocks were soon depleted that winter. Soon there was no bread. They could brew no beer. Once more the pot on Mary's fire, as those on the other hearths in Plymouth, relied entirely on seafood. Had it not been for the abundance of the bay, she and the others would have starved.

Then, in the last quarter of May 1623, they experienced their last rain for two months. Precious corn in the fields wilted under the New England sun. The ground cracked. Disaster loomed. And once again the situation was made worse by the arrival of new settlers. The arrival of the ships the *Anne* and the *Little James* in July brought another ninety new settlers. These included Alice Southworth, whom William Bradford married soon after her arrival. Less positive, though, was the increased numbers without their bringing additional provisions. There were now somewhere in the range of 180 colonists at Plymouth. Of the newcomers, thirty had paid for their own passage and were under no obligation to work for the common good of the colony. The rest were a mixed bunch. William Bradford contrasted those who were "very useful persons" with others, "so bad as they were fain to be at charge to send them home again the next year."[17]

Faced with a crisis occasioned by drought and more mouths to feed, a Day of Humiliation was declared, when, through fasting and prayer, the colony could repent of its sins that had caused God to close up the clouds as a judgement. For some nine hours they prayed under a cloudless sky. Then, by evening, the clouds were gathering. The next day it rained and did not stop for two weeks. Seeing the revival of their withered corn, the Pilgrims called for a Day of Thanksgiving. Although today we focus on that harvest celebration in 1621, this event in 1623 was, arguably, the first Thanksgiving Day (as the Pilgrims would have termed it) in the history of Plymouth Colony. What is clear is that Mary Chilton was present at both these events.

The later life of Mary Chilton

We know that when Mary was sixteen, she was given three shares in the land division of 1623. This was one share for herself and one each for her dead father and mother. Those who had died had not been forgotten. Her property was sited between those of Myles Standish and John Alden, which suggests that she was under the oversight of one of these leading Pilgrims.

Her plot was also close to that of the Winslow family, with whom she became more closely associated; it seems that love blossomed between her and John Winslow. The brother of the leading Pilgrim Edward Winslow, John had come to Plymouth on the ship *Fortune* in 1621. Sometime around 1626 John Winslow and Mary were married. John would have been aged twenty-nine and Mary nineteen.

In the 1627 Division of Cattle they received a share in the "lesser" black cow, which had been transported to Plymouth in the ship *Anne* in 1623. They also received two female goats. At this point they had no children.

Mary and John eventually had ten children: John, Susannah, Mary, Edward, Sarah, Samuel, Joseph, Isaac, an unnamed child who probably died in infancy, and Benjamin. Of these children only the birth of the youngest, Benjamin, is listed in the Plymouth Colony records:

> *1653. Plymouth Regester of the Beirth of theire Children . . .*
> *Beniamine, the sonne of Mr John Winslow, born the 12th day*
> *of August.* [18]

Sometime after the birth of Benjamin in 1653, the family moved to Boston. Mary was the only *Mayflower* passenger to do so. Despite being of the godly, her husband, John Winslow, was more intent on business than on public service. Although appearing in the tax records for Plymouth in 1633 and 1634 and being listed in the 1643 census as one of the men capable of carrying arms to defend the colony, along with positions within the court of the colony, he was not overly active in public office. He left this kind of thing to Edward, his elder brother. Instead, he prospered in trade, acquiring part ownership of two ships: the *Speedwell* (significant name) and the intriguingly named *John's Adventure*. The later description of the *Speedwell* as a ketch indicates that she was a two-masted vessel that probably carried coastal freight or was involved in the fishing industry off the North American coast.

Despite the move to Boston, the connections of Mary and John with Plymouth remained strong, as it was as late as June 1671 that they finally transferred their Church membership from Plymouth Colony to the Third Church in Boston. What was then termed the Third Church is now called the Old South Church or the Old South Meeting House. The current building of the Old South Meeting House was not built until about fifty years after the death of Mary Winslow, née Chilton.[19]

The family thrived in Boston, with John Winslow prospering to become one of the wealthiest merchants in the town. In 1671, he bought, for the sum of £500,

> *the Mansion or dwelling-house of the Late Antipas Voice with the gardens wood-yard and Backside as it is scituate lying and being in Boston aforesaid as it is nowe fenced in And is fronting & Facing to the Lane going to mr John Jolliffes.*[20]

The house site, on today's Spring Lane in Boston, no longer exists. Mary was by now the wife of a prosperous trader in a growing town. Compared with Boston, Plymouth was something of the poor relation, but Mary and John had become Bostonians. For Mary, the first winter, with its family tragedies and the cold, rickety homestead in the hastily built colony, were now things in a very distant past. Though taught from childhood to be wary of the worldly snares of wealth and possessions, a tidy number of these were growing around her. She was the mistress of a comfortable household. Clearly, God had blessed the enterprise of her husband and also her own areas of responsibility in the home.

John Winslow died in 1674. He left to Mary their house, gardens, yards, all of the household goods, and £400 in cash.[21] The cash in hand was an impressive sum of money, given that the value of a good horse might be £4 by the 1670s.[22] The house and lands were to be hers for the remainder of her life and would then pass down to their eldest son. Among much else bequeathed, John Winslow left the children of his son, John Winslow junior, the "katch [ketch] *Speedwell*," of which John Winslow senior had become the sole owner. He also instructed that the cargo be divided among these grandchildren on the return of the vessel to Boston. Also in the will was a statement that a "Negro girl" named Jane should be freed after twenty years of service. But before that, she should serve Mary and on Mary's death could "be disposed of" as thought best by the executors of the will. This clearly meant that the girl would be sold and converted into cash. So Jane probably had many years of servitude ahead of her in 1674.

Mary herself made out her will in 1676 and died, probably in late April, in 1679. Both John and Mary are buried in King's Chapel Burying Ground in Boston.

When Mary made out a will on July 31, 1676, she became one of only two female passengers from the *Mayflower* to do so (Elizabeth Tilley being the other). In it we can gain an intimate glimpse into both her preparation for death and the acquisitions of a lifetime.

Regarding herself, she wrote:

> *I Mary Winslow of Boston in New england widdow being weake of Body but of Sound and perfect memory praysed by [be] almighty God for the same Knowing the uncertainety of this present life and being desirous to settle that outward Estate the Lord hath Lent me. I doe make this my last will and Testamt . . .*

Among the many items bequeathed to various family members the ones that were first on her mind perhaps reveal those that she valued the most.

> *Item I give and bequeath unto my Sone John Winslow my great Square Table Item I give and bequeath unto my Daughter Sarah Middlecott my Best gowne and Pettecoat and my silver beare bowle and to each of her children a Silver Cup with an handle: Also I give unto my grandchild william paine my Great silver tankard: Item I give unto my Daughter Susanna Latham my long Table: Six Joynes Stooles and my great Cupboard: a bedstead Bedd and furniture there unto belonging that is in the chamber over the room where I now Lye; my small silver Tankard: Six Silver Spoones, a case of bottles with all my wearing apparell: (except onely what I have hereby bequeathed unto my Daughter Meddlecott & my Grandchild susanna Latham . . .)*[23]

These were tangible symbols of God's provision. Yet Mary kept these signs of worldly success in proportion, for her principle aim, according to her will, was to commend her soul into the hands of Almighty God. Recognizing the passing nature of worldly things, her focus was on the hope of receiving full pardon for all her sins. In this, her training at Leiden (and later) stood her in good stead. For she knew the insufficiency even of good works to achieve such forgiveness, and, of course, she had long renounced the popish rituals (as she saw them) of the Church left behind in England. As she herself made clear, her eternal hope was based on nothing other than her faith in Jesus Christ.[24]

Yet, for a girl who had suddenly found herself alone on an unknown continent, things had turned out well. The estate that she bequeathed to those she left behind came to an impressive total, in 17th-century terms, of £212. Not bad, given that much had already been distributed on the death of her husband, five years earlier. However, more enduring than the gifts of her "great Square Table" or her "Best gowne and Pettecoat" was her legacy to the mythology of the United States of America. For, whatever the real status of the stone now revered on the shore at Plymouth, Mary Chilton will continue to be celebrated in art, poetry, and story as the girl who was the first to step onto Plymouth Rock.

7

The Exiled Little Servant's Story: Mary More, Unwanted Four-Year-Old

A number of the Pilgrims who sailed on the *Mayflower* in 1620 left members of their family behind in Leiden. This was especially so with regard to their daughters and little children of both genders. There was a good reason for this. They realized that the early years in the colony were likely to be tough ones. They were quite literally going to have to carve out homes in an alien and dangerous land. This was more than just emigrating; this was pioneering in all its raw and risky manifestations. So, it seemed safest to leave the most vulnerable behind and then bring them over once things settled down and life seemed a little more secure.

This was particularly so with regard to the weakness associated with girls.[1] The Saints of the *Mayflower* were fairly representative of their wider society in their belief that girls were the weaker sex. They remembered how in one of the New Testament letters it was written,

Likewise ye husbands, dwell with them as men of knowledge,
giving honor unto the woman, as unto the weaker vessel, even as
they which are heirs together of the grace of life, that your prayers
be not interrupted. (1 Peter 3:7)

This passage was all about husbands treating their wives decently, but it also drew attention to the weakness of women. But in what sense were women "weaker vessels"? The Pilgrims saw in this a reinforcement of their belief that men were the (strong) authority figures and leaders in marriage and in the world generally. But it went further than that, as they could see in the day-to-day experiences of life how men seemed physically stronger than women too. As a result, it is not surprising that many of the Pilgrims left their girls at home. There were exceptions, of course, like Mary Chilton (she of Plymouth Rock fame). But overall the rule generally stood out as being followed by those who boarded the *Mayflower* at the start of its epic journey. Some girls were left back in the Netherlands, some in England. It was with this in mind that William Brewster (an elder of the Leiden church) brought over his two sons, named Love and Wrestling, but decided to leave behind his two daughters, named Patience and Fear. He was not alone in this decision. Richard Warren had no fewer than five daughters. These were named Mary, Ann, Sarah, Elizabeth, and Abigail. And, with ages ranging from two to ten years, they were both young and female. So, it is not at all surprising to discover that he left all of his daughters behind. Both Thomas Rogers and Francis Cooke took their sons (Joseph Rogers and John Cooke), but each left their two daughters at home (Elizabeth and Margaret Rogers and Jane and Hester Cooke). To give one final example, Degory Priest (an ironic surname for one of the godly) had two daughters, but neither Mary nor Sarah set foot on the *Mayflower* when the ship departed the shores of Europe. The pattern is fairly clear: leave girls at home, especially the little ones.

It was a pattern but not an absolute one, since some families clearly did not want to be separated from their daughters. Mary Chilton was one of eleven girls, aged one to seventeen years old, who were taken across the Atlantic with their families in 1620. And these girls bucked the mortality trend that first terrible winter. While 75 percent of the women, 50 percent of the men, and 36 percent of the boys on the *Mayflower* died, only two girls who had come aboard that previous summer were to die and be buried in unmarked graves in the snow-covered earth of Cole's Hill. As a result, the girls of the *Mayflower* suffered 18 percent casualties. Terrible as this was, they seem to have been the toughest of all the passengers. This was against all expectations. This might have been helped by the fact that the girls stayed on board the *Mayflower* while the men went out exploring and hunting. This meant they were almost always on board the ship from its arrival in November 1620 until the completion of building the settlement at Plymouth at the end of March 1621. Boring and smelly though the ship was, it was less ruinous to health than freezing ashore or wading backwards and forwards between the *Mayflower* and the beach. However, men died on the *Mayflower* (as Mary Chilton discovered when she lost her father) and women died on board the ship too (as Mary Chilton also discovered when she lost her mother). Mary Chilton was not the only girl orphaned. Elizabeth Tilley lost both parents (John and Joan Tilley) and her uncle and aunt too (Edward and Ann Tilley). Remember and Mary Allerton lost their mother (Mary Allerton, who had herself lost a child, stillborn, while the *Mayflower* was moored in Plymouth Harbor).

Even after the worst of the winter was over, the girls outlived those around them, as was seen in the case of Desire Minter, who lost her adopted parents, John and Katherine Carver, in April 1621. Death stalked every family that first winter except that of Stephen and Elizabeth Hopkins, who survived along with all their children: Constance, Giles, Damaris (who was just two years old), and Oceanus (born during the Atlantic voyage). There is the possibility that little Oceanus died that first winter, but things are not clear about when his short life ended. Given these terrible stories of suffering and death, the survival of the girls is remarkable. Even one-year-old Humility Cooper survived.[2] The girls were tougher than anyone had imagined.

Yet two little girls *did* die that first winter. Ellen More died, aged eight years old, and so did her little sister named Mary, who was just four years old. The deaths of these two little girls opens a window onto one of the most unexpected and tragic of the stories of those who sailed on the *Mayflower*. For both these little girls were traveling without any adult members of their family. Both were unwanted and being despatched into exile in a strange and dangerous land. And both died. The connection between these two factors seems disturbing. . . .

The tragic story of little Mary More and her siblings

The short life and tragic death of Mary More is tangled with a complex weave of scandal, family breakdown, paternal cruelty (and perhaps neglect).

Mary was one of four children traveling without any family whatsoever. These four were all siblings: Ellen, Jasper, Richard, and Mary. When the *Mayflower* sailed from England, Ellen was aged eight, Jasper was seven, Richard was six, and Mary was just four years old. All had been effectively abandoned, although the matter had been carefully dressed up in order to cloak such a heartless reality. But abandoned they had been. They were going into exile; out of sight, out of mind, as the old English saying has it. Among the mixed community of Saints and Strangers, these four were certainly Strangers, and ones tarred with the sins of those who had given them life. Even among the Strangers, these children were on the very edge.

Of these four children only Richard survived the traumas of the winter of 1620–21. We will come across grizzled—and licentious—old Captain Richard More in our final Mayflower Life, in a story that links Plymouth to Salem of the witch hunts and a whole lot in between. But the other three children all died early in the *Mayflower* story. Jasper died while the ship was moored in Provincetown Harbor, about a week before the Mayflower sailed across the bay to Plymouth. Ellen and Mary died at Plymouth (sometime between January and March 1621), before spring finally brought an end to the cold season of suffering that took the lives of so many Saints and Strangers. However, we might ask what they were doing on the voyage in the first place. To answer that, we must return to England in the decade leading up to the sailing of the *Mayflower*. For the answer to this question lies in the western Midlands, where England meets Wales, and in a tempestuous story of marital disharmony, adultery, betrayal, and revenge.

All four children were baptized in the parish of Shipton, in Shropshire. The baptismal register (mandatory in all churches of the Church of England since 1538) clearly states that they were the children of Samuel and Katherine More. These two were cousins and came from a wealthy landowning family in the county. As a result, Katherine carried the same surname both before and after she married Samuel in February 1611. Katherine was twenty-five years old and Samuel was seventeen. The relative difference in their ages was significant, since, in time, it would be revealed that Katherine had had a "life" before she married Samuel, but it was one that she kept to herself for understandable reasons.

The marriage settlement was noteworthy because Samuel's father (Richard More) paid Katherine's father £600 in order to take control of her family's estate at Larden, which was near Much Wenlock, in Shropshire. This transfer occurred immediately after the marriage took place in 1611. Consequently, Samuel and Katherine looked set to eventually hold both the More estates at Larden and Linley. This looked a very satisfactory state of affairs, as it promised to safeguard the More family's power in the English borderlands and entrench the influence of a Puritan dynasty (Samuel's father would eventually go on to support the parliamentary cause in the civil wars of the 1640s).

If the matter had ended there, then the four More children would not have ended up on the *Mayflower*, but things were far more complex than that, and the baptismal register did not reveal the half of it. Under the surface of its straightforward entry was a set of relationships that were anything but straightforward.[3]

Samuel and Katherine were not happy in their marriage. Although all marriages in 17th-century England required the consent of both parties, it was not at all uncommon for the union between members of wealthy families to be, in effect, arranged. The expectation was that those so arranged to marry would fall in line with their parents' wishes. After that they could learn to love each other. Or not. What Samuel

More was blissfully unaware of was that his bride was already involved in a long-standing relationship with a local man named Jacob Blakeway. And that relationship continued after her marriage with Samuel. The career pursued by Samuel inadvertently assisted the continuation of the relationship between Katherine and Jacob, as Samuel was away from home for very long periods of time; while the cat's away, the mice can play. What took Samuel away was his decision to work in London as the secretary to a courtier and diplomat named Lord Edward Zouche. Lord Zouche was also very active in the affairs of the Virginia Company, which, in time, would become involved in Samuel's resolution of his marital and family problems.

As the marriage progressed, so children were born to Katherine and (ostensibly) Samuel More, four of them in all. It was then that a worrying realization dawned on Samuel: none of them looked like him. More alarmingly, they did, in his opinion, look like somebody that he knew. That person was neighbor Jacob Blakeway. Blakeway was closer in age to Katherine and was one of the tenants holding land on the More estate at Larden Hall, which belonged to Katherine's branch of the family. This apparent resemblance only reinforced a growing suspicion that his wife and Blakeway seemed somehow involved with each other. It was a suspicion regarding adultery that only grew every time he looked at "his" children.

Incensed at the realization, Samuel embarked on a bitter divorce, which started in 1616. The dispute dragged on for four long years, from 1616 to 1620. All in all there were twelve court appearances as the whole matter was played out in public. During this time the four children were placed in the custody of Samuel's father. In April 1616, Samuel acted to ensure that none of the Larden estate would be inherited by the children, whom he now publicly accused of being bastards and products of his wife's adulterous relationship with Blakeway.[4] The whole matter became even more complex when Katherine declared that she had indeed had a relationship with Blakeway—and continued to do so—but that there existed a former betrothal agreement between them. If true, this would make Blakeway her actual husband and would render invalid her marriage to Samuel. When Samuel laid out his divorce declaration, he quoted his wife's own statement, which declared that

though she could not sufficiently prove by witnesses yet it was all
one before god as she sayed.[5]

It was all getting very messy and complicated, and Samuel's public humiliation was growing at the same time as his determination to be revenged, both on the woman who had betrayed him and on the children who were the fruits of that betrayal.

When the legal matter was finally settled in Samuel's favor, he gained custody of the children. Given that the whole premise of the divorce was that they were not his, this can only be read as a determination to be revenged on his wife and to use the children as the means of achieving this. Samuel must have reasoned, as he reflected on the ruin of his marriage and the humiliation of having been duped over many years, that if his wife kept the children, then she could achieve emotional happy-ever-after with the man she truly loved. Samuel was going to ensure that such a happy ending was not enjoyed by Katherine.

Against Katherine's expressed wishes he arranged for the children to be sent to North America on a colonial expedition. In the matrimonial power politics of Stuart England, the law was heavily tipped in his (male) favor, and the power of bitter revenge was in his hands. He was determined to use it. In this plan he was assisted by his relationship with Lord Zouche. There was past practice in this area, in that orphaned children and poor children supported by parish relief had already been shipped to the growing British colonial empire as a way of getting rid of economically dependent people and relieving the taxes paid by the better-off to support them in England. Since Lord Zouche was a member of the governmental Privy Council, there was not much chance of a successful legal challenge to this brutal practice. This did not mean that Katherine tamely accepted the transportation of her children. She certainly did not. A document, dated 1622, details Katherine's petition to the Lord Chief Justice against the forcible removal of her four children. The document reveals that Katherine had earlier attempted to take back her children by force, "and in a hail of murderous oaths, did teare the cloathes from their backes"[6] (clearly in a violent attempt to wrest them from those charged with keeping them from her).[7] In this atmosphere of violence and recriminations, Samuel More and his father were only too keen to "shunne the continuall sight of their [the children's] great grief" and to permanently get rid of "such a spurious broode."[8]

The "answer" lay in forcible transportation of the children to America as indentured servants. How long their indenture would last is not clear. Since Richard More's indenture appears to have ended in 1627, when he was fourteen years old, this might have been the term applying to all the More children had they survived. Katherine lost her final appeal to get her children back in July 1620, even as the *Mayflower* was being hired in London by the Merchant Adventurers, before sailing to Southampton to begin loading food and supplies for the voyage to the Virginia Colony. The children's fates were being sealed.

With the last legal avenue closed down to their mother, the four tearful and bewildered children were moved from Shropshire down to London. There they were placed in the charge of the penny-pinching Adventurer William Weston, whom we have met in other Mayflower Lives. From there they were placed in the charge of John Carver and Robert Cushman, who were the representatives of the Leiden Pilgrims in their negotiations with the Virginia Company representatives in London. While this was happening, their mother, Katherine, was oblivious regarding their fate, since all had been kept secret from her. By the time she realized what was happening, the ship had sailed and the children were in the guardianship of members of the Leiden Separatist church. She had lost her children, which was exactly as Samuel More intended it to be. His revenge was complete: his wife was broken, and the children, who were the living embodiment (though personally innocent) of his pain and humiliation, had been shunted across the Atlantic.

Is there any evidence that Samuel felt any remorse? The answer is: none whatsoever. Did he know he had secured a likely death sentence for such little children? We cannot tell, and no doubt he could satisfy his conscience with the thought that their fate was in the hands of God and he was blameless with regard to whatever befell them. He had his revenge and yet could console himself that no sin was attached to his actions. No doubt that was the story he developed for himself, and it clearly satisfied him. Furthermore, he would certainly have added that the sin of the mother (and father) had been visited on the children. In this way he could both point the finger of blame for their fate at Katherine and Jacob and, at the same time, classify the children as so tainted by sin and depravity that they were little more than objects of judgement. There could be some very cold and self-satisfied judgmentalism in the calculations of some Puritans, which tarnished the impressive spiritual zeal that was otherwise such a feature of this great movement. We can be fairly sure that Samuel More was unconcerned about the fate he had secured for the children. There is certainly no evidence that it troubled him.

Given the young age of the victims of Samuel's feud with his ex-wife, they could not travel alone. Instead, they were placed in the care (*in loco parentis*) of leading members of the Leiden church. Richard and Mary More were placed as servants with the family of Elder William Brewster. Jasper was placed as a servant with future first governor John Carver. Finally, Ellen was placed as a servant with Edward Winslow, another leading member of the godly. The little Strangers had been distributed among the Saints.

Little Mary More has left little to show for her short life. We know that she was baptized at Shipton on April 16, 1616. We can only guess what she made of the forced separation from her mother, being parcelled out to strangers, the cold and fear of the Atlantic crossing, and the cold winter shore of Massachusetts. But it does not take much imagination to conclude that she must have been traumatized. A four-year-old is a four-year-old whether from 1620 or 2020, and the emotional impact must have been devastating. That is why this May-flower Life is in her name. For in the terrible upheavals and suffering that first disrupted, and then ended, the life of such a little girl we can see something of how a little innocent could get crushed between the turning iron wheels of legal and historical events; the determined actions of adults; and the cold ambitions of others. Mary More deserved better and deserves at least a chapter named after her. It is more than she achieved on the inscribed Pilgrim Memorial Tomb now to be found in Plymouth, at the southern end of Cole's Hill (now part of Pilgrim Memorial State Park). For there, on the monumental sarcophagus erected in 1921, which contains bones thought to be those of early Pilgrims, is inscribed, among the many names, this misidentification:

ELLEN MORE AND A BROTHER (CHILDREN)

Clearly, something has gone wrong here. The answer lies in an error found in appendix 13 of William Bradford's journal, *Of Plymouth Plantation*. When compiling a list of all the *Mayflower* passengers, Bradford wrote, in the list referring to the family of William Brewster,

And a boy was put to him [as a servant] *called Richard More, and another of his brothers.* [9]

This is a mistake. Richard had only one brother, and we know (and Bradford states this) that he was assigned to the household of John Carver. As Bradford compiled his history, looking back to recall all those names, he forgot that the other little person put as a servant to William Brewster was not Richard's brother but his sister—four-year-old Mary More. She was so small and easily forgotten in all the momentous events of the voyage and the settlement. Mary More was all too easy to slip from the mind.

Back in England, though, was someone who had certainly not forgotten her; indeed had not forgotten any of the More children. Early in the year 1622, Katherine More made one more legal attempt to get her children back. It failed, but it was during that final court hearing that Samuel revealed where the children had been sent, and why, and in that record we learn the details of this terrible tale of betrayal and revenge. The bitter irony of it all is that when Katherine made her final attempt to retrieve her children, three of them had been dead for a year and she did not even know it.

In 1625 Samuel More remarried, although the next year he had to obtain a royal pardon (to allow the marriage to continue), as technically he was not free to marry again while Katherine was still alive.

He got his pardon. So, in the end, he got his happy-ever-after. We do not know when Katherine died, and Jacob Blakeway vanishes from the records as well. Perhaps they finally found some happiness together. Nobody knows.

During the civil wars, Samuel More held Hopton Castle, in Shropshire, for Parliament. When it was stormed by Royalist forces, in 1644, the parliamentary garrison was massacred. All, that is, except for Samuel More. He was taken prisoner and later released as part of a prisoner exchange. Once again, others had died, but Samuel More carried on. He lived until 1662.

The great sickness

Mary More's life and death reveal something of the gender politics and sexual relationships of the early 17th century. Her experience also reminds us how children had no rights of their own and were subject to the decisions made by others. Indeed, they could be parcelled up and shipped off as indentured servants even if they would not be old enough to start school in a modern Western society. It also raises questions over what killed so many of the early settlers who traveled on the *Mayflower*. In short: Why did Mary More die?

It is striking how well the adventure started, given the length of the voyage and the difficulty of the Atlantic crossing. When the *Mayflower* anchored off Cape Cod on Saturday, November 11, 1620, of the 102 passengers who had initially sailed from Plymouth, England, only one had died. This was William Butten, who was apprenticed to Samuel Fuller. Since one had been born—Oceanus Hopkins—there were still 102 passengers. One death and one birth had numerically cancelled each other out. However, it was after this that things started to go wrong. While the ship anchored in Provincetown Harbor, four more passengers died. These were Dorothy Bradford (possibly in suspicious circumstances), James Chilton, young Jasper More, and Edward Thompson. At the same time one more was born; this was Peregrine White. This meant that by the time the ship arrived at Plymouth

Harbor on Saturday, December 16, 1620, there were ninety-nine "first comers" on board. Then the death toll rose inexorably. William Bradford records the deaths of forty-four passengers over the next three months. As if that was not enough, five more settlers died after the *Mayflower* returned to England on April 5, 1621. These included the first governor, John Carver (who collapsed from heat stroke after working in the fields), and his wife. These final deaths reduced the number of first comer *Mayflower* survivors to just fifty.[10] The losses had been devastating.

Neither was the crew of the ship spared, for, as William Bradford later put it, "almost half of their company died." Physical strength seemed no defense, for "many of their officers and lustiest [strongest] men" were among those who fell victim to the catastrophe.[11] This finally caused Master Christopher Jones to send beer ashore to the passengers suffering there. Earlier the crew had refused to do so, as they said they needed it for their journey home. No doubt they remembered the scummy green water they had been forced to drink from the foul barrels on board ship during the westward journey, and they had no wish to repeat the experience when they sailed home again in the summer of 1621. But their own experience of sickness finally caused them to show pity to the suffering passengers.

When the spring finally came it was clear that the deaths had cut a strange demographic swathe through the community. Of those who lived, only three were definitely older than forty. Adult males outnumbered adult females by five to one. Children and teenagers now made up 50 percent of the colony. Orphans and widowers were present in significant numbers, since fourteen of the eighteen wives who had initially embarked on the *Mayflower* had died by the spring of 1621. Of those who had lost parents, bereavement was particularly acute for Mary Chilton, Samuel Fuller, Priscilla Mullins, and Elizabeth Tilley, since each had lost both mother and father. Richard More had lost all three of his siblings. Yet young women had survived, as we have seen, to a quite remarkable degree.

The strong faith of a man like William Bradford could allow him to look back on this devastation and still determinedly write,

Faint not, poor soul, in God still trust, Fear not the things thou suffer must; For, whom he loves he doth chastise, And then all tears wipes from their eyes. [12]

Only four married couples survived, and one of these couples consisted of Edward and Susanna Winslow, (who had previously been married to William White), who had only married in May 1621 after both of them had lost their previous spouses. [13] So great was the number of deaths that the Pilgrims concealed the graves to avoid signalling to the Native Americans how badly the colony had been depleted. James Thacher, in his *History of the Town of Plymouth* (1835), quoted a contemporary of his, who had heard it from an old man, who in turn had heard it from Elder Faunce, that the early graves had been leveled and corn planted on them in order to conceal them from hostile eyes. [14] The devastation was undeniable, but the question remains: What caused it all? Why did so many Pilgrims die?

Looking back from the perspective of four hundred years it is difficult to be entirely sure what lay behind the terrible mortality of the first winter. It is probable that it was a combination of things that caused so many deaths. Malnourishment certainly played a major part; of this, scurvy was probably the biggest identifiable killer. William Bradford wrote that the disaster was down to "scurvy and *other* diseases," which suggests that once people were weakened, a whole host of problems could then carry them off without there being one clear identifiable cause of all the deaths.

Less dramatic but probably as important was exposure. New England winters in the 1620s were particularly hard. All across the Northern Hemisphere the so-called Little Ice Age lowered temperatures and impacted on many communities. This situation was made worse by the need to wade to and from the *Mayflower* because the ship could not tie up close to shore, either at Provincetown or at Plymouth. This is probably why the death rate was particularly high among older people. For those already brought low by a hard sea crossing and poor diet, this wading through icy seawater was the final straw. The cramped and unhygienic conditions on board the ship did not help either. We can be sure that for a four-year-old like Mary More, this combination was lethal. And one also wonders if the traumatized little girl had just given up and had simply lost the will to live. However, this does not explain why the older women succumbed before the girls. There will always be something of a mystery about it.

Yet, when it comes to Mary More, there is something else that leaves a nagging doubt in the mind. Try as one might, one cannot ignore the fact that the only two young girls to die that winter were Ellen and Mary More. That seems just too coincidental. Rather like the shadow that falls across the death of Dorothy Bradford (who "fell" from the ship and drowned), one just wonders whether there was more to it than meets the eye. Not that one has to suggest foul play or anything like it—more a situation of casual neglect. After all, everyone else was very busy just staying alive themselves that winter. And how were these little children regarded? We hope they were carried and cuddled, comforted and loved. But how likely is that, really? Everyone knew why they were aboard. People looked, nudged each other, raised eyebrows, frowned at the very thought of what they embodied. These were the little bastards. The living proof of the corruption of adultery. If everyone was tainted with original sin, which was a given, then how much more so were they? If every human being's nature was irretrievably contaminated and depraved, how much more so was theirs? It was woven into their very being and existence. We do not have to suggest active abuse or active unkindness to imagine a situation where they were just "the alien others," the Strangers among Strangers. William Bradford could not even remember Mary's name. When he compiled his journal he recalled she was a boy, an anonymous boy-child. One has a feeling that maybe, just maybe, one of the main reasons why Ellen and Mary More died was that they were not loved.

That left just one of the More siblings alive, come the summer of 1621. It was that one who became an American and never returned to the country whose legal system had failed him and abandoned him. We know that Richard More was still living with the Brewsters in 1627, but we will learn more of what happened next to him when we finally come to explore the events of his life.

Behind him, though, in 1627, he left a devastated family, having lost all his siblings. The death of each is a tragedy, but perhaps the most poignant is that of four-year-old little Mary More, the exiled little servant; an unwanted child whose life ended in early 1621 and whose unmarked grave lies somewhere among the others buried on Cole's Hill, overlooking Plymouth Bay.

8

The Man Overboard's Story:
John Howland, Indentured Servant,
Negotiator, and Fur Trapper

For those familiar with the 1995 Disney film *Pocahontas*, a memorable episode involves a man falling overboard from the ship that was sailing in 1607 to start the colony at Jamestown, Virginia. This occurs while a terrible storm is battering the ship, named the *Susan Constant*. Apparently doomed, he is saved by Captain John Smith, who grabs a rope, leaps overboard, and swims out to the drowning man. Seizing him before he sinks, Smith and the man thus saved are hauled back on board by those on the ship. This episode is a piece of creative fiction designed to emphasize the heroic nature of Smith, the English military man. No matter, it is all dramatic stuff and great entertainment. In fact, the only man to be fished out of the water during John Smith's time in Virginia was the legendary captain himself. This occurred in 1609 when a powder bag he was wearing exploded, burning him and setting fire to his clothing. In order to douse the flames, he leapt from a boat into the James River. From there he was saved by his companions, who hauled him back into the boat.[1]

Well, truth is sometimes stranger than fiction. Something rather reminiscent of this cartoon episode really occurred during the voyage of the *Mayflower* to North America in 1620. Then the near disaster and remarkable rescue involved a man by the name of John Howland, and he is our next Mayflower Life. His experiences reveal the remarkable life of an indentured servant who survived an accident at sea, became personal secretary to the first governor of Plymouth Colony, negotiated treaties with local Native American tribes, took on the colony's debts owed to its London backers, developed the fur trade, and fought other European settlers from rival colonies. This is the Man Overboard's Story.

John Howland was born in Fenstanton, Huntingdonshire, England. He was baptized in the parish church of Saints Peter and Paul there. The date of this event has been suggested as having been around 1592,[2] by working backwards from his stated age of eighty, when he died in 1673, as revealed in the surviving Plymouth church records. Not everyone is convinced about this, though; it has been suggested that his age at death was a little overstated, since his status as a servant suggests he was younger than twenty-five in 1620, and it seems a bit unlikely that William Bradford would have described him as a "lusty young man" if Howland was twenty-eight in 1620 (Bradford being thirty years old then). It has, consequently, been postulated that Howland's age at death has been exaggerated by at least five years.[3]

Be that as it may, we can say with more certainty that he was the son of Henry and Margaret Howland, and the brother of Henry and Arthur Howland, who late emigrated from England, ending up at Marshfield, Massachusetts (just under ten miles northwest of Plymouth). The family came from the Puritan end of the 17th-century Christian spectrum, having broken from the established Church of England. Henry and Arthur Howland ended up as Quakers, a sect condemned by the godly in Massachusetts. However, John himself held to the original faith of the separating Puritans, which was in line with the faith outlook of the Saints in Plymouth Colony.[4]

William Bradford, the governor of Plymouth Colony for many years and compiler of the record entitled *Of Plymouth Plantation*, informs us that Howland was a manservant of the leading Saint, John Carver. Carver, as we have already seen (in 'The Master's Story'), was a leading member of the church that transplanted on the *Mayflower*. He had risen to prominence while it was located in Leiden in the Netherlands. His role was that of a deacon within this Separatist congregation. In the summer of 1620, when large numbers of the Leiden congregation left the Netherlands on the (soon to be abandoned) *Speedwell*, Carver himself was in England. His role was that of representative of the church as it prepared for the movement to the New World. As such, he approved the investment from the London Adventurers, negotiated for the addition of other passengers to join the enterprise, and, eventually, chartered the *Mayflower* for the journey to New England. We do not know if John Howland was with him in London or whether, instead, he accompanied Carver's household as it moved from Leiden, when the *Speedwell* sailed from Delfshaven in July. If it was the latter, then Howland would have been reunited with his master in Southampton. If it was the former, then he would have gained some useful insights into negotiations with the London Adventurers, which would stand him in good stead for the future development of Plymouth Colony. Given the close relationship of John Howland to John Carver, and Howland's later influential role in the colony, it is likely that he acted more like a secretary or assistant to Carver than a servant. Bradford's use of the rather vague label "manservant" may unintentionally give us too lowly an impression of Howland's place in the Carver household.[5]

Saved from drowning on the *Mayflower* voyage

John Howland nearly did not make it to his new home in Massachusetts. During the voyage across the North Atlantic he was almost lost during one of the fierce storms that made the *Mayflower*'s voyage so miserable. Astonishingly, John Howland fell overboard. More astonishing still: he survived.

Life between the decks of the *Mayflower* was cramped, stinking of vomit and the chamber pots of those confined there. If the *Mayflower* had ever been a "sweet ship"—so called from the spilled wine that affected the smell below decks of vessels employed in the wine trade—then those days were long past. The sweat, and worse, of 102 passengers saw to that. So it was that John Howland climbed the rough ladder and ventured out onto the heaving deck timbers to escape the smell, while others stayed below to weather the storm. But his search for fresh air inadvertently put his life on the line.

William Bradford, when recalling the event as he wrote *Of Plymouth Plantation*, remembered how on that particular day the wind and waves were so violent that the crew of the *Mayflower* had been forced to allow the ship "to lay at hull in a mighty storm." This meant that they shortened sail and let the ship be driven by the wind and sea. We do not know exactly what happened next. Did Howland lean over the rail to vomit and relieve seasickness? Did the ship swing wildly upward as a wave crashed into its side? Did a great cascade of seawater sweep him overboard? Bradford says that the ship experienced "a seele," meaning it rolled or pitched, which is certainly easy to imagine in such foul weather. Whatever exactly caused it, Howland was flung over the low rail that provided some safety to those on deck; he was hurled headlong into the North Atlantic.

As he tumbled from the ship, he managed, through remarkable presence of mind, to seize hold of a rope. It was one of the topsail halyards that, good news for John, was trailing in the rolling seawater. Used to raise the upper sail, the trailing rope now provided the only chance of escaping catastrophe. It should have been carefully tied to a cleat, but it was not secured. And due to that piece of untidy seamanship, John Howland survived. In the desperate lunge that ended with him grabbing the twisted, slippery rope, he saved himself from drowning. He clung on even though he found himself, in Bradford's words again, "sundry fathoms under water." Back on the *Mayflower* there was a hurrying of men to the side of the pitching vessel. Many hands took up the shipward end of the rope and hauled him back towards safety. As the exhausted and drenched man was pulled from the waves and up against the rough timbers of the rolling *Mayflower*, someone grabbed a boat hook and, by catching it in his coat, helped pull him back on board.[6] It had been a close call. Had the trailing rope not been there, had Howland failed to catch it, he would have been swept away by the white-crested waves and lost. As it was, he lived. It was an almost unbelievable event; an astonishing cheating of death. All of the godly who witnessed it or who heard of it would have felt convinced that it was possible only by the providential hand of God. Jonah-like, John Howland had been both thrown into the stormy deep and also rescued from it (though without the intervention of a great fish) by the will of God. His, clearly, was a life marked out for future importance in the story of the colony about to be founded. Heads would have nodded as word of the event spread among the godly passengers on the ship. Here, clearly, was a man in the hand of God. A man blessed and marked out by the action of the Almighty. The crew, though, probably winked and swore as they considered the naivete of a landsman taking the air in such a storm. For them it was just the latest evidence that these passengers were doomed to disaster; they lacked the edge and awareness needed to survive what lay ahead of them. And those less godly among the passengers might also have been less willing than some of those around them to assume the certainty of providence acting in the events. Which of these would be proved right—faithful Saints, profane seamen, uncertain Strangers—only time would tell. But one thing was certain: the name of John Howland was on everyone's lips. And he himself was being written into history.

Having survived the storm-tossed adventure that nearly cost him his life, Howland went on to become part of the decision to settle in what would become Massachusetts, rather than settling to the south in Virginia. On November 11, 1620, John was among the forty-one men who were signatories of the Mayflower Compact, while the ship was anchored off Cape Cod, in Provincetown Harbor. He was, apparently, the thirteenth to sign.[7]

John's rise to prominence in Plymouth Colony

Having finally arrived in North America, John Howland was soon active in establishing the colony there. He was one of those closely involved in the exploration of Cape Cod once the *Mayflower* finally anchored in Provincetown Harbor. He was among the men—such as William Bradford, Myles Standish, Edward Winslow, and Stephen Hopkins—who set out in the shallop on December 6, 1620, on an adventure that would end two days later in the fight at First Encounter Beach. Since John Carver, recently elected as the first governor, was there too, it is no surprise that his trusted assistant, John Howland, was beside him in the boat as it pushed away from the *Mayflower*. Also there was a man named John Tilley, whose daughter Elizabeth would eventually become Goodwife (i.e., Mrs.) Howland, not that John knew this as they set out that Wednesday morning into the cold unknown to explore the shoreline within the arc of Cape Cod.

In keeping with his role as an assistant to the first governor of Plymouth Colony, and as a single young man, Hopkins lived with the Carver family when they eventually erected their house in the early months of 1621 overlooking Plymouth Bay. In contrast to many others, who were struck down by death, Carver's family survived the dreadful winter of 1620–21, which otherwise halved the colony. But death had not finished its work. In the spring—on an unseasonably hot day in April 1621—Governor Carver left his cornfield feeling terribly ill. It was almost certainly a case of severe sunstroke afflicting a man who was already exhausted by the privations of the previous four months. He quickly lapsed into a coma as his distressed household gathered around him in the cooler confines of the wooden house; but John Carver, in the shocked words of William Bradford, "never spake more." Not long after this shockingly sudden death, Carver's wife, Katherine, also died. William Bradford poignantly recorded that she died from a broken heart. The longed-for new home in the New World had, instead, simply provided two graves for the hardworking governor and his wife. Since the Carvers' only children had died while the church community was located in Leiden, there was no immediate family to inherit their estate or their share of the land in Plymouth. It is not absolutely clear, but it seems that John Howland inherited their estate and land. This is even more likely if he was, as has been suggested, related to Carver in some way. In 1621, following Carver's death, Howland was recognized as a freeman, holding land in his own right and now one of the pillars of the new community. By 1624, he clearly headed the Carver household, since it was then that he was given oversight of the grant of an acre of land for each member of that household. Those benefitting from this included himself, and also the household members named as: Elizabeth Tilley, Desire Minter, and a young boy who was named William Latham.

One of these—Elizabeth Tilley—became John Howland's ward after the death of John and Katherine Carver. Until the rediscovery of William Bradford's *Of Plymouth Plantation* in the mid-19th century, it was often assumed that Elizabeth Tilley was the adopted daughter of the Carvers. This erroneous identification even informed the grave-stone that was originally erected for the Howland family on Burial Hill, in 1836.[8] But this was not so. William Bradford explains that she was, actually, the daughter of John and Joan Tilley and had traveled with them as passengers on the *Mayflower*. Elizabeth, further research has shown, was baptized in August 1607, at Henlow, in Bedfordshire. Both John and Joan Tilley died the first winter. This left Elizabeth without family, since during the same period of time her uncle and her aunt—Edward Tilley, brother to her father, and Edward's wife, Agnes—also died. It was this devastation of the Tilley family that took Elizabeth into the wardship of John and Katherine Carver, until they too succumbed and died. Once more we have a shocking insight into the suffering of the little community during their first winter in New England, and we can only feel admiration for their faith and courage, which upheld them through such a tragic introduction to their longed-for new home. When Elizabeth was left without family she was just thirteen years old. John Howland was at most twenty-five but probably nearer to twenty years in age. With the sudden deaths of her parents, near relatives, and then her guardians, she and Howland were thrown together in adversity. And from that throwing together, mutual affection grew, for they later married, probably in 1624 and certainly before 1627, and had no fewer than ten children.

John Howland became one of the leaders of Plymouth Colony. After becoming a freeman, he served in various posts of responsibility there: as selectman (on the governing board of the town); assistant and then deputy governor; surveyor of highways; and (as we shall shortly see) a member of the fur committee.

As early as 1626, he was one of eight settlers who were asked to take on responsibilities for the colony's debt to its investors back in London. By that year the Merchant Adventurers had disbanded, but those who had inherited the rights to collect their debts still looked towards New England for a profit. These debts were stifling the colony. It was impossible for the settlers to pursue their own agenda in developing the settlement, as they were constantly at the financial beck and call of the relentless financiers back in London. If only the settlers could be free from this burden, they could start making a profit in their own right and invest it in further developments, instead of watching all their profits being shipped eastward back to England.

These brave Undertakers, as they were known, paid the London investors £1,800 in order to have them give up their claims on the land in New England. In addition, they also took on the burden of an additional £2,400 to cover other debts. It was a bold decision, and John Howland was there in the middle of it. He was only in his middle twenties, but he was taking on responsibilities that would have daunted many men twice his age. In return for this action, those who took on this burden also gained the potentially huge benefit of holding a monopoly in the colony's lucrative fur trade for six years. John and the other men took a risk, but it was a calculated one, since the trade in beaver pelts had the potential to be a very profitable one indeed. In time it would save Plymouth from financial collapse.[9] Nevertheless, the action still took courage but was in keeping with the grit and determination of those early settlers carving out a new life in Plymouth Colony.

Given his leadership in the debt resolution issue, it is not surprising that John was elected to act as deputy to the General Court of the colony between 1641 and 1655, and then again in 1658. He was also a leading member of the Separatist church at Plymouth. John Howland was a man who got things done.

John Howland: frontiersman

Life on what was then the western frontier of settlement—the movement westward that would characterize the next 250 years was only beginning—was hard, but there were highly profitable natural resources to be harvested from the land for those willing to explore, trade, and take risks in what was, to them, the American wilderness.

It was on one of these explorations, in 1628, that John Howland went with Edward Winslow along the Kennebec River, in what today is the state of Maine. They were hoping to locate sites for fur trapping; they were also assessing other possible resources of the area. This was only the beginning of John's work in this region, as he later led the way in setting up a trapping and trading post there.

The possibilities of trade with Native American tribes had been greatly assisted by something that occurred in 1627. It was in that year that a Dutch trader named Isaack de Rasieres visited Plymouth, where he familiarized the colonists with the means of exchange known as wampum; he also left us a detailed record of life in the colony in that year. [10] Wampum consisted of white or purple colored beads and discs, which were made from two different seashells. The white beads were fashioned from whelk shells, while the purple ones were made from the quahog clam. Finely ground and then polished into small tubes, using a stone drill called a *puckwhegonnautick* by Native Americans, the finished products were the result of many hours of hard, skilled work. The beads had great symbolic significance for some local tribes, with the white ones representing purity and light and the purple ones representing war and death. Wampum was given as a gift to accompany events as significant and diverse as births, marriages, agreeing treaties, and the remembrance of dead family members. Huge strings of wampum could also be won by teams engaged in inter-communal tribal games. In 1622 (two years after the *Mayflower* arrived at Cape Cod) wampum came to have a new importance, and this was as a medium of exchange. It was then that the Dutch demanded a ransom for a Pequot *sachem* whom they had seized; they received 280 yards (256 meters) of wampum in order to secure his release. This was not so much a cash transaction as the declaration of the symbolic value of a *sachem*. For the Dutch, though, it was a game changer, because they were more interested in the cash value of wampum than the symbolic worth and suddenly realized that they now had the possibility of trading for furs using something far more valuable to Native Americans than the Venetian glass beads they had hitherto used. According to legend, the Dutch trader Peter Minuit purchased Manhattan Island for twenty-four dollar's worth of glass beads, but beads were about to become yesterday's means of exchange. Wampum was the coming thing. After 1622, it became the common medium of exchange used by the Dutch in return for beaver fur traded to the coast from the interior.

They were so successful in this that they seriously destabilized the existing trade between northern fur-trading Native Americans and the French. This was because the Dutch were proving more attractive trading partners than the French. The Dutch had stumbled onto a veritable gold mine (or rather, fur mine), since this new form of trade opened up previously unimaginable quantities of beaver fur that was worth a fortune on the European market. Globalization was drawing the native peoples of the East Coast into an (initially) mutually advantageous trading system but one that would, eventually, undermine Native American society and culture and finally destroy it. The Narragansetts and Pequots were soon producing huge amounts of wampum for the Dutch and, as a consequence, were benefitting from an advantageous position in the new and growing trade networks that were developing along the coastal areas. Tribes locked out of this could not exploit the trade in European goods that was enjoyed by the Narragansetts and Pequots as these two tribes initially cooperated with the Dutch.

Enter: the settlers of Plymouth Colony. As the Dutch trading network expanded, they began to operate as far north as Narragansett Bay. In 1627 they set up a trading post near what is today Warren, Rhode Island. A potential conflict was avoided with the settlers at Plymouth

Colony, who were alarmed at Dutch activity in what they considered their back yard; each side agreed that they would desist from trading with the Native American allies of the other. It was this same year that Isaack de Rasieres visited Plymouth and the Pilgrims were introduced to the wonders (from their point of view) of wampum.

As William Bradford informs us, it took a while for the tribes in the hinterland of Plymouth Bay and Massachusetts Bay to accept wampum as a currency. After all, that was not how it had originally been used. But persistence paid off; wampum soon became a universally recognized form of exchange throughout New England, and it drew the tribes into ever-increasing dependence on European trade. We should not underestimate the attractiveness of European metal tools, cauldrons, and kettles to Native Americans, any more than we should underestimate the value of beaver to the Europeans. At first, at least, it seemed to be a win-win situation for those directly involved in the trade.

This accelerated in 1630, when a huge number of Puritan settlers (non-separating Puritans this time) arrived at what would soon become Boston and established a colony—Massachusetts Bay—that would dwarf the venture farther south at Plymouth. They too were soon dealing in wampum. In 1650, wampum was officially recognized as a currency in Massachusetts Bay Colony, and this continued, with a fairly stable rate of exchange, until about 1660. After this, increased trade with the West Indies for raw materials such as Caribbean cane sugar and tobacco became more profitable than the fur trade. This new trade was one in which coinage was used, and, consequently, the once-stable wampum currency collapsed. Those tribes that had come to rely on it and the now much-depleted fur trade were soon facing huge difficulties, with no alternative on which to fall back. That lay ahead, but even in the 1630s, the negative impact of these new trade networks on Native American peoples was beginning to emerge.

All this complex maneuvering and jockeying for position eventually led to the appalling violence of the Pequot War (1636–38), which we will address a little later in the Mayflower Life of Myles Standish. The Narragansetts would initially benefit from the crushing of their Pequot rivals, but in time they would themselves be destroyed in the later violence associated with King Philip's War (1675–78). After the Pequot War, the Dutch abandoned southern New England, which was now seeing increasing activity by the English, and concentrated their efforts on trading with the Iroquois nations farther to the north. These tribes still had access to quality furs, which were now greatly depleted in the over-trapped south. [11] However, when Plymouth Colony first entered the fur trading business in the late 1620s, it looked as if this trade would carry the colony for the foreseeable future, for it promised large rewards if sufficient furs could be obtained.

As we have seen, the prize for which Europeans competed (French, Dutch, and eventually English) was beaver fur. This soft but water-resistant fur was much sought after in Europe for the making of felt hats. This trade grew massively from the 1580s. The fur was also used in the making of coats. A form of beaver pelt known in France as *castor gras* (greasy beaver) and in England as "coat beaver" was especially sought after for felt-hat making. *Castor gras* was beaver fur that had been worn by Native Americans for up to eighteen months. This caused the long outer hairs to be rubbed off and revealed the more valuable wool beneath. This fur was both shiny and pliable, which made it easier to work with when manufacturing European luxury fashion items.

The demand for beaver was so great that it eventually led to an ecological collapse in areas once rich in these animals. In fact, it has been estimated that while approximately twelve million beavers are to be found on the North American continent in the 21st century, there might have been as many as four hundred million of them before Europeans impacted their population. [12] It was European trade that caused this reduction, and it was already apparent in the 17th century, for as the production of wampum increased in the south, trapping accelerated massively in the north. For some Native Americans, the hunting of beaver soon dominated their lives and undermined age-old patterns of land use. The Abenaki people of Maine and southern Quebec, for example, became so intent on acquiring massive amounts of fur in order to trade it for wampum that they caused a collapse in the populations of fur-producing animals. Of these, the populations of beaver and marten were the hardest hit.

It was this trade that the Pilgrims of Plymouth Colony were seeking to exploit. And if the colonists could not get their hands on sufficient wampum or trade goods, they could always export corn. They found that the tribes of northeastern Maine were willing to trade beaver for corn, since European diseases had devastated their population of skilled native farmers.[13] Looming famine made them open to trade with Plymouth for corn. By the early years of the 1630s, Plymouth had set up a series of trading posts, which ran from the Connecticut River to Castine, in Maine. After his earlier exploration of the Kennebec River, John Howland also established a trading post on that same river, at Cushnoc, at what is now Augusta, the state capital of Maine. The site was located just below the falls on the Kennebec River. The trading house had been constructed at Plymouth and then shipped up the coast. There it was erected within a palisade to protect the traders from wolves and hostile attacks.[14] In the 1980s, archaeologists digging there discovered the remains of a wooden house that almost certainly dates from when Howland worked there. They also found broken pieces of red pottery jugs that had once held cider. The pots were of a type known to be used at Barnstaple in Devon, England, and on oceangoing voyages. It was a strange reminder of the globalizing nature of 17th-century trade, which linked Devon with a tiny settlement below the falls on the Kennebec. Unlike the home settlement at Plymouth, down in Massachusetts, this one at Cushnoc/Augusta was better sited, on a major river that gave access to the interior.[15] However, its attractive location had not only been spotted by the explorers from Plymouth. Others too had noted its potential for making big money.

It was there, in 1634, that a violent confrontation occurred, reminding us of the complex politics of settling and seizing resources that marked aspects of life on this dangerous frontier. It was an incident that William Bradford was later to judge "one of the saddest things that befell them" there, and it directly involved John Howland. For the trappers and traders from Plymouth were not the only ones seeking to harvest the valuable resources of the Kennebec area. Another group of traders had traveled there from a coastal settlement that they called Piscataqua but which is now Portsmouth, in New Hampshire. These men were led by a man called John Hocking. As he and his companions came into the area, they entered the trading lands that had been granted to Plymouth by an official English patent and thus were theirs by legal right (from an English perspective, anyway). It was this right that was challenged by the explorers from Piscataqua. Their disregard for the position of the traders from Plymouth was revealed in their pushing on up the river beyond the trading post set up by the Plymouth men. It was clear that the party from Piscataqua had no intention of allowing the Plymouth Colony to exploit the lands farther up the Kennebec. Instead, the interlopers clearly intended to intercept that trade before it even reached the trading house established at Cushnoc. As far as the newcomers were concerned, it was land open to be harvested by whoever chose to do so. This was a direct challenge to the legal position of the Plymouth men, and John Howland had no intention of letting the provocation pass without resistance. However, he could never have imagined the violent confrontation that was about to explode.

Howland challenged Hocking and ordered him to leave the Plymouth territory. Hocking was having none of it. Back in London and in the coastal settlements there might have been lines on maps and detailed clauses penned by lawyers and courtiers, but on the frontier there was a different set of rules, and here the right of an individual was expressed in his determination and his weaponry, not in his possession of a charter on parchment. So it was that Hocking waved his loaded pistol and poured a torrent of "ill words" in the direction of John Howland and the others from Plymouth. He was calling Howland's bluff in no uncertain terms. Howland too was not backing down. The situation ratcheted higher in intensity as legal rights and testosterone faced off beside the river. Howland ordered his men to cut adrift the vessel being used by the men from Piscataqua. If successful, the current of the river would force the intruders back down the way they had so recently come. Things were spiraling wildly out of control. With difficulty, the Plymouth men slashed one of the ropes with their knives; the next move would have cast the Piscataqua vessel adrift. It was then that Hocking revealed that his earlier armed threats were no bluff. Hocking thrust his pistol against the head of Moses Talbot, one of the Plymouth men. In a moment all was confusion as the gun's report, the flash and smoke of the discharged pistol, and Talbot's spattering blood signalled how far Hocking was prepared to go. Talbot was hurled back, dead, his head shattered by the pistol ball fired at point-blank range. Then it was Hocking's turn to die. One of the other men with John Howland raised his musket and dispatched the interloper-turned-killer from Piscataqua. Now it was Hocking's turn to tumble lifeless into the river. From hurled insults to discharged firearms was just a matter of a few minutes.

It took some time for the Plymouth men to get their side of the story out into the public domain; in the meantime, a very one-sided account got back to England. It omitted the fact that Hocking had been the first to use violence. So incensed were others who heard of Hocking's death that those in Massachusetts Bay even seized and imprisoned a Plymouth man—John Alden—who had been at Kennebec bringing in supplies to the Plymouth trading house and was later in the Boston area, which facilitated his arrest there. It seems that many in New England were keen to see "justice" done, especially as the settlers at Piscataqua had influential backers in London. Alden's arrest occurred despite the fact that the site of the killing was outside the jurisdiction of the Massachusetts Bay settlers at Boston. They were acting without authority and without ascertaining the true facts of the bloody altercation on the Kennebec. After a flurry of letters and representations to London and the magistrates and ministers at Boston, the matter was finally settled in Plymouth's favor, and Alden was released.[16] Nevertheless, as William Bradford later concluded, it "brought us all and the Gospel under a common reproach of cutting one another's throats for beaver."[17]

The fur trade offered huge rewards, but the violence on the Kennebec River revealed to Howland and others that it was not easy to control. And fellow Englishmen were not the only ones trying to muscle in on the action. In 1635, the French forced them out of their trading post at Castine. Clearly, they were not going to be left to enjoy the rich hinterland of Maine, unmolested. Plymouth Colony did not grow rich on the fur trade. Despite William Bradford's estimate that between 1631 and 1636 they shipped £10,000 worth of beaver pelts back to England, the debts of the colony remained as large as ever. Bradford blamed the mismanagement (even perhaps deliberate insider trading) of Isaac Allerton, who supervised relations with London merchants. But it is as likely that Bradford and the others were just not financially savvy enough to make the most of the market, especially when faced with possible sharp practice employed by some others. Life in the New Jerusalem of the New World was not easy when one still had to trade with Babylon. Things only improved when Boston replaced London as their main trading partner, as this made it easier for the Plymouth colonists to keep an eye on transactions. Even then, in 1648, Bradford, Howland, and others were forced to sell off some of their hard-won land in order to finally pay off their massive debts. [18]

Later life, at Duxbury and Kingston

In Plymouth the Howlands lived on the north side of Leyden Street, on the four-acre spot granted to the family by the Division of Land in 1623. There the Howland family lived on a plot next to one occupied by Hobbomock, who acted as guide for the colony following the death of Squanto. [19] It must have all seemed a very long way from Leiden in the Netherlands. Then the family lived for a short time in Duxbury, where they farmed eighty acres. While located there, John was one of the Duxbury citizens on a committee that met in March 1636 to decide where to locate the new Duxbury church. Then finally, in 1639 or 1640, they moved to Kingston, where they had a farm on a piece of land still known as Rocky Nook. Here the family took ownership of a farmhouse, with its barn and outbuildings; they farmed the uplands there, along with five acres of meadowland, from which they could cut hay for feeding livestock over the New England winters. [20] Four of their youngest children—Ruth, Jabez, Joseph, and Isaac—were born at Rocky Nook.

For John Howland it was a move that brought him full circle with the first nervous exploration of the land around Plymouth Bay way back in the cold, early winter of 1620. For it was then that the third exploratory party from the *Mayflower* (including John) had ventured "three English miles" up a creek that could take a fair-sized boat at high tide but drained so low at low tide that even the shallop struggled to navigate it. At that time its distance from the planned fishing grounds, and the close bordering woodland that could provide cover for native attacks, had caused them to give up the place in favor of the site that would become Plymouth. But they did not forget the place and promised that when they had finally paid off their debts to the Merchant Adventurers, some would return and settle there.[21] It is rather fitting that of those who did finally establish the village of Kingston, one would be John Howland, who had taken part in the original exploration of the area around the creek and also taken on the debt owed to the London speculators.

The site is now owned by the Pilgrim John Howland Society, and archaeologists have carried out a number of excavations there.[22] Among the artifacts discovered is a spoon tentatively dated to between 1680 and 1710.[23] It is a simple connection to the world of John and Elizabeth Howland. Within the landscape at the site it is still possible today to trace the course of a surviving stone wall that marked the boundary of the land farmed from the Howland homestead back in 1639. The original farm was burned down in 1675, during the savage conflict known as King Philip's War.[24] By that point in time, John Howland had died, and it was then that Elizabeth Howland moved in with their son, Jabez. Today, the Jabez Howland house can still be found in Plymouth. Built in about 1667, John and Elizabeth Howland lived there with Jabez, their son, during the cold winter months; Elizabeth then moved there after the death of her husband in 1673.

John Howland died on February 23, 1673. The Plymouth church records state that he was eighty years of age. As we have seen, he might have been a little younger, but whether eighty or seventy-five, he outlived most of the other male passengers who had originally traveled on the *Mayflower*. It was an impressive achievement for one who had almost drowned before he'd even caught a glimpse of North America.

In 1672, when John Howland eventually made his will, he was still, as he stated,

> *of whole mind, and in Good and prfect memory and Remembrance praised be God.*

He is presumed to have been buried on Burial Hill in Plymouth, although the exact site of his grave is unknown. In keeping with the faith of his community, his will declares how:

> *I Will and bequeath my body to the Dust and my soule to God that Gave it in hopes of a Joyfull Resurrection unto Glory.* [25]

Among his possessions was a book that reveals a lot about the mind-set of the man. It was entitled *Annotations upon the Five Books of Moses*, and it was written by Henry Ainsworth, who, like John Howland, had also lived in self-imposed exile in the Netherlands. It was a book that searched every word, every line of the Bible for layers of meaning that might otherwise be missed in a simple reading of the text. For John Howland, and for his fellow Pilgrims, this was how they read both the Bible and their own lives. At every point they sought to find God's meaning and message in all its aspects and layers of truth. Looking back on his life, John could see it again and again: saved from a tempestuous sea, preserved from harm at the conflict on the Kennebec, raised to posts of responsibility. It was all there to be read, for a man who possessed eyes to see it; to see how God had guided a Pilgrim from Leiden to a New Jerusalem in a foreign land. And to see how in this latter-day Canaan, the beginnings of a Promised Land had been wrested from the wilderness in the face of great adversity. For a man like John Howland, the work of God was there to be read in the events that had brought him so far. [26] The faithful reading of providential events by the godly had seemingly proved more accurate than the doubts entertained by others.

Elizabeth Howland outlived her husband by some fifteen years and eventually died, on December 21 or 22, 1687, in the home of her daughter, Lydia Brown, who was then living in Swansea, Massachusetts. Elizabeth is buried in the Little Neck Cemetery, in what is now East Providence, Rhode Island.

A tombstone was erected in John's memory on Burial Hill in 1897 to replace a stone erected about 1836. It ends with words that sum up something of the significance of John Howland:

> *Here ended the Pilgrimage of JOHN HOWLAND who died February 23, 1672/3 aged above 80 years. He married Elizabeth daughter of JOHN TILLEY who came with him in the Mayflower Dec. 1620. From them are descended a numerous posterity. "Here was a godly man and an ancient professor in the ways of Christ. Hee was one of the first comers into this land and was the last man that was left of those that came over in the Shipp called the Mayflower that lived in Plymouth."* [27]

Since all of the ten children of John and Elizabeth Howland lived to adulthood and married, they may have more descendants living today than any other of the *Mayflower* passengers who raised a family in the New World. This is not surprising, since John and Elizabeth had no fewer than eighty-eight grandchildren from which future generations could spring. [28] Among these many later descendants we can name three presidents of the United States (Franklin D. Roosevelt, George H. W. Bush, George W. Bush); Hollywood actor Humphrey Bogart; founder of the Mormon Church, Joseph Smith; poet Ralph Waldo Emerson; and pediatrician and Olympic gold medalist Dr. Benjamin Spock. [29] Quite an impact for a man who nearly never made it to New England in 1620.

9

The Preacher's Story:
William Brewster, Saint,
Diplomat, and Preacher

One of the leading Leiden Saints was William Brewster. He was the only Pilgrim who had political and diplomatic experience in England; and he was the only university-educated member in the colony that was eventually set up in New England.

Due to his education and existing status within the godly congregation from Leiden, Brewster became a regular preacher and one of the leaders of the little community in Plymouth Colony. In fact, he was the colony's religious leader during some rocky periods as they tried to find a suitable church pastor. William Brewster's Mayflower Life opens a door into the nature of this little community of the godly as they struggled to establish their New Jerusalem. It also allows us an opportunity to explore how life in Plymouth was different when compared to the bigger community of Saints that was established a little farther north at Boston, after 1630.

From Cambridge University to godly exile

William was born around the year 1566, in Scrooby, in the English county of Nottinghamshire. He was the son of William and Mary Brewster. His actual home lay on the lands of the manor of Scrooby, which was owned by the archbishops of York. The Church of England, then as now, was overseen by two archbishops. The senior one was based at Canterbury, in Kent, and the other at York, in Yorkshire. Scrooby came under the authority of this second archbishop, and the manor there was leased to the son of the archbishop of York. William Brewster's father was one of the bailiffs of the archbishop. As well as being responsible for the running of the lands of the manor, he was also the postmaster. This was an important job, providing horses for the mail riders who conducted official business along the Great North Road, which ran from London to Scotland. Scrooby lay on this major artery of communication and travel.[1]

William Brewster stood out from all the other Pilgrims who sailed on the *Mayflower* due to his impressive level of education. He could read both Greek and Latin and studied at Peterhouse College, Cambridge University, although he never actually completed a full degree there. He entered Peterhouse in December 1580, when he was aged about fourteen. The last mention of him in the college records is from December 1581, when he would have been sixteen at the most.[2] It was not at all unusual at the time for young men (and it was only men) from families with sufficient resources to support them, to benefit from a period of time at Cambridge or Oxford without necessarily getting a full degree. William Brewster was certainly no "college dropout" simply because he left without one. That is clear from what came next.

In 1584, he entered the service of a man named William Davison, who was at that time one of Queen Elizabeth I's secretaries of state. While working for Davison, Brewster made his first visit to the

Netherlands, in 1585. He accompanied Davison, who had been tasked with negotiating an alliance with the government (the States-General) there. It was an important mission and gave William Brewster his first taste of life in a country that one day would be his temporary home.

He remained in Davison's service when his boss was advanced, in 1586, to the role of assistant to Queen Elizabeth's spymaster, Francis Walsingham. However, in 1587 Davison fell out of favor with the queen and ended up in prison. It seemed that William Brewster had hitched his wagon to the wrong man. As a result, he went back to Scrooby, where he took on his father's job as postmaster and bailiff. It looked like William Brewster had experienced his fifteen minutes of fame and was about to vanish back into rural obscurity, even if it was a fairly comfortable life. But history had not finished with William.

It is clear that while he was at Cambridge, William had been influenced by Puritan ideas. Then, while traveling to the Netherlands, he had been given the opportunity to experience a society where there was greater religious freedom to practice the kind of reformed Christianity longed for by Puritans in England, but blocked there by the Crown and the bishops and archbishops of the English Church. Clearly, seeds had been sown that were soon to germinate. The time at Cambridge, and then with Davison, were crucial in the making of Brewster.

As we have seen, William was living in a period of growing dissatisfaction, in some quarters, with the Church of England. While the majority of people had adapted to the kind of moderate Protestant Church that had emerged under the rule of Queen Elizabeth I, a growing minority was anything but happy. From the 1550s, reformers (often termed "Puritans") had argued in favor of further reforms in the English Church. They opposed anything (ceremonies, decoration, style of service) they considered "popish" and wanted a stripped-down Church that only reflected things specifically mentioned in the Bible. By 1600, things were heating up as those governing the Church blocked these demands and some of the more radical among the self-proclaimed godly Saints were even considering splitting from it entirely. It was these separating Puritans (at the time called Brownists after an early spokesperson) who had begun to influence the outlook of William Brewster. It was a revolutionary influence, and it would change his life.

It is clear that William came from a family where these rebellious thoughts were brewing. These thoughts were already affecting his brother, James. In the 1590s James Brewster became the vicar of the Parish of Sutton and Lound, near Scrooby. After 1594 he began appointing curates (trainee assistant ministers) to Scrooby church who were of a Puritan persuasion. But William Brewster went further than this. Losing faith in the ability of the Church of England to reform itself, he drifted beyond the law and became a leading member of a congregation of separating Brownists, which met at his home from 1602 onwards. By 1606 he had jumped ship entirely and set up a Separatist church in Scrooby, in collaboration with a man named Richard Clyfton. He was on a collision course with the law. As a result of their radicalism, both William and James Brewster were summoned before the Church courts for their dissenting opinions and activities. By 1607, with more and more restrictions being imposed on them by the Church authorities, and with the threat of fines and imprisonment mounting, the Separatist group at Scrooby made the momentous decision to emigrate illegally (i.e., without official permission) to the Netherlands.[3] They finally left in 1608, on their second attempt. Their destination was Amsterdam. Little did Brewster know that this was only the start of a journey that would eventually lead to a new home in North America. While at Scrooby, Brewster virtually adopted the young William Bradford (later the long-serving governor of Plymouth Colony), who was an orphan, the care of whom had fallen to uncles unsympathetic with his religious idealism. In Brewster, Bradford found a more suitable role model and lifelong father figure. As a result, William Bradford left England in the company of his surrogate father and his radical church community.

In 1609 the Scrooby group moved on to Leiden. It was there that William Brewster was selected to act as the assistant to the Rev. John Robinson, who shepherded the little flock of exiles. In a short period of time William became the elder with particular responsibility for overseeing the lifestyle of the Saints as they lived among their Dutch neighbors in an environment that, though freer than in England, brought its own temptations to drift from the path of godliness. This remained his role when he sailed to North America in 1620.

In Leiden, William (now married) lived near the Pieterskerk (St. Peter's Church) with his wife, Mary, and their growing family. It was there that he collaborated with Thomas Brewer, Edward Winslow, and other exiles, in printing religious books and pamphlets, which they then illegally shipped to England. This printing operation lasted from 1617 to 1619; modern historians refer to it as the Pilgrim Press, although it had no such name at the time. Several of the books that were published in Leiden by the Pilgrim Press carry Brewster's badge, the so-called Brewster bear. The Library of the Pilgrim Society, in Plymouth, Massachusetts, contains a number of the books published by them, and some are on display in Pilgrim Hall Museum, in Plymouth, where they are a reminder of this key phase in Brewster's life.[4] Brewster was also employed by the University of Leiden teaching students English.

What became very clear was that Brewster and his co-publishers were sailing very close to the wind. And a legal storm, as great as any that would one day threaten to shred the sails of the *Mayflower*, was about to descend on them. This happened in 1618 because Brewster and his friends printed two books, written by a man named David Calderwood, which criticized King James of England and his bishops. The book that caused the biggest storm was entitled *Perth Assembly*. It protested James's imposition of the Five Articles of Perth on the Church of Scotland, which enraged Puritans by such things as insisting on kneeling to receive the bread and wine of communion (which they thought a popish practice), the authority of bishops to confirm Church membership, and observance of traditional holy days. This incendiary little publication soon attracted the attention of the London authorities.

The English government was getting tired of seeing books they considered seditious turning up in England after being printed in the apparent safety of the Netherlands. As a result, they increasingly leaned on the authorities in the Netherlands to put a stop to these irritating activities, and they used their agents there to ferret out those responsible. The English ambassador went into overdrive to discover the whereabouts of the printers responsible for producing these trouble-some books and pamphlets. As a result, William Brewster was forced to go into hiding for two years; his house in Leiden was searched by the Dutch authorities; and the offending printing press was seized. Thomas Brewer was arrested by the University of Leiden authorities and held in the University of Leiden's prison. It is no surprise that with things heating up in the Netherlands, the emigration on the *Mayflower* occurred just one year later. Curiously, the Pilgrims of Plymouth Colony never set up a printing press in North America. There was no printing press in Plymouth until the late 18th century. Perhaps they had had enough of the troubles it could cause. Alternatively, they were probably just too busy staying alive!

The Netherlands was not proving to be the safe haven the exiles had expected, at least not for those who insisted on fishing in the troubled waters of English Church politics. And so the plan of emigra-tion to North America emerged. With William Brewster in hiding, the Leiden congregation turned to their deacon, John Carver, and to another leading church member, Robert Cushman, to negotiate with the Merchant Adventurers in London. This also threw up another Scrooby connection. The treasurer of the London Virginia Company was a man named Sir Edwin Sandys, and he was the brother of the man who held the manor of Scrooby from the archbishop of York, where the Brewster family had been bailiff and postmaster. Sir Edwin obtained what was known as a patent, which granted colonists the right to settle on land in Virginia. He did this, partly in his own right, and also on behalf of the Leiden Pilgrims.[5]

When the Leiden congregation was finally ready to send the first group of colonists, it was decided that their pastor, the Rev. John Robinson, would stay behind in Leiden with the majority of the com-munity. He would emigrate later with the remainder. This raised the matter of who would provide the spiritual oversight for those who were emigrating. Elder William Brewster took on this role, as he was second in seniority within the church. This was despite the fact that at age fifty-four, he was one of the oldest passengers on the *Mayflower*.[6]

When the time came to leave Leiden, Brewster took with him his wife, Mary, and their two youngest children, boys named Love and Wrestling. Their daughters, Patience and Fear, and their eldest son, Jonathan, traveled to North America later. When the illegitimate More children were divided up among members of the Leiden congregation, Richard and Mary More were placed as servants with the Brewster family on the *Mayflower*. So, the Brewster family and their immediate servants set sail into the unknown. Their flight from Babylon (first from England and then from the Netherlands) was entering a new and dramatic phase. The Old World fell away to stern. The New World beckoned, with all is potential and all its unknown. They were going to create a new community with their strange combined passenger list of Saints and Strangers. And William Brewster was charged with its spiritual direction; no small matter for those seeking to make a godly community in a distant and strange land.

What the Mayflower Compact reveals about the community at Plymouth

What kind of community was Elder Brewster going to lead in the New World? We can get a glimpse of it in one of the great foundational documents in the history of what became the United States of America: the Mayflower Compact.

On November 11, 1620, the passengers on the *Mayflower* faced a potential crisis. Everyone on board had signed up to settle in the colony of Virginia (at its then northern edge, on the Hudson River). But, when storms and shoals forced them to turn back to Cape Cod, all their plans were thrown up in the air. It was not just a matter of geography, since some of the more unruly Strangers started muttering that if they were not going to Virginia, then the rules and regulations that they had signed up to for living *there* did not apply to them anymore. In effect, they no longer had a government over them. Everyone was free to do as they wished. Things were set to fall apart. William Bradford later described the scene as he remembered it when compiling *Of Plymouth Plantation*:

*the discontented and mutinous speeches that some of the strangers
amongst them* [the passengers on board] *had let fall from them
in the ship.*[7]

To avoid a disaster, William Brewster and the other leading passengers gathered together all the adult male passengers in order to
sign up to a new arrangement. It would be one that would provide
an organizational foundation for the community they were about to
establish. This was a key moment in the history of the *Mayflower*
voyage and Plymouth Colony. William Brewster is the strongest
candidate for the person who wrote the agreement. This Cambridge
University student was the best educated of anyone on board, and as
a former diplomat, he was no stranger to treaties and formal documents. It is reasonable to assume that he was the man who put quill
to parchment and created this most famous of Mayflower-related
documents.

It is not a long piece, and a few key words of Brewster's stand out
to give a flavor of what kind of people and community it represented.
They were carrying out the venture principally "for the Glory of God
and advancement of the Christian faith." They intended to "Covenant and Combine ourselves together into a Civil Body Politic, for
our better ordering and preservation." They would then be empowered
to create laws and set up public offices, "for the general good of the
Colony, unto which we promise all due submission and obedience."[8]
Just a few words . . . but powerful sentiments.

Shortly before dawn, forty-one men signed it. The die was cast.
They were in it together: for better or for worse. The original document
is long gone, so we can no longer see those names hurriedly penned, by
the light of a lantern within the cramped confines of the *Mayflower*.
However, its wording survived, first in the account of the early colony
known as *Mourt's Relation*, which was hurriedly published in London
in 1622; then in William Bradford's *Of Plymouth Plantation*, which he
compiled (but did not publish) up to about 1650; and finally in *New
Englands Memorial*, published by a man named Nathaniel Morton
(Bradford's nephew) in 1669, together with the names of those who

signed it. The two earliest versions are almost identical, so we can be confident that we know what was signed. [9]

William Brewster was, apparently, the fourth to sign. He did so after John Carver, William Bradford, and Edward Winslow. This is now where his name stands in most modern publications of the document. His importance is also seen in the fact that he is described as "Mr." William Brewster, one of only eleven men accorded a title (ten differentiated with "Mr." and Myles Standish with "Captain"). However, this is misleading. It was not until 1669 that a published version of the compact gave names of signers, and we have no idea how accurately it represented where the names actually appeared on the original. And even if we had that original, there is no way of knowing the order in which the signatures were written on it. As for the numbers that often appear in modern lists beside the names, they did not appear until an edition of 1736. [10] It was also then that the eleven titles were added, based on a list of passengers (where *some* were given titles) that is found at the end of the manuscript *Of Plymouth Plantation*.

We can, though, be fairly confident that William Brewster was foremost in the venture, having almost certainly penned that important document, which bound the group together and gave them a new identity. When William Bradford later recorded it, he first wrote how they were formed "into a Civil Body Politic, for *ye* better ordering and preservation." Then he thought twice and made a small alteration by scratching out one word and replacing it with another, so that it finally read: "into a Civil Body Politic, for *our* better ordering and preservation." [11] He was probably just bringing his version into line with the original document, but the difference is telling. What William Brewster had written—and what the forty-one had signed—was "*ours*." It was what defined *them*. It was what made them stand apart. It was foundational.

For the Saints of the gathered congregations of the godly, compiling and signing such a compact was in their spiritual DNA. [12] It was the kind of thing they did when they formed their congregations as they consciously broke away from the Church of England and created a separate community. Now they were doing so again. It was like a kind of rebirth; a reformation, even. Having crossed the Jordan River (as it were), they were establishing their identity in the New World, which they hoped would become a Promised Land. It also settled the matter of the grumbling by the Strangers too of course, as now they had a governing identity to replace that which had been rendered null and void by the decision to abandon the plan to settle in the Hudson River area. But there was more to it even than that. This compact was signed by Saints *and* Strangers. It made no demands that its signatories agree with a particular sectarian outlook, and, in that feature, it was remarkably encompassing and inclusive.[13] While the religious character of New Plymouth would be decided mostly by the godly, they were not the only ones who would be making an input. Neither would they alone constitute its responsible citizens, its workers, and its lawmakers. This New Jerusalem would find room for more than just the inner core of the elect. In time that character would differentiate Plymouth from the more sharply defined—and excluding—semi-theocracy that would emerge, for a time, at Boston. We should not exaggerate the difference, but it was important, as we shall see. And William Brewster played a key part in creating that character in the predawn of November 11, 1620, as the *Mayflower* lay at anchor in Provincetown Harbor. Cultural history was being made.

Now that the passengers had agreed on a new legal identity, they could proceed with the actual settlement in their revised location. As a key next step they elected John Carver as their first governor on November 21, 1620. The constitutional features of Plymouth Colony were coming into existence. It had been a difficult process, but, with these in place, they could take their next, tentative, steps towards establishing their settlement.

Leading the Saints in Plymouth: preaching, pastoring, and a sex scandal

Brewster continued his work as senior church elder throughout his life at Plymouth Colony, and he was a key adviser to Governor William

Bradford. This continued a neighborly connection that went right back to England, since William Bradford was born at Austerfield, only three short miles from Scrooby, and, as we have seen, Brewster acted as a father figure to the younger man.

Brewster's spiritual leadership was crucial, because the Rev. John Robinson never made it to the New World, and the first contingent of Leiden Pilgrims—though still deeply loyal to him—never enjoyed his wise and moderate leadership. He was still living in Leiden when he died in 1625. We cannot be entirely sure why he never emigrated. The needs of those remaining in Leiden would have weighed heavily on such a caring man, along with the possibility of personal illness, which made it difficult for him to make the move. On the other hand, the Merchant Adventurers in London might have been unwilling to encourage the formation of a Separatist community in New England, and hoped that a non-separating clergyman might eventually take over the role of spiritual leader there and so bring the colony back under the authority of the Church of England.

In the meantime, it would be William Brewster who would provide spiritual oversight of the colony until a minister could be appointed. And the need to appoint such a person was pressing, since there were limits to what Brewster could do as an elder. He could lead services, teaching twice every Sunday when there was no other minister, on top of his day job working in the fields. But he could not administer the only two sacraments acceptable to a Puritan congregation: baptizing children and administering the Lord's Supper (the bread and wine of communion). These were crucial to the functioning of the congregation and relied on the presence of what they considered to be a regularly ordained minister who had a theological education.[14] Since the Leiden congregation had been used to the Lord's Supper every Sunday, its absence grieved them deeply, as did their inability to baptize any new babies born to the community. William Brewster and the others needed a minister to lead them, and they needed one quickly.

In 1623 it looked like this might be about to happen. It was then that the Rev. William Morrell was brought over from England by Captain Robert Gorges (who briefly acted as the royally appointed governor-general of New England from 1623 to 1624). Gorges was charged with extending the area of colonization to the north of Plymouth; his efforts failed.[15] Nothing better emerged from the work of Rev. Morrell, who was supposed to have oversight of all the churches in New England. This attempt at getting the place back under the authority of the Church of England came to nothing. Well, not quite nothing. In the year that he spent in Plymouth he wrote some very fine poetry in Latin hexameters; when he returned to England in 1624, he published an English-language version of these, which appeared in 1625 under the not-exactly-catchy title *New-England, or a briefe Enarration of the Ayre, Earth, Water, Fish, and Fowles of that Country. With a Description of the. . .Habits and Religion of the Natives, in Latine and English Verse.* He was not exactly a substitute for the Rev. John Robinson.

William Brewster must have been torn between disappointment that no permanent acceptable minister had been appointed and relief that such an unsatisfactory clergyman had gone back to England. But all was not lost, for in the same year that Morrell left, another clergyman arrived. Here at last, perhaps, was a minister who could shoulder the burden currently carried by Brewster. If that was what William Brewster hoped, then he was about to have a rude awakening. A very rude awakening indeed!

The Rev. John Lyford arrived in 1624, probably on the ship *Charity.* He accompanied a new group of colonists led by a man named John Oldham. These newcomers had their own personal and particular reasons for emigrating, which were unlike those which had led to the Pilgrim Leideners moving: they became labelled as "Particulars."[16]

The Rev. Lyford's arrival posed a problem for William Brewster and all the Saints at Plymouth. In their (separating) version of the Church, a clergyman was only legitimate if chosen by a particular congregation and commissioned by the laying on of hands by those acting as elders and deacons in that church. They did not accept the authority of a man who was ordained by a bishop, since they rejected the authority of bishops of the Church of England. Even non-separating Puritans (who wished to remain within a reformed Church of England) had problems with accepting the authority of bishops. There was going to be trouble, because William Brewster and the other Saints simply did not accept that Lyford had any legitimacy at all. This came to a head when Lyford privately baptized a child of one of the new colonists who had arrived with him.[17] This baptism of one of the Particulars, when Lyford was not regarded as a real minister anyway, was a double red rag to a bull. But that was not the half of it. Not for nothing did a later historian of the Pilgrim colony refer to him as the "Lewd John Lyford"![18] A sexual scandal was about to explode in the colony.

John Lyford was awarded his master's degree from Oxford University in 1602 and became the Protestant minister at Leverlegkish, Armagh, in Ireland. There he ministered to one of the Protestant communities that had been settled in Ireland as part of the English attempts to hold down the majority-Catholic island.

When he first appeared at Plymouth, he seemed sympathetic to the Separatist congregation there, but in reality he was favorable to the Church of England despite what he told his new congregation. The congregation allowed him to preach but not to administer the sacraments, which clearly annoyed him. Lyford began writing letters to England criticizing the administration of Plymouth. Suspicions arose about the man, and some of these letters were impounded by Governor Bradford before they were sent to England. When they were opened, their contents shocked the godly of the colony. Lyford also championed the rights of the Particulars and set up a second church. Such diversity was unacceptable to the colony's leadership.[19] Lyford apologized for what he had done, but his contrition was feigned, because soon he wrote a similar letter criticizing the colony's separatism. It was also intercepted before it could get back to England. After this, in 1625, he was sentenced to banishment from Plymouth.

It was then that the real bombshell landed. Lyford's wife, who was named Sarah, revealed that Lyford had fathered an illegitimate child with another woman before his marriage to her. But this was only the start of his sexual offenses. Sarah—who had clearly had quite enough of her philandering husband—then revealed that after their marriage he was constantly having sex with their female servants!

Even worse was to follow, as eventually it was revealed exactly why the Rev. Lyford had decided to emigrate to New England. While counselling an unmarried female member of his Irish parish, Lyford had raped her. Later the poor girl, now married, told her new husband, who decided to bring justice down on the head of the sexual predator. Faced with the vengeance of this man and his friends, Lyford had made a quick getaway in the direction of the New World.

After this sexual scandal erupted, Lyford was expelled from Plymouth Colony. From there he moved to Nantasket (southeast of Boston). Then he moved to Cape Ann (now near Rockport, Massachusetts, northeast of Boston). Finally, he relocated south to Virginia, where he died.

All of this threw more responsibility back onto William Brewster to provide spiritual stability at a time of real crisis and distress within the colony. This continued until a new pastor, one Ralph Smith, finally arrived in 1629. Unlike the previous two ministers, he was a Separatist in outlook and therefore acceptable to the godly of Plymouth, who ordained him as their leader. He led the congregation at Plymouth for seven years, from 1629 to 1636. However, a depressing note found in the Plymouth church records lamented that "he proved but a poor help to them in that, being of very weak parts."[20] The strong and capable leader they so wanted to have still eluded them.

For three years the Rev. Smith was assisted by an associate pastor named Roger Williams. In many Separatist churches, it was the associate who provided most of the teaching and preaching, while the senior minister devoted more time to prayer and direction of the community. However, this associate pastor soon gained a notoriety of his own, which once more unsettled the colony. In this his backstory should have alerted them to the likelihood of trouble.

In 1631 Roger Williams arrived in Boston, where a large new colony had been established in 1630. There he refused an invitation to lead a local church because that congregation had not separated itself from the Church of England. As we shall shortly see, in the community at Boston, it was non-separating Puritans who predominated. This meant that Williams was on a collision course with the civil authorities there, who prevented him from accepting a post at the church at

Salem because of his Separatist outlook. The colonists at Boston rather looked down on the "wrong sort of Puritans" who had earlier settled at Plymouth, and they had no intention of encouraging such Separatist tendencies in their own back yard. This was exacerbated by Williams's belief in the complete separation of Church and state. This did not go down at all well in Boston.

As a result, Williams moved south to Plymouth Colony (where the Separatists were his kind of Puritan). However, his antagonistic personality soon caused him to fall out with them too. Eventually he moved back north, in 1635, and took up the post at Salem. This, despite the clear opposition from the authorities based in Boston. Having settled in Salem, he then proceeded to further annoy the authorities by preaching that the Church of England was so sinful that membership in it constituted a sin. This was hardly likely to go down well with non-separating Puritans. He added to this by stating that Charles I (head of the English Church) was not a real Christian. Furthermore, Williams insisted that no oaths should be imposed by civil authorities, as this contravened the clear teaching of the Gospel of Matthew chapter 5, verses 34–37. After this the General Court of the Massachusetts Bay Colony expelled him in 1636. From there he founded the colony of Providence Plantations, where freedom of religion was allowed.

Then he drifts out of our story, but it is worth noting that for a while Williams became a Baptist and established the first Baptist church in North America. Since both separating Puritans and non-separating Puritans believed in infant baptism, this only confirmed their opinion of Williams as a dangerous radical, a real loose cannon. But true to his belief in freedom of religion, he welcomed the Quakers (when some others were hanging them), even though he disagreed with them. In addition, he developed a ministry to the local Native Americans and translated the scriptures into native languages. Finally, he rejected even the Baptists and became what was termed "a Seeker," one who had given up on all formal Church structure and belief systems and, instead, sought inner spiritual enlightenment.

Roger Williams and Ralph Smith had both left Plymouth by 1636. Once more William Brewster was left carrying the burden of preaching, and once more there was no one capable of leading communion or baptizing babies. It was then that Edward Winslow located a Mr. Glover, in England, who agreed to take up the role. However, he died before he could travel, so the effort was frustrated. Finally, Winslow located a possible minister in the form of John Norton, who agreed to travel to New England on the understanding that he would then decide if the situation seemed right for him. If it was not suitable, then he would repay the community for the expense of bringing him over (this came to £70). According to William Bradford,

> *He stayed about a year with them after he came over, and was well liked of them and much desired by them; but he was invited to Ipswich* [on the Massachusetts coast, north of Salem], *where were many rich and able men and sundry of his acquaintance. So he went to them and is their minister. About half of the charge was repaid, and the rest he had for the pains he took amongst them.*[21]

It looked like they would never find a man to ease Brewster's burden and minister to the community. Then, just as frustration mounted, they found the man! And one who stayed with them for eighteen years. This was John Rayner, whom Bradford described as "an able and a godly man . . . and of a meek and humble spirit, sound in the truth and every way unreproveable in his life and conversation."[22] All must have breathed a collective sigh of relief. If so, it was a little premature.

Rayner was accorded the role of teacher and was initially the associate of another minister named Charles Chauncy, who emigrated to North America in 1637, having faced conflict in England due to his Puritan views. However, Chauncy only spent three years in Plymouth. During his time there he sparked controversy over his beliefs regarding the exact nature of baptism. Chauncy insisted that the only legitimate baptism was by dipping (immersing the whole body under water). He insisted that the form usually used with babies—sprinkling—was unacceptable. In contrast, William Brewster and the other church elders believed that sprinkling was acceptable, as it was a symbolic act representing a spiritual truth. Chauncy had an altogether more literal outlook and was not one to accept complexity. Over such things did the godly in New England divide. To give a further flavor of Charles Chauncy's outlook, back in England he had gotten into trouble for opposing communion rails in churches. These items of church furniture might seem of minor importance, but to Puritans like the Rev. Chauncy, they were popish, since they focused attention on the front of the church, where a communion table might therefore become considered to be an altar and so encourage latent Catholic beliefs in transubstantiation.

Back to total immersion baptism. With some reluctance, the elders at Plymouth (including William Brewster) accepted Chauncy's form of the rite, but as William Bradford noted,

> *The church yielded that immersion or dipping was lawful but in this cold country not so convenient. But they could not, nor durst not yield to him in this, that sprinkling (which all the churches of Christ do for the most part use at this day) was unlawful and an human invention . . .*[23]

Brewster and the other elders offered a flexible solution. Rev. Chauncy could baptize by dipping all who desired this, while the Rev. Rayner would baptize by sprinkling and pouring all those who desired that. The matter was made more pressing because the Pilgrims of Plymouth were not Baptists. Unlike those particular Separatists, the ones at Plymouth believed in infant baptism. In this they were in agreement with a lot of other non-separating Puritans and also (not that they found any comfort in this) with the doctrine of all shades of the Church of England and even with Roman Catholics. That it was infant baptism in question made the matter more complex, as Chauncy's belief resulted in little babies being put completely under water; potentially very cold running water. Consequently, the elders and civil authorities at Plymouth wrote to other congregations in Boston, Connecticut, and New Haven asking for their advice. The response was that both forms of baptism were valid; this vindicated the flexible outlook of men like

William Brewster but did not go down at all well with the inflexible Charles Chauncy, who held that only his strict interpretation was acceptable. Eventually, after three years at Plymouth, Chauncy moved to Scituate (on the Massachusetts coast, north of Marshfield) in 1641, where he continued to be fairly divisive in his views. It was there, in 1642, that Chauncy led a spectacularly eventful open-air baptism service involving his own twin sons. One passed out due to the cold. The mother of another child due to be baptized refused to allow it and, in the ensuing altercation, nearly re-baptized Chauncy by pulling him into the water. Despite this he went on to become the second president of Harvard College, although only on the condition that he kept his rigid views on baptism to himself. From this we can conclude that the fiasco at Scituate had done nothing to dent his confidence in his own superior interpretation of how to carry out the rite.

During all these stressful times of uncertainty the one continuity was the faithful ministry of William Brewster. He continued to preach, when required, until his death in April 1644.

Together with the other church members (and with the clergy when they had a minister), the congregation met at first in the meeting house they built in 1621 near the shore, on the street they called First Street, but which today is Leyden Street in Plymouth. Then, from 1622, they met in the fort, located on what is today Burial Hill. In 1648 (some sources say 1637) they finally built a simple square meeting house on the north side of what is now Town Square, at the top of Leyden Street. This lasted until 1683, when they built their second meeting house on the highest point of Town Square, looking down Leyden Street towards the shoreline. Today this is the location of First Parish Plymouth Church, with its records dating back to 1606 in England. The second meeting house built here served both the religious and civic needs of the town until 1744, when the town gave the meeting house to the church and the unity of Church and state that had been the legacy of the first Pilgrims finally ended.[24] On the site of the first meeting house (just across from First Parish Plymouth) is located the Church of the Pilgrimage, built in 1840 after a split from First Parish Plymouth. But that is part of another and later story. . . .

Keeping to the narrow way of holiness

Looking at Plymouth Colony from a 21st-century perspective, we are often struck by the limits to their tolerance of views different from their own. But in this they were very much representative of their age, in which there was a strong belief that only a particular way of life was acceptable to God and that what was necessary was both discovering the boundaries of that narrow way (as they would have put it) and insisting on its being adhered to by all, for the good of the whole society. For them, it was this that acted as a glue to hold the whole community together and which prevented it fragmenting. And in this, as we will see a little later through comparing Plymouth Colony with that of Massachusetts Bay, the Saints at Plymouth were much more tolerant of difference than some of their contemporaries were. We have already seen this in the flexibility of William Brewster regarding baptism.

In addition, at Plymouth the Saints and Strangers generally got on to a surprising degree. This did not mean that they always saw eye to eye, but these differences did not lead to conflict. This was very apparent at Christmas 1621. William Bradford later recorded the events of this year and then wryly wrote,

> *I shall remember one passage more, rather of mirth than of weight. On the day called Christmas Day, the Governor called them out to work as was used. But the most of this new company excused themselves and said it went against their consciences to work on that day. So the Governor told them that if they made it matter of conscience, he would spare them till they were better informed; so he led away the rest and left them.*

This was very open-minded, even liberal.

> *But when they came home at noon from their work, he found them in the street at play, openly; some pitching the bar, and some at stool-ball* [a game like modern English cricket] *and such like sports. So he went to them and took away their implements*

and told them that was against his conscience, that they should play and others work. If they made the keeping of it [Christmas] *matter of devotion, let them keep their houses; but there should be no gaming or reveling in the streets. Since which time nothing hath been attempted that way, at least openly.* [25]

The Christmas problems of 1621 reveal a relatively live-and-let-live attitude among the Saints of Plymouth towards the Strangers living among them, so long as the Strangers did not overplay their hand. And, while the so-called Strangers were rather an alien element on board the *Mayflower*, most of them eventually joined the church in Plymouth. Also, the Strangers knew that they were partnering with Saints, so what emerged was hardly a surprise. Even the indentured servants knew what they were joining and could have opted for something more secular "à la Virginia."

But this was not the case in every area of religious difference. Antagonism to Quakers and Baptists (often termed Anabaptists at the time) was absolute. Neither the Baptists nor the Quakers were welcome in Plymouth, in Massachusetts Bay, or in any other English colony. So the attitude toward these groups by the Plymouth colonists is little more than a reflection of widely held views. Adult-baptizing Anabaptists had first emerged in the 16th century, and their refusal to accept infant baptism, to take oaths, recognize secular law courts, hold secular offices—alongside pacifism in some groups and millenarian revolutionary excesses in some other groups—had gained them a very bad press indeed. [26] By the 17th century, calling a person an Anabaptist was akin to calling someone a Red in the United States of Senator McCarthy. By the time of the *Mayflower* voyage, most moderates who believed in adult baptism preferred to call themselves Baptists, not Anabaptists, and posed no threat to social order. But the mud had stuck, and in Plymouth there would have been a fear that such people threatened moral dissolution and would undermine community cohesion. They also undermined trust in the clergy, since they repudiated the validity of infant baptism. Baptists were lumped together with Anabaptists, and little or no differentiation was made between them.

We are told that one of the *Mayflower* passengers, named John Cooke, "fell into the error of Anabaptistry" (that term!), despite being a deacon in the Plymouth church under Elder William Brewster. The Plymouth church records state:

> *This John Cooke although a shallow man became a cause of trouble and dissension in our Church and gave just occasion of their casting him out; so that Solomon's words proved true in him that one sinner destroyeth much good.* [27]

Eventually, Cooke left Plymouth and took up residence in Dartmouth (on the coast southwest of Plymouth, facing Buzzards Bay), where he died in 1695.

Like the Baptists, Quakers were not welcome either. This applied to many communities in England and New England, with the exception of Providence Plantations, where Roger Williams was more open-minded. [28] Like the Anabaptists/Baptists, these early Quakers were feared as a threat to social order. Unlike the Baptists, the Quakers were a new phenomenon when they first appeared in the 1650s, in the decade after the death of William Brewster. And some of these early Quakers really did challenge social norms in a way that put most Baptists in the shade. They did not accept the ultimate authority of the Bible, they would not swear oaths or serve in the military. Some were so confident in their inner spiritual enlightenment that they behaved in ways that others considered heretical or blasphemous. They could also be disruptive and very challenging, a long way from the gentle pacifism of modern Quakers. In 1657 two Quakers were tried before the General Court of Massachusetts Bay. They were uncowed; one called the judge a liar, while the other labelled him malicious and mere "dust beneath my feet." This went down very badly, as one can imagine. Both were whipped and banished to Rhode Island, which was regarded as a dumping ground for heretics! Along with Providence Plantations, it had been established by settlers who had been expelled from Massachusetts Bay Colony due to holding religious opinions judged unacceptable by their fellow colonists there. Another Quaker disrupted the church meeting at Cambridge, Massachusetts, by smashing bottles on the floor and declaring that, in a similar way, God would smash them! All of this wound up opponents and seemed to justify harsh responses.

Nevertheless, they had sympathizers. In Plymouth Colony these sympathizers included Captain James Cudworth, from Scituate, and Arthur and Henry Howland, who were brothers of John Howland of the *Mayflower*. This was despite the fact that any Quakers who articulated their radical beliefs were sure to be hauled before the colony's court. Nevertheless, the situation in Plymouth was less hard-line than up the road in Massachusetts Bay Colony. Somewhere in the region of ten Quakers were deported from Plymouth, with five of them being whipped before their expulsion. Yet none of them was hanged or branded, as occurred in Massachusetts Bay and also in England. They could even meet if they kept their heads down. Consequently, by 1690, there were several Quaker groups, or "Meetings," along the border with Rhode Island, at Rehoboth and Swansea. There were others at Falmouth, on the southern coast of Cape Cod, and also in the eastern settlements of Dartmouth (now New Bedford). No attempt was made to hunt them out. It was a policy akin to don't ask, don't tell. This brings us to the question of the relationship between the Saints living in Plymouth Colony and those in the colony of Massachusetts Bay to the north.

Relationships between Plymouth Colony and the colony of Massachusetts Bay

Most of the early colonists in 17th-century New England were what we would now call non-separating Puritans, who did not wish to set up separate congregations distinct from the Church of England. Instead, they wished to enjoy semiautonomy within their individual church communities, while still holding allegiance to a loose Church system. Most of the godly who emigrated to North America traveled there in the decade after the *Mayflower* voyage (1630–1640) and were non-separating Puritans.

As a result, it was non-separating Puritans who played key roles in establishing the Massachusetts Bay Colony in 1629, New Hampshire Colony in 1629, Connecticut Colony in 1636, and New Haven Colony in 1638. The most striking influx of these non-separating Puritans occurred in 1630, when John Winthrop led the so-called Winthrop Fleet, consisting of about seven hundred colonists carried on eleven ships to Massachusetts Bay. This movement was encouraged by the fact that the Plymouth Colony had survived and it seemed that a godly New England really was possible, despite the fact that the Plymouth Saints were separating Puritans and represented the "wrong kind" of Puritan.

As Winthrop explained to his companions, as they sailed to the New World, their colony was going to be a "City upon a hill" (quoting Matthew 5:14–16). In Massachusetts Bay he and those with him were determined to create a theocracy where voting rights were restricted to those in the godly congregations—people who had publicly confessed their experience of conversion and whose lifestyles were acceptable to their godly neighbors. Those who fell out with this strict system included Roger Williams, whom we met earlier, and Anne Hutchinson, who denounced local ministers for being too focused on works contributing to salvation, in contrast with a "covenant of grace." She also antagonized those in authority by claiming that God had spoken directly to her through a revelation and by being too assertive as a woman. In 1638 she was banished and helped found a breakaway colony at what became Portsmouth, Rhode Island, part of what developed into the colony of Rhode Island and Providence Plantations.

The Massachusetts Puritans generally favored a Presbyterian-type of Church government (of semiautonomous congregations), while still remaining in full communion with the Church of England. To them, the Separatists, such as those down south in Plymouth Colony, were suspect, even schismatic. This did not make conflict inevitable, but it could lead to tensions. Compared with this, the regime at Plymouth was relatively liberal. Overall, though, there was a fairly cordial relationship between the two groups. When a church was established at Salem, in 1629 (the second New England congregation to be established and officially part of the Church of England), Governor

Bradford and some others from Plymouth journeyed there in order to "extend the right hand of fellowship, wishing all prosperity and a blessed success unto such good beginnings." On top of this act of fellowship, the Separatists of Plymouth Colony would worship alongside other Protestant Christians, including members of the Church of England.[29] This owed a great deal to the attitudes of men such as the Rev. Robinson in Leiden and William Brewster in North America. Under other men, with harder attitudes, it could have been very different.

This was illustrated in the 1640s. The British civil wars threw a great stone into the political and religious pond of the mid-17th century, and its ripples affected North America. At the Westminster Assembly in London, called in 1643 to advise the parliamentary government about how best to reform the Church, it was agreed that some form of national system should survive the current upheavals. Both Scots Presbyterians and moderate parliamentary members of the Church of England set their face against Separatists. That left the members of Plymouth Colony very exposed, especially as a Scottish Presbyterian minister named Robert Baillie opened up a broadside of criticism against Anabaptists and Separatists generally and mentioned the ex-Leiden Pilgrims explicitly. It may have been this unexpected storm of abuse that stung William Bradford into action to complete *Of Plymouth Plantation*, in order to defend the godly experiment there. Other New England Puritans put quill to parchment at the same time in defense of their relative independence.

Bradford might have been feeling particularly vulnerable, as the venerated William Brewster had recently died and, within four years, Rev. John Cotton of Boston had gone on the record attacking both Presbyterians *and* Separatists and making some very negative comments about the community at Plymouth. Cotton insinuated that their sufferings and poverty were signs of God's displeasure. In contrast, things were going rather well in Boston. In reply, Bradford's conclusion was that, in fact, it was little Plymouth that had kept alive the idea of independent godly churches for Massachusetts to pick up and, in turn, inspire people like Cromwell in England too.[30]

In the long run, though, Plymouth was always going to be in the shadow of Boston. The Puritan settlers in the Massachusetts Bay area outnumbered Plymouth's population by about ten to one by the late 17th century and finally absorbed them into its jurisdiction in 1691. But the days of Boston's experiment in semi-theocratic government were over by then. Massachusetts Bay had also been eclipsed by events. In 1684 the British crown annulled the existing charter of the Massachusetts Bay Colony. Furthermore, from 1686 the scattered colonies were finally unified in the Dominion of New England, under royal control. In 1691, King William III issued another charter, which unified the colonies of Massachusetts Bay, Plymouth Colony, Martha's Vineyard, Nantucket, and the territories that constitute present-day Maine, New Brunswick, and Nova Scotia. This became the Province of Massachusetts Bay. As if this was not enough to make it clear that the Crown had replaced the meeting house as the arbiter of affairs, the same action extended voting rights to non-Puritans. The godly semi-theocracy of Massachusetts Bay (including the much looser version existing at Plymouth) was effectively at an end. [31]

Family life in Plymouth Colony and the legacy of William Brewster

Although the Brewster family had been divided by the *Mayflower* voyage, they were eventually reunited in the New World. Their son Jonathan (then aged twenty-eight) rejoined the family in November 1621, when he arrived at Plymouth on the ship *Fortune*. Their daughters, Patience (then aged about twenty-three) and Fear (then aged about seventeen), arrived in July 1623 aboard the ship *Anne*.

Together they farmed the land allocated them. In addition to plots at Plymouth itself, William Brewster was granted land among the islands of Boston Harbor, where four of the outer islands still carry his name: Great Brewster, Little Brewster, Middle Brewster, and Outer Brewster. In 1632, he was granted further lands at Duxbury (on the coast south of Marshfield). As a result, the family moved from Plymouth to farm there.

Life was not easy though. In 1634, the diseases of smallpox and influenza killed many among both the settlers and Native Americans in the area. William Brewster and Mary lost their two daughters, Fear and Patience, who were by then married to Isaac Allerton and Thomas Prence respectively. It was a terrible blow for a family who had managed to survive the first terrible winter of 1620–21 without loss. More than ever, it was clear that only faith could carry a family through the uncertainties of life. Only in the way of holiness was there a route through the tempests of this world to an eternal home. Even before this, less traumatic difficulties had beset the family when Fear's husband, Isaac Allerton, had run up debts of more than £200 on William Brewster's account. Life could be stressful in families, then as now.

William Brewster's wife, Mary, died in April 1627. Mary's burial place is unknown. William never remarried, although he lived to be almost eighty years old. He died in April 1644, at Duxbury, in Plymouth Colony. He had experienced a short illness but only took to his bed on the day he died. In the afternoon his speech finally failed him, and he died peacefully, shortly before 10:00 P.M. that evening, surrounded by his loving friends. He was buried on Burial Hill in Plymouth, where a memorial stone was later raised, which declares that it marks the burial of "Elder William Brewster Patriarch of the Pilgrims and their Ruling Elder 1609–1644." The inventory of his estate lists the titles of several hundred books that he left behind. As a mark of respect, William Bradford compiled a short biography of Brewster but mistakenly lodged it under 1643 in his compilation. Of Brewster, Bradford commented, "He was wise and discrete . . . of a very cheerful spirit . . . undervaluing himself and his own abilities and sometimes overvaluing others . . . tenderhearted and compassionate of such as were in misery . . ."[32]

Since 1620, in the absence of the beloved Rev. Robinson, and despite the upheavals involved in finding a replacement, William Brewster had been like a rock for the godly of Plymouth. His death was something of a watershed. Within a few months of it, leading colonists such as Myles Standish and Edward Winslow set up homes away from the main focus of Plymouth. Members of the next generation shifted to Cape Cod and set up farms there. Plymouth remained, but something significant had changed. William Bradford compared

William Brewster and the older first comers to the Old Testament patriarch Jacob, who traveled "from one nation to another people and passed through famine, fears and many afflictions, yet he lived till old age and died sweetly and rested in the Lord."[33] Something of that inspiration outlived him, despite the changes that occurred after his death, and those who had known him were well aware of that. Elder William Brewster had passed over, but his legacy of faith lived on.[34]

10

The Pamphleteer's Story: Edward Winslow, Pilgrim Leader, Colony Agent, and Lobbyist

Sixteenth-century New England did not know the term *lobbyist*, but if it had, it would undoubtedly have been used to describe Edward Winslow, one of the Saints, a senior leader on the *Mayflower*, and then later in Plymouth Colony.[1] He eventually served as assistant governor, acted three times as governor, and was also the colony's agent in London. He wrote several important pamphlets designed to acquaint people with life in New England and encourage future settlement. It is no exaggeration to describe him as "New England's First International Diplomat."[2] In 1655, on a mission for Oliver Cromwell, he died of fever while on a British naval expedition against the Spanish in the Caribbean. He is the only Plymouth colonist with a surviving portrait. From exploring his life, we have access to something of a portrait of what it was like to lead this remarkable New England colony.

Edward Winslow was born in 1595, the eldest son of Edward and Magdalene Winslow of Droitwich, in the English county of Worcestershire. Like William Brewster, he was well educated; between April

1606 and April 1611, he attended the King's School, which was located at Worcester Cathedral. There have even been suggestions that, like Brewster, he spent a short time at Cambridge University, but that is uncertain.

What is clear is that in August 1613, he became an apprentice in London. In this capacity he was signed up for eight years to a man named John Beale, who was a stationer in London. A little later there was some legal wrangling with John Beale over the details of the arrangement. Eventually, Winslow's contract was revised in October 1615 with him being apprenticed for eight years from that date. As he set off to London he must have felt both excitement and trepidation at the move to the big city, but what he did not realize at the time was just how much it was going to change his life. The move to London was to be so important both in Winslow's life and the future life of Plymouth Colony because it introduced him to the publishing trade: he would eventually become the most widely published member of the colony as he sought to extoll the benefits of life in North America, encourage more migrants to settle there, and—when necessary—defend the godly colony against its detractors.

Despite this important career choice, something did not work out right. Perhaps there are hints of some ongoing disharmony in that renegotiation of the apprenticeship contract. We would like to know more about it, but the evidence is lost. However, it is clear that something went wrong, because Edward Winslow did not complete his contracted time with Beale. It should have lasted until 1623. But just two years after the renegotiation, in 1617, he left the work and relocated to Leiden, in the Netherlands. There he joined the Separatist church which was located in the city and which is so crucial in the *Mayflower* story and the history of Plymouth Colony. If he had worked out his contract, then he would have still been busy in the London stationery and publishing trade when the *Mayflower* sailed to the New World. He might, then, have gone on to be influential in the "pamphlet wars" that led up to the British Civil Wars. Instead he became the key pamphleteer of the godly in New England.

There is no clear evidence that he was a member of any Separatist congregation in London, but his mind must have been moving in that direction well before he abruptly left the city and moved to the hothouse atmosphere of the exiled congregation in the Netherlands.[3] Today we might say that the young man had been radicalized. And in that, he was in the company of a growing number of English men and women. Not all of those who were disenchanted with the status quo would go as far as Winslow and the Leideners in cutting themselves off from the established English Church and leaving their homeland, so it is clear that Edward was in the most radicalized core of the movement. The kinds of literature that he was reading and helping to publish probably challenged his outlook to the extent that he made the move in 1617. Today such radicalization might be affected by access to the internet, social media, and online forums; in 1617, access to radical and revolutionary pamphlets spread such ideas and gave them traction.

The extent to which Edward Winslow had been affected by what he read can be traced through the fact that he ended up in Leiden (clearly not a random geographical choice) and that there he became a close associate of Elder William Brewster and his illegal printing activities. Indeed, it might well have been through reading one of the publications of the so-called Pilgrim Press—with its Brewster logo of the bear—that young Edward was finally won over to the cause. In Leiden his interest in publishing grew into a passion for spreading the ideas of the Saints. With his intelligence and experiences in London, he was a confident and skilled member of the underground publishing group. But it was a confidence and self-assurance that was about to lead him to step over the line!

In 1618 they pushed things too far when Brewster, Winslow, and others were responsible for the publication of a pamphlet critical of the English monarch and his bishops. A furious King James ordered Brewster's arrest, leaned on the Dutch to disrupt the radicals, and even sent English government agents to the Netherlands to locate and arrest those responsible. The hammer fell on Brewster, who, as we have seen, went into hiding, but it was clear that trouble was brewing for all those associated with him in Leiden. And this included the 23-year-old Edward Winslow.

That year was one of great importance in the life of this particular young man, since—as well as seeing his publishing partner go into hiding—he married a woman by the name of Elizabeth Barker on April 27, 1618. In the wedding records of Leiden, Edward described himself simply as "a printer" from London. It was an identity that would shape his future as well as his current role.

While in Leiden, Winslow became one of the leading members of the English exiles there. This is no surprise, since he was clearly devout, educated, and committed to the cause. In June 1620, he was one of four leading men among the Leiden Saints (the others being Isaac Allerton, William Bradford, and Samuel Fuller) who represented the Leiden congregation in a letter written to their fellow Saints John Carver and Robert Cushman, who were representing the Leideners in London. These two men had been charged with negotiating with the Merchant Adventurers concerning the movement to America and the financial terms of this arrangement. It is clear that Edward Winslow was at the center of these historic events, and it is, therefore, no surprise that he and his wife were among the forerunners sailing to North America, when the rest of the congregation remained in the Netherlands with the Rev. Robinson.

So it was that they set off from Delfshaven, late in July 1620, aboard the ship *Speedwell*. Traveling with the Winslows on the *Speedwell* and then on the *Mayflower* were Edward's brother, Gilbert, a family servant named George Soule, and a youth by the name of Elias Story. When they reached England the family took on additional responsibility for the illegitimate eight-year-old Ellen More, who was being sent to North America along with her equally illegitimate siblings. The More children were divided out among three different families from among the Saints. Like her younger sister Mary, Ellen More would not survive that first terrible winter moored first off Provincetown and then off Plymouth.

Both Edward Winslow and his brother, Gilbert Winslow, were among the men who signed the Mayflower Compact on November 11, 1620, when the ship was at anchor in Provincetown Harbor. Soon events would reveal that Edward would be an even more important figure among the Saints in New England than he had been among them in Leiden.

Pilgrim Leader in the New World

Edward Winslow was soon active at the center of events in the new settlement and was given the responsibility of negotiating with Native Americans living in the vicinity of Plymouth. This was the tribal confederacy that we often describe today as the Wampanoag. In this task he succeeded in winning the friendship of their chief, the *sachem* named Massasoit, whom we have met in earlier Mayflower Lives. When Massasoit first visited the Plymouth settlement in March 1621, it was Edward Winslow who was chosen to go out and personally greet the chief. He acted as hostage in order to assure Massasoit that it was safe to go over the stream the Pilgrims called Town Brook in order to meet with the governor (who was then John Carver). Edward's confidence had never been more severely put to the test than when he took his place among Massasoit's warriors and found himself looking back the way he had come, as he watched the *sachem* pass through the ranks of musket-carrying men. Without his weaponry, he knew that his own life depended on the success of the negotiations. And yet his confidence was one underpinned by faith in the mission to which he had been called. As he stood there among the Wampanoag warriors, Edward Winslow was a man who was certain in his convictions and, undoubtedly, waited it out without fear. All this is clear from his later traveling in the woods with only one guide accompanying him; one guide and his undergirding beliefs.

This hostage arrangement happened again when Massasoit returned with his brother as part of further negotiations with the newly established incomers. From this developed a close friendship with Winslow, which would prove crucial in the development of the colony. And in that development, Edward knew both sorrow and success.

Winslow's wife, Elizabeth, died on March 24, just two days after the second visit by Massasoit. She was one of the last to die that first winter. Then, just a month and a half later, Edward married Susanna White on Saturday, May 12. When this occurred (as we saw in her Mayflower Life), they became the first couple to marry in Plymouth Colony. Following the marriage, Edward adopted Susanna's boys as his own sons; and he and Susanna went on to have five children together (three boys, one girl, and one whose gender is unknown). Of these five, just two—their son Josiah and their daughter, Elizabeth—outlived their parents. Similarly, Edward's daughter Margaret, by his first wife, died in 1655, the same year as her father. As we will shortly see, it was the Winslows who eventually established one of Plymouth's daughter settlements, that at Marshfield, in 1632, located about twelve miles north of Plymouth itself.

After early 1621 Winslow became one of several key leaders on whom the newly appointed governor, William Bradford, relied, following the death of the first governor, John Carver, in April. William Bradford appointed Winslow as his assistant. From there his role developed considerably. Edward served as a member of the governor's council from 1624 to 1647. The only breaks from this were in 1633–34, 1636–37, and then 1644–45, when he was the governor of Plymouth Colony.

His leadership role had been clear from the first meeting with Massasoit, so it is no surprise to discover that he played a crucial part in ongoing relations with the Wampanoag peoples. In July 1621, it was Winslow, accompanied by Stephen Hopkins (who had gained experience working with local tribes in Jamestown), who journeyed to Massasoit's village of Pokanoket. The name they used for this village was also the name of the particular tribe to which Massasoit belonged; it lay near what is today Warren (Rhode Island). Edward was almost certainly also one of the group who, later that same month, traveled to Nauset on Cape Cod to negotiate the return of a boy named Edward Billington, who had gotten lost in the woods and been picked up by a tribal hunting party.

In November 1621, when the ship *Fortune* arrived carrying more colonists, it was Edward Winslow who took the opportunity to send a letter back to England, in which he provided the earliest account of the first Thanksgiving that had recently occurred (although he never actually used the word *Thanksgiving* to describe the Harvest Home that had taken place in the company of Massasoit and ninety of his warriors). But he did take the opportunity to describe the good relations with the local tribe, which he had played a major role in establishing. Thinking back over the events of that year, he wrote of how the "Indians" were both loving and cooperative, and that some of the settlers had gone deep into the interior accompanied by them. By some of the settlers, he had himself in mind. He added that "it hath pleased God so to possess the Indians with a fear of us, and love unto us."[4] However, he was too modest to explain that within the outworking of providence, he had played a major role through his open-mindedness and fair dealing. It was an approach that had been reciprocated in the constructive attitude shown by Massasoit. The two men, from such different origins, had come to like and respect each other.

The fact that Edward was regarded as a key member of any negotiations with the local tribes is revealed in the fact that, in March 1622, he accompanied Myles Standish when the captain journeyed north in order to trade with the Massachusett people. His negotiating skills were similarly revealed in his being selected by the governor to travel even farther north, to Maine, in order to attempt to trade for provisions with English fishermen who put into shore there, at a place they called Damariscove (not that he was successful in this venture). Then, through no fault of his, the situation in Plymouth became even more difficult later in 1622 when two ships, the *Charity* and the *Swan*, stopped at Plymouth on their way to setting up the ill-fated Wessagusset Colony.[5] The newcomers stealing of corn from their hosts at Plymouth was a prelude to their later theft of corn from Native Americans. All of this only emphasized to Edward that a better provisioning of the colony from England and an extending of the colony's trading role were essential if Plymouth was to survive. It was this that led to him being heavily involved, in 1623, in negotiations between Plymouth and London. But, before that could happen, he was to play yet another important part in the relationship that developed with his friend Massasoit.

In March 1623, news reached Plymouth that the *sachem* was seriously ill and likely to die. Edward Winslow was the man chosen to go to him and ascertain what was happening. By now he was an experienced traveler into the interior, although he went in the company of Hobbomock, one of the Native Americans who lived with the Pilgrims at Plymouth. Hobbomock acted as his guide. Together they headed out to the winter village of the *sachem*. Here the *sachem* and his people had gathered together and spent the winter hunting, while awaiting the coming of spring, the return of the herring shoals and dispersal to the coast.

On the way they heard that Massasoit had died, but when they stopped in the village of a *sachem* named Corbitant, they learned that in fact Massasoit was still alive—just. This spurred them on to get to him as quickly as possible. When they arrived, they found his home in a state of uproar as those about the *sachem* engaged in rituals aimed at healing the dying man. Within the dark interior of the longhouse—with its cedarwood frame, oak bark covering, walls hung with insulating mats and woven bags containing possessions—the smoke from three fires drifted lazily upwards to the smoke-holes. Raised up from the bulrush mats on the floor, the *sachem* lay on one of the fur-covered bench beds.

To Edward, who had become used to the beliefs and customs of the Native American tribes, the sound of the rituals was still disconcerting. He later was to wryly comment that the level of noise made ill those who were well and was not likely to heal the sick man. Those about Massasoit would have seen things differently from Edward's Christian and European eyes. Clearly, Winslow was not impressed but was determined to do what he could to save his ally. It also transpired that Massasoit had not slept in two days, nor had he passed a stool in five. Looking back in 1624, when he wrote *Good Newes from New England*, he recalled how Massasoit—unable to see—had spoken to him the words *"Keen Winsnow"* (Is that you, Winslow?). Looking at the pale and dying man, with his eyes shadowed by illness, Edward had quietly replied, *"Ahhe"* (yes). Moved by the knowledge that his friend was so close, but burdened by sickness, the *sachem* had lamented, *"Matta neen wonckanet namen Winsnow"* (I will never see you again, Winslow). [6]

Edward sprang into action. First he washed out Massasoit's mouth and scraped his heavily furred tongue. Those gathered around their dying chief paused in order to see if there was any positive outcome as a result of the visitor's strange intervention. Then Winslow gave him a medicine that had been brought from Plymouth. We have no idea what it contained, only that Winslow later described it as "the confection" and that it was dissolved in water in order for Massasoit to drink it. Those watching were duly impressed when Massasoit began to recover his sight. One can imagine the intakes of breath and the sudden buzz of conversation at the improvement. It looked like, maybe, he would not die after all. The next day Winslow took his musket and, on the request of Massasoit, did a bit of fowling and prepared a soup for the *sachem* from the bird he had shot, flavored with strawberry leaves and sliced sassafras root. The *sachem* seemed to particularly want the kind of soup he had tried at Plymouth, rather than the traditional *succotash* of corn and beans. This duck pottage (often now referred to as chicken soup in modern accounts of these remarkable events) had a striking effect, which amazed everyone even more than the confection and the tongue-scraping of the previous afternoon. Massasoit passed three stools as his digestive system started moving again. Despite his total lack of medical training, the ex-printer and pamphleteer had enough practical experience to know the importance of a nourishing and easily digested meal for a man hovering on the brink of death. And it worked. The result was a deepening of the relationship between Massasoit and the Plymouth Pilgrims to the extent that he revealed that he had gotten wind of a native conspiracy to extirpate the thieving colony at Wessagusset, and also the other English settlements too. It was useful information and came as a direct result of the medicinal intervention.

On the way back to Plymouth, Winslow and Hobbomock stopped off with Corbitant, who was so impressed by the recovery of Massasoit that he asked for similar assistance from Plymouth if he ever fell dangerously ill. Edward promised that he would come. This went down very well with Corbitant, who was already impressed with the courage of his visitors, who traveled—just the two of them—through the woods without fear. However, he commented that he was less impressed with the colonists' custom of pointing their muskets (clearly presenting arms) at him when he visited the settlement at Plymouth!

The meeting with Corbitant was so cordial that it provided Winslow with an opportunity to talk about his Christian faith, since Corbitant was intrigued when he saw how Winslow prayed over his food before commencing to eat. In the animated conversation that followed, their only area of disagreement was over the seventh commandment, "Thou shalt not commit adultery" (Exodus 20:14). Corbitant and his friends were not at all convinced about the restrictions involved in that one, as it seemed to them to involve "many inconveniences," since it tied a man to just one woman. But, apart from that, there seemed a high level of agreement.

Edward was convinced that he had gotten his head around Native American beliefs, but he had not really grasped the differences between Christian beliefs and those of his tribal friends. He looked at the world through a lens that filtered between "good" and "evil," but these were not concepts known in native beliefs. Talking with Corbitant, as he had with other native people, he was sure that the being they named Kietan was the equivalent of the Christian concept of God, while the mention of a "spirit of darkness" was a reference to the devil. In fact, these ideas concerning opposing spiritual forces were not really part of Corbitant's religious culture, which tended to emphasize complementary (if contrasting) spiritual forces.[7] Consequently, Edward and Corbitant were actually talking past each other. But at least they were doing it amicably, in a spirit of friendship. By a strange irony, both of the Native Americans who lived among the Pilgrims and who became friends with Winslow and Bradford—Squanto and Hobbomock—were named after a being whom the Puritans would probably have understood (wrongly) to be the devil. Hobbomock was named after a manifestation of a spiritual force (*manitou*); in native mythology, Kietan had cast a spell upon *manitou* to keep it from causing havoc. Similarly, Squanto/Tisquantum's name[8] meant something like 'anger of the *manitou*.' It was all for the best that Edward was ignorant of this as he engaged in friendly theological conversation with Corbitant on his way home from Massasoit's village.

The year 1623 continued to be an eventful one for Edward. He gained four acres on the northern side of town in the Division of Land.

Then, in September, he was charged with returning to England on the ship *Anne* to deliver a load of clapboard and beaver skins. With the money gained, he was to buy urgently needed provisions. As agent of the colony he set off for England. He returned in 1624 on the ship *Charity* and brought with him three heifers, a bull, some articles of clothing, and other items. Edward Winslow was the man to get things done.

Edward knew that as long as the colony labored under the weight of its debt to its creditors in London, it would never truly prosper. And so, in 1626, he joined with seven others to take on responsibility for the debt as long as they also gained a monopoly in the fur trade. It was a move that was both generous and wise, since the trade in beaver pelts promised to be very lucrative indeed. As part of this venture, Edward accompanied John Howland in exploration of the Kennebec River area (in Maine), although that would eventually lead to a fatal confrontation with rival English fur traders in 1634. But that lay ahead.

His own position in the colony was further advanced, in 1627, at the Division of Cattle, when his family gained a share in the "red cow" and two female goats. The value of this is revealed in the fact that in 1628, he sold his share in the cow to Myles Standish for five pounds and ten shillings. In 1631 he bought up nine acres of land in adjoining lots from various neighbors. He was becoming a wealthy man and could certainly say that the movement to the New World had been blessed by God. In the Plymouth tax return for 1633 he was the second wealthiest man, and in 1634, he was the wealthiest. It is little surprise, then, that he acted as assistant to the governor and even managed to get elected instead of the usual incumbent (William Bradford) in 1633, 1636, and 1644.

In 1635 he made another trip back to England in order to petition for better protection for the English colonists from the Connecticut Dutch and from the French operating out of Maine. Edward was clearly something of a New World statesman and was bold enough to ask for the granting of rights to the colonies to defend themselves against these other European rivals. To his surprise this all got unexpectedly complicated when the subject was changed from defense strategies to the theology and Church practices of the colonists. When his petition for defense rights was blocked, he resubmitted it again—only to find himself the subject of attention by no less a person than Archbishop Laud himself, the head of the Church of England. As a result, he was arrested and held in the infamous Fleet Prison in London, as it was alleged that he had performed marriage ceremonies without being an ordained minister. This was correct, since the godly of Plymouth viewed marriage solely as a secular contract to be overseen by the civil magistrates and not by the churches. This seems a strange position to adopt, given that they believed that all of life should be lived in a spirit of godliness and that the Saints should oversee the workings of society. Consequently, their determination to deny any Church role in the formation of a marriage looks rather odd and surprisingly secular for such a spiritual community. Arguably their rigid stance on this was fueled by their bitter opposition to what they described as the "sacramentalism" of the established Church and its rites and services. It rather looks as if on this one, the Puritans threw out the baby with the bathwater, as the saying goes. Be that as it may, Edward was probably guilty as charged and would have been unrepentant. He stayed in prison for about four months until he could finally arrange to be released. It was an example of the way in which debates about religious practice cast a shadow over the reputation of New England back in London.

Having gotten out of prison, he secured a passage home. We know that in 1643, he relocated from Plymouth to Marshfield, north of Duxbury. The next year he began his third and final stint as governor of Plymouth Colony. In 1643 he was also appointed as one of the commissioners of what became known as the United Colonies of New England, to represent the interests of the colonies of Plymouth, Massachusetts Bay, Connecticut, and New Haven. Edward Winslow must have felt real satisfaction in this achievement. He looked back on his time in the Netherlands and could recall how a union of independent states had not only prospered there but had also provided a place of exile for the godly from England. It was this experience that he now brought to the table as a unique contribution, based on his experiences in Leiden. Clearly, Plymouth had its own important role to play in New England, even if Massachusetts Bay now overshadowed it. And Edward knew that the need to better organize New England was pressing, for he could point to two threats to the colonies: mounting Native American frustrations with their expansion, which showed itself in rising tensions towards the English from the tribes of the Mohegans and the Narragansetts; and the need to defend the reputation of New England back in London. At a time of increasing tension in England between King Charles I and Parliament, and between different parliamentary factions, Winslow's role as far back as the Fleet Prison incident had been to defend the colonies of Plymouth and Massachusetts Bay against charges that they were fractious Puritan strongholds who repressed others and were at odds with the power politics of London. Only in this way could unwanted interference be fended off. This need to defend the colonies continued even as royal power collapsed in England, since some, even in Parliament, were unsympathetic towards the Separatists in New England and also towards those who, while not Separatists, were still keen to resist supervision from England. To these critical parliamentarians, Winslow and his allies represented rather the wrong sort of Puritan.

Edward realized that in such troubled times, unity was strength. He was not alone in this realization, as the forming of the United Colonies revealed. Much later, no less an American patriot than John Quincy Adams would point to the formation of the United Colonies of New England as inspiration for the North American Confederacy, which was formed in 1774 as a precursor to the United States of America.[9] One wonders what Edward Winslow would have made of that in 1643, since his "American" identity was inextricably mixed with his "English" one. And it was to the mother country that duty once more called him to travel.

He returned to England again, in October 1646, on his last mission on behalf of those colonies in the vicinity of Massachusetts Bay. By this time there were allies of New England in power in London, and he represented New England on a number of parliamentary committees. He could rest assured that he would not again be flung into the Fleet Prison on the instructions of Archbishop Laud, since the archbishop had been executed, on the orders of Parliament, as recently as 1645. Winslow did not return to New England for the remaining nine years of his life, but he was occupied in English affairs relating to the colony and the wider issues relating to godly rule, since this was during the British Civil Wars between Parliament and King Charles I, which resulted in the king's eventual execution in January 1649.

It was during this time that Edward published a couple of pamphlets in defense of the New England colonies. These were *Hypocrisie Unmasked* (1646) and *New England's Salamander Discovered* (1647), both of which we will examine in more detail shortly. He also penned an introduction to another work, entitled *The Glorious progress of the Gospel amongst the Indians in New England* (1649).

Spreading the word

As we have just seen, Winslow was the author of a number of important pamphlets that promoted or defended the settlement in Massachusetts. These included one entitled *Good Newes from New England, or a True Relation of Things very Remarkable at the Plantation of Plimouth in New England* (1624), which he cowrote with Governor William Bradford. It is an account of events between 1622 and 1623, in which the Pilgrims triumphed over adversity, including that posed by unfit emigrants who had followed them. It called for people of worthy character to continue the work. As Edward concluded,

> *I write not these things to dissuade any that shall seriously upon due examination set themselves to further the glory of God, and the honor of our Country, in so worthy an enterprise, but rather to discourage such as with too great lightness undertake such courses . . .* [10]

He also penned the early description of life in the colony which we now know as *Mourt's Relation*, which gives us our earliest account of the first Thanksgiving, in 1621, and also extolls the natural riches of New England to encourage the farmer and the hunter who might be considering emigration.

Then there was *Hypocrisie Unmasked; by a True Relation of the Governor and Company of Massachusetts against Samuel Gorton, a Notorious Disturber of the Peace* (1646), in which he presented the case against a man who had been expelled from Plymouth Colony for insubordination towards the magistrates and minister but who had gone on to win some influential backing, in England, for his breakaway settlement south of the Pawtuxet River, in Rhode Island. The attack was continued in another pamphlet entitled *The Danger of Tolerating Levelers in a Civil State* (1649), which drew negative parallels with a group in England (the Levelers) who argued for major political change. Clearly, Edward Winslow was no political or social radical.

The curiously titled *New England's Salamander Discovered* (1647) defended the colonies in New England against criticisms concerning their standards of government, and marshalled evidence such that the administration "is shewed to bee legall and not arbitrary."

Finally, *The Glorious progress of the Gospel amongst the Indians in New England* (1649), which he cowrote with John Eliot and Thomas Mayhew, publicized Christian missionary activities among the Native Americans and emphasized the providential nature of the settlement as a way to spread the Christian faith. However, its description of the unconverted as "poor creatures" reveals a rather dehumanizing attitude, very different from the way Edward actually appeared to interact with native people. [11] It reveals something of his mental world, and he was not alone in this.

Serving the cause of God: in the New Jerusalem or in the Old Country?

Edward never returned to New England after the year 1646. He was now refocused on England in a way that had not happened before, as he tried to discern what God was doing in these strange times. It seemed as if the New Jerusalem he had labored so hard to build in North America was now becoming something of a backwater. As he studied developments in the Old Country, which he had once so decisively left, he could not help but wonder if it was actually there, of all places, that the promises and prophecies of God were going to be fulfilled. He could certainly rationalize the need to be there to promote America. New England's future was uncertain now that the upheavals of civil war in Britain had caused a collapse in the market there for American produce.[12] Then there were New England malcontents who presented petitions and complaints about the colony before the authorities back in London. He could assure himself that being there allowed him opportunities to put the case for the colonies at this critical juncture. But it was more than just pragmatic requirements that held him in London. For one who had so passionately believed in God's Providence pointing to North America, an uncomfortable question was arising: What now was New England for? The focus of providence had seemingly moved elsewhere. And so, he postponed his return to North America again and again. Despite his wife and his lands being three thousand miles away in Marshfield, it was in the corridors of power in Whitehall, London, that he now trod, not along the deer paths that wound through the woods of New England. He could justify this to himself, since that was where the epicenter of events now lay, not in Massachusetts. But others did not see it so clearly. Writing in 1650, William Bradford unhappily noted in *Of Plymouth Plantation*, under the year 1646, how Winslow "fell into other employments there" and that his absence "hath been much to the weakening of this government, without whose consent he took these employments upon him."[13] Clearly, Bradford was not impressed and had a bone to pick with his erstwhile right-hand man. But Edward Winslow had bigger fish to fry now, for his skills had been spotted by the government of Oliver Cromwell, which had replaced that of the executed king; in Edward's view, England was moving from being a Catholic-inclined monarchy to being a godly republican commonwealth.

Others were more outspoken than Bradford regarding Winslow. Reading between the lines, it seems that perhaps Edward had become rather too much the polished diplomat. Samuel Maverick certainly described him unflatteringly as a

> *Smooth tongued Cunning fellow, who soon gott himselfe into Favour of those then in Supreme power, against whom it was in vaine to strive.* [14]

Edward would have argued that Maverick was just a non-Puritan New England planter who could not read the signs of the times and was as out of joint with events in the revolutionary London of the late 1640s and early 1650s as he was regarding the godly experiment in New England. And Edward clearly felt that he had lost nothing of his godly ardor; it was just that providence had dictated that the cause needed him in London. He was now sure that it was as a diplomat there that he now served the cause of godly rule. If God told him to, he would swiftly return to North America if the cause of the Saints required it.

However, in 1655 he was sent by Lord Protector Oliver Cromwell as one of three Commonwealth grand commissioners to superintend the English military expedition against the Spanish colonies located in the West Indies. It was while he was on this mission, in support of the wider cause of the godly, that Edward died of yellow fever while at sea near the island of Hispaniola, on May 8 of that same year. It was the end of a momentous and a challenging life that had been lived in turbulent times.

On reflection it must be said that life was not always easy for a man who was acting on such a broad stage as Edward Winslow. And not everyone appreciated his priorities, which took him away from New England for so long. We have seen how William Bradford was unhappy at his absences, but Edward was clear about the fact that his duties were trans-Atlantic in order to promote and defend the wider cause of the Saints. We do not know what those most intimately united with Edward thought of all this, but we can surmise that the huge periods of enforced separation were hard. When Edward eventually died, on that mission for Oliver Cromwell's government, he had been apart from his wife, Susanna, for almost ten years. While he had visited England several times (in 1623, 1624, 1635, and 1646) on business either for Plymouth Colony or that of Massachusetts Bay Colony, there is no evidence that Susanna ever left New England to accompany her husband. Their marriage was not one that saw them traveling together. Instead, she remained back at the family home in Marshfield, while her husband was on the move. It is telling that the only portrait of Edward Winslow (the only surviving one of any Pilgrim) was painted in London in 1651. He is portrayed as a well-dressed member of the London Commonwealth elite. He holds a letter from his wife, but this is as close as she got to him in nine years.

The words of Edward's will (dated December 18, 1654) reveal a man on the move whose earthly sojourn was always likely to be interrupted by the needs of the cause of godliness.

> *I Edward Winslowe of London, Esquior, being now bound in a voyage to sea in the service of the comon welth do make publish & declare this to be my last will & testam't touching the disposing of my estate.*

But even then his thoughts were ranging from those closest to him to his wider responsibilities within the community. For, while he started with those nearest and dearest to himself . . .

> *ffirst I doe give will devise & bequeath all my lands & stock in New england & all my possibilities & porcons in future allotm'ts & divicons to Josia my onely sonne & his heires, hee allowing to my wife, a full third parte thereof for her life also . . .*

He was soon looking to the wider areas of his influence . . .

> *I give to the poore of the Church of Plymouth in new England Tenn pounds & to the poore of marshfielde where the chiefest of my estate lyes Tenn pounds.*

The peripatetic nature of his life, on the move and carrying his possessions with him, is revealed in the next section of his will.

I give my lynnen wch I carry wth me to sea, to my daughter Elizabeth & the rest of my goods wch I carry wth mee I give to my sonn Josias, hee giving to each of my brothers a suite of apparel.[15]

From this, as from so much else, it is abundantly clear that Edward Winslow remained a Pilgrim to the very last.

The prominent (and later) Bostonian Cotton Mather—a theologian and writer—summed up something of how those living in the generation after Edward Winslow assessed his importance. Mather, writing in 1702, described Winslow as a "Hercules" due to his strength and resilience in tackling the many and varied challenges that had faced the Plymouth settlement and, in time, had faced New England as a whole. Edward Winslow had played a key role in building alliances with local Native Americans who were willing to partner with the newcomers, but also in squaring up to those other tribes who were hostile to the newly arrived colonists and their local allies. He had worked tirelessly to promote the colony through his pamphlets, his travels, and his negotiations with the conflicting political and economic factions in England. From the simple supplying of the colony, to defending its role within the English colonization of North America, Edward Winslow had played a key role. In this role he had faced extended periods of separation from his wife and family and from the colony whose cause he promoted. Many later writers, like those at the time, have come to marvel at his dedication and energy in waging these battles, which were not conducted in the woods of Massachusetts against hostile tribes but instead were "fought in the corridors of power and the court of public opinion back in England." Not for nothing has this remarkable man been described as "the equivalent of a modern-day lobbyist."[16] The term would, of course, have been unfamiliar to Edward Winslow, but a brief moment getting this 17th-century pamphleteer up to speed on 21st-century political terminology would, no doubt, have led to him embracing it as an appropriate one with which to describe himself. For he was, indeed, the advocate of the godly colony in New England. This seems a fitting place to leave Edward Winslow's Mayflower Life.

11

The Soldier's Story:
Captain Myles Standish,
Commander of the
Plymouth Colony Militia

I t was dim in the one-roomed house. The small window opening was shuttered, and smoke from a low fire gathered in the rafters under the low ceiling. The room was poorly furnished. Benches ran alongside a rough trestle table on which a rudimentary meal was laid on wooden platters. None of the other houses in Wessagusset was any better furnished. The whole place, the entire settlement, was makeshift, untidy, down at heel. The meal consisted of a little sliced smoked pork brought from Plymouth, some flat cornbread with the black marks from the crude oven visible even in the low light, and water in a pewter pitcher. Captain Myles Standish looked about the room and exchanged a curt nod with each of the Plymouth men who were with him. Glancing around the room, he thought how badly built it was and how the copious stains of beer on the rough planks of the walls spoke volumes about the kind of place this was: mean, badly disciplined, and poorly maintained. The whole place was quietly desperate. Standish grew tired of pacing the earth floor and finally sat down on the bench. He had removed his breastplate; it leaned against the wall beside his propped-up musket.

Outside there was the sound of movement, and conversation in English and another tongue. Then the door opened and a little light broke into the room, though the lowness of the lintel prevented much from invading the inner space. Standish nodded to the first man to enter. It was the Pokanoket guide and interpreter Hobbomock, whom Standish had brought with him from Plymouth. Behind him came four Massachusett warriors, the first of whom was tall and strongly put together and clearly their leader. One was younger than the others; an adolescent boy, but with the look of one who reflected the warrior status of his older companions. They had some women with them, but these were motioned to wait outside. Standish stood up and was forced to look up at the leading Massachusett. There were a few terse words of greeting exchanged, for the tall man had learned sufficient English. But Standish noticed the slight smile on the other man's face as he looked down at the diminutive captain. Well, Standish thought, we will soon see who is smiling in a short while from now. Among the other warriors was one who had, in recent past, twice threatened Standish, and he and the captain appraised each other coldly. Standish motioned the newcomers to sit down and take food with them.

Together they began to eat. Standish was careful to position himself near the head of the table, at the end of the bench and opposite the tall man with the mocking look. The Massachusetts used their hands to break open the bread, and Standish saw how they had laid down their knives in order to do so. He motioned with one hand, and one of the Plymouth men, who had not yet taken a seat, walked over to the door with quick steps and shut it. The light dimmed again. The Massachusett warrior opposite him looked up. He sensed something. Then it all happened very fast. Standish seized the other man's knife and was across the table stabbing him in the chest again and again. The meager meal was scattered to the floor. Elsewhere in the room the other Plymouth men were similarly engaged in brutal execution. Hobbomock watched them as they did so. Then it was done. The three older warriors were either dead or in the final stages of dying. The adolescent boy was taken captive. Great pools of blood were spreading across the floor. Spreading and joining to form a dark shadow. It had been done in a few short minutes. And with scarcely a cry from those killed.

There was now no time to lose. Striding outside into the daylight, Standish saw to it that the young Massachusett captive was swiftly hanged. The women cowered against the wall of the building, terrified of the muskets pointed towards them. The captain then ordered the deaths of any other Massachusetts about the settlement. Two other warriors were elsewhere, with Plymouth men. The order arrived from Standish. Once more knives went to work and two more were dead. Standish found two other Massachusetts and killed one, but the other escaped.

Beyond the badly built palisade of the settlement there were more scores to settle with others of the Massachusett band. But first, Standish took an axe from one of his men and went back into the house. With a rain of well-aimed blows he severed the head from the body of the warrior who had once threatened him. Carrying it outside, by a braid of thick black hair, he held it up to the approving murmurs of his men. Blood dripped from the gruesome item, and a trail of it ran along the ground, marking the path that Standish had taken from the doorway. Then he laid it down on the ground and motioned for his men to follow him out of the stockade, to finish the business with those outside in the woods.[1]

The origins of Myles Standish, soldier and "semi-Stranger"

The slaughter that occurred at Wessagusset—to which we will return—is not how we like to imagine Myles Standish. We have a very different image in mind, the product of later artworks and a famous poem written by Longfellow in 1858, *The Courtship of Miles Standish*. A portrait, which was first published in 1885, claimed to be a likeness of Standish painted originally in 1625; however, its authenticity is far from certain. But it shows him as he is often now imagined: with a handsome face and a full head of hair waving down over his ears, fully bearded and wearing a prominent lace ruff and a dark jacket. But it is just that—"imagined"—for we have no idea what this prominent member of Plymouth Colony actually looked like! But what is clear is that the handsome visual image and the poetic impression of a diffident admirer of a local beauty is in stark contrast with the bloody events at Wessagusset. Myles Standish was more complex than he might first appear.

That complexity starts at his beginnings, for there is something of a mystery concerning the very origins of Myles Standish. In his will he left land to his son Alexander,

> in *Ormistick* [Ormskirk] *Borsconge* [Burscough] *Wright-ington Maudsley* [Mawdesley] *Newburrow* [Newburgh] *Crawston* [Croston] *and the Ile of man* [Isle of Man] *and given to mee as right heire by lawfull Decent but Surruptuously Detained from mee my great Grandfather being a 2cond or younger brother from the house of Standish of Standish*[2]

All the named manors are in Lancashire, in northwestern England, so it has often been assumed that he originated there or, perhaps, was from the nearby Isle of Man, since land he owned there is mentioned in the will. Standish later named his home in New England "Duxbury," and this might have been a nod towards Duxbury Hall, Lancashire, where a branch of the Standish family owned the manor. An origin in Lancashire for Standish was certainly the conclusion drawn by Nathaniel Morton, who was later the secretary of Plymouth Colony and wrote a history entitled *The New England's Memorial*, in 1669. He also added some information that explains the later trajectory of Standish's life.

> *In his younger time he went over into the low countries, and was a soldier there, and came acquainted with the church at Leyden* [Leiden] . . .[3]

Here we have the crucial evidence regarding Myles Standish, the soldier. Exactly what role he played in the warfare of the Low Countries (what we now know as the Netherlands and Belgium) is not entirely clear. During the time that he served there, the Protestants of the Dutch Republic were engaged in the terrible bloodshed of the Eighty Years' War fought against Catholic Spain. It was part of the process by which the Netherlands broke free from Spanish control and developed into an independent state. It was a war in which the Protestant government of England also played a significant part. The English queen, Elizabeth I, was sympathetic towards the Protestant Dutch and had become the bitter enemy of Catholic Spain. After all, it was from Spain that the famous Armada had sailed in 1588 with the sole purpose of deposing this "heretic queen" and reestablishing Catholicism in England. So, in order to stoke up trouble for Spain and give assistance to the Dutch, Elizabethan England had sent military assistance to the Netherlands, either in an official capacity or as Protestant mercenaries. As a result, we are not sure whether Standish served as a mercenary[4] or as an officer in an official English military unit.[5] But whether he was a mercenary in the pay of the Dutch, an English lieutenant promoted to the rank of captain in the Netherlands, or serving there under Sir Horatio Vere (who had apparently recruited English troops in Lancashire and the Isle of Man), Myles Standish gained military experience in one of Europe's bitter wars of religion.

However, if warfare built his early career, peace was more of a challenge. Between 1609 and 1621 the bitter fighting was temporarily halted by the Twelve Years' Truce. For a man such as Myles Standish there was little by way of a peace dividend to enjoy, since the cessation of hostilities also meant the cessation of pay. What was he to do? One possibility was soon revealed. By 1620 he was living in Leiden and, as a fellow Englishman, was known to the émigré community there. Standish never quite nailed his colors to the mast when it came to his exact religious position. On one hand he was clearly sympathetic to the principles of the godly adventure of the Leiden Pilgrims. On the other hand, there is no clear evidence that he ever formally became a member of the Separatist church in New Plymouth.[6] As such, he was something of a semi-Stranger. Or if that is rather a glass-half-empty view of his standing, perhaps a more positive category might be semi-Saint. What is clear is that he was known to the Leiden congregation gathered around the Rev. Robinson and was clearly regarded as acceptable. As a result, they hired him as their military adviser. By 1620 Standish was regularly using the title of captain and was clearly well aware of both his military experience and its marketable value.

On this matter, though, he had to accept the fact that he was not the first choice of these Pilgrims planning emigration to the New World. It seems that their first choice had been to buy the services of a more prestigious military adventurer. This was Captain John Smith, who had been one of the founders of the English colony at Jamestown, Virginia, in 1607, for the Virginia Company. He had also extensively mapped the coast as far north as the intended destination of the Hudson River. When approached, he showed an interest, but his price was rather too high (clearly he knew his market value too). This posed a problem to the cash-strapped Leideners. In addition, he made them nervous. He was famous, autocratic, and strong willed, and they feared he might attempt to dominate their colony.[7] Furthermore, his godly credentials were a little on the thin side. So it was that instead of Captain John Smith, the Leiden congregation contracted with Captain Myles Standish instead. A reduced-price military expert would accompany a reduced-price ship (the *Mayflower*). Both, though, would prove ready for the demands that lay ahead. And so, they sailed.

Military command in the New World

We already met Captain Standish in the Mayflower Life of Stephen Hopkins, and we saw how Standish led the exploration along Cape Cod that culminated in the clash with Native Americans of the Nauset people at First Encounter Beach on December 8, 1620. This was just the beginning of his military role as the Pilgrims chose their new home. After exploring more of the coast within the hook of Cape Cod, the settlers eventually chose the site for their settlement on the edge of

Plymouth Bay in December 1620. Then it was that Myles Standish advised on the location of the small fort to protect the little settlement. Using his military experience, he advised where the cannons should be mounted and how the first houses should be sited in order to enhance the defense of the place. As he looked down from the little fort to the settlement site below, he could envision the attackers streaming out of the nearby woods and descending on the place. To prepare for such an eventuality, each house needed to be strong enough to be defended and its proximity to the other houses set so that each was assisted by the field of fire from its neighbors.

Today the site of the fort lies on top of Burial Hill, among the later graves of Plymouth citizens. What was once its line of fire down the town's first street is blocked by the building of First Parish Plymouth Church on the top side of Town Square.[8] By the time that the original church in this location was constructed in 1683, defense was no longer a pressing priority in Plymouth. So the modern visitor, standing on the site of the old fort, no longer has the same sense of its strategic positioning that would have been in Standish's mind back in the winter of 1621–22.

But before his military skills were called on again, there would be a battle against sickness which almost destroyed Plymouth Colony even as it started. The settlers had built just one house, and it provided the shelter of just one large communal room, when disease struck the settlers that winter and took the lives of half those present. Standish's own wife, named Rose, died in January 1621 and was buried in an unmarked grave located somewhere within Cole's Hill Burial Ground. In her final resting place she lay alongside the others who died that first grim winter. Though her exact burial plot is not known, she is named on the Pilgrim Memorial Tomb on Cole's Hill simply as "Rose, first wife of Myles Standish." They had no children.

Perhaps he was used to the kinds of pathogens that killed the others? Perhaps he was just physically stronger and better withstood the rigors of hunger and the threat of exposure from wading through the icy waters of the bay? Whatever the reason, Myles Standish was one of the very few new arrivals who did not fall ill during that first winter.

Looking back, William Bradford—who became the second governor following the early death of Governor Carver—recalled the care offered by Standish, and how his example and assistance comforted those colonists who were suffering and dying. Bradford particularly recalled how the captain helped him when he fell ill.

Though very different personalities, it was the beginning of a friendship that would last for the rest of their lives. That mutual bond through suffering would always act as a foundation which gave common ground to two men so temperamentally at odds: Bradford, reflective, thoughtful, and slow to judgement; Standish, the man of action and so quick to anger that William Hubbard (one of the first Harvard graduates in 1642 and later the author of *History of New England*) memorably reported that his temper was like a "chimney soon fired." However, despite their differences they came to value each other. Bradford appreciated the man of action who got things done. And Standish knew the value of one who thought things through and provided stability at the heart of the community. It was a bond that was forged in that grim winter of 1620–21, and it held even when Bradford disapproved of some of the captain's precipitous and violent actions.

By February 1621, the colonists were increasingly glad that the captain was with them. They had seen Native Americans several times near Plymouth—although without contact—and their depleted numbers made them fearfully aware of the shadows that occasionally flitted through the trees, which indicated they were being watched. As a result of this sense of threat, on February 17, 1621, the armed men of the Plymouth Colony militia elected Standish as their first commander. They would reelect him to that position of authority for the rest of his life. For Standish it was a welcome reaffirmation of his role. He could not forget how, back in November after a faltering start to the premature exploration of Cape Cod, he had been temporarily replaced as exploration leader by Master Christopher Jones of the *Mayflower*. While nothing could permanently dent the self-confidence of the captain, it was an irritant that was now removed by the settled recognition from the others that he alone offered the military expertise and fighting leadership that they needed.

As the newly appointed captain of the Plymouth militia, it was Standish who drilled the men in the use of their muskets and their pikes. Soon they were proficient in standing to arms and using heavy long guns, with their musket-rests to support the weight of the gun when firing. Myles was in his element, like a fish in water, watching the men drill. What was unfamiliar to some of them was second nature to him, whether it was shielding the smoldering matchcord of a matchlock musket, or maintaining the flint and steel of a firelock. He knew that a matchlock was less dependable than a firelock, understood the need to keep powder bone dry, and knew how to use pikemen to shield the flanks of the musketeers and protect them as they loaded their weapons in a complex coordination of the cartridge-bandoleer, powder flask, and lead ball.[9] He could close his eyes and watch it all play out perfectly. Then he could make it happen in real life so that, in time, it could even be done when arrows hissed past, fire raged through a torched building, and hostiles screamed and shouted. For it would be then that the Plymouth men would most value these hours of drill. Not that everyone appreciated this, though. While overseeing drill in March 1621, Myles was subjected to verbal abuse from one reluctant soldier who objected to taking orders. This minor mutiny was the work of John Billington, a source of trouble in the colony. He challenged the captain's orders because he had "contempt of the Captain's lawful command with several speeches," and he was swiftly punished for it. It was not an isolated incident.[10] Billington would remain a source of trouble until he was hanged for murder in 1630—we shall shortly return to that in his own Mayflower Life.

Captain Standish was determined to brook no opposition, because he knew that disobedience and disunity spelled disaster in battle. And battle was coming, because, despite the treaty of friendship that had been agreed with the Wampanoag *sachem* Massasoit, not every native leader regarded the Pilgrims so positively; others were envious of the status that (the once rather marginalized) Massasoit had gained from his alliance with the musket-wielding English colonists. Only five months after Billington challenged Standish's authority and the formation of an alliance with Massasoit (which had happened on March 22,

1621) the Plymouth militia were in action. Captain Standish's musket drill was about to be deployed in anger.

Among his own Pokanoket people, within the loose alliance of tribal groups we now remember as the Wampanoag, Massasoit did not always have things his own way. In August 1621, news reached Plymouth of a rebellion against him being prepared by another *sachem*, named Corbitant, whom we met in the Mayflower Life of Edward Winslow. The center of this rebellion lay fourteen miles west of Plymouth in the Pokanoket village of Nemasket (now Middleborough, Massachusetts). This was very bad news, as the continued survival of Massasoit was crucial for peace and stability. On top of this, if the people of Plymouth stood by and did nothing when their key ally was deposed, then there was no value in an alliance with them. Bradford and Standish knew that their credibility was at stake.

First, though, they needed to know what was happening. Bradford sent two trusted interpreters to find out: these were Squanto (Tisquantum) and Hobbomock. Both were closely associated with Massasoit (this was especially true of Hobbomock), and both had developed a relationship with the Pilgrims. It was then that things became even more complex. When the two scouts arrived in Nemasket, Corbitant seized Squanto, threatening to kill him, while Hobbomock escaped from the village and set off to warn the people of Plymouth.

Bradford and Standish heard the news with alarm. Now they had two allies in danger. They quickly conferred and decided on action. On August 14, the captain led a militia detachment of ten men to Nemasket. Here lay the summer camp of Corbitant, situated to harvest the fish runs on the nearby river in spring and, after that, to tend the corn, gourds, and beans growing in the fields around their summer encampment. The militia's objective was to kill Corbitant. Hobbomock acted as guide; Standish was impressed by his skills as they made their way along the woodlands paths. It was the start of a relationship of mutual respect, which would eventually see Hobbomock joining Standish's household.

The little expedition reached Nemasket at nightfall. Scouting the village, Standish decided on a night attack to shield their movements and to add shock to the surprise action. Under cover of darkness Standish and Hobbomock led the musket-carrying Englishmen into the heart of the sleeping village. Hobbomock threaded his way between the cattail-mat-covered, circular *wetuash* dwellings,[11] to the one within which Corbitant was thought to be sleeping. When they reached it, he and Captain Standish broke in, shouting for Corbitant. Then all was confusion as sleeping people leapt from their mats and burst out of the house in panic. Outside, muskets flashed. A Pokanoket man and woman fell before the musket balls. But Corbitant had fled at the news of the expedition from Plymouth.

However, Standish had every reason to be pleased with the outcome of his bold intervention. Squanto was released unharmed, and on September 13, no fewer than nine local *sachems* came to Plymouth to sign a treaty of loyalty to the English ruler, King James. A penitent Corbitant was among them.

Despite this, Standish's success at Nemasket also had unintended consequences. For, now that Plymouth had become a significant player in the complex intertribal politics of the area, there were others who took an interest in them. This was not always a friendly one, and an antagonistic approach to the new kid on the block who was throwing his weight around explains why the Narragansetts made their move just two months after the September submission of the nine *sachems*. The Narragansetts were one of the leading tribes of what is now New England, dominating the western parts of Narragansett Bay in present-day Rhode Island, and also parts of Connecticut and southwestern Massachusetts, from the Providence River on the northeast to the Pawcatuck River on the southwest. At the time when the English colonizing of New England began in 1620, the Narragansetts were the most powerful tribe in the southern part of that region, because they had escaped the epidemics that had devastated neighboring tribes. Massasoit had allied himself with the English at Plymouth in order to gain protection from the Narragansetts.

When the Narragansetts made their move, it was both simple and dramatic. In November 1621, a Narragansett messenger arrived in

Plymouth with a parcel. The man delivered a bundle of arrows wrapped in a snakeskin. As Bradford, Standish, and the others examined the sinister gift, Squanto and Hobbomock explained (in case anyone had missed the meaning) that it was a threat and an insult combined. The "gift" had been sent by the Narragansett *sachem*, Canonicus. Famously, Governor Bradford sent back his own version of the gift: the same snakeskin filled with gunpowder and shot. Plymouth was not intimidated. Canonicus was struck with a dread of the powder and shot, would not touch it, and had it cast into a nearby river. [12]

Watching the Narragansett warrior leaving, Standish was acutely aware of the vulnerability of the colony, despite all that he had done to influence the siting of its fort and mutually defensible houses. As a result, he urged his fellow colonists that now was the time to encircle the whole settlement with a palisade of tall, upright logs: a wooden wall more than half a mile in length, with strong gates and platforms erected for shooting over the wall. It was a daunting task—even with reinforcements provided from a recently arrived ship, the *Fortune*, there were still just fifty men to build it. Despite this, they completed Standish's palisade in just three months, finishing it in March 1622. In the fall of 1622 a visitor to Plymouth, John Pory, described it as "a strong palisado of spruce trees of some ten foot high." [13] Another visitor, Emmanuel Altham, writing home in September 1623, described

> *a strong fort . . . with six pieces of reasonable good artillery mounted thereon . . . pale* [palisade] *of eight foot long, or thereabouts, and in the pale are three great gates.* [14]

A later visitor described how, in addition to the palisade and the fort on the hill, a square stockade stood in the center of the settlement (beside the governor's house), equipped with four *patereros* (swivel guns), which could fire along the streets at any intruders who broke through the walls. [15]

With the palisade in place, the captain next divided the militia into four companies: one company to man each wall. The drills, so bitterly derided by Billington just one year before, were now intensified but with greater urgency. Assembled by beat of drum outside the captain's door, the men made an impressive sight armed with muskets and firelocks, cloaked and in order three abreast, the captain with his sidearms, cloak, and small cane; "constantly on their guard night and day."[16] The very sword that Standish bore at these musters can still be seen in Pilgrim Hall Museum, in Plymouth.

Militant and armed, the militia's willingness to defend the colony through bloodshed became indelibly linked to the character of Myles Standish in March 1623. The conflict at Wessagusset Colony would always cast a shadow over his career through its shocking display of premeditated violence.[17] The roots of this conflict lay in the arrival, in April 1622, of the first of a new colony sent by Thomas Weston (the Merchant Adventurer behind the original *Mayflower* voyage) to establish a new settlement on the Fore River (today Weymouth, Massachusetts), some twenty-five miles north of Plymouth. Weston had been very disappointed at the financial returns from the more religiously motivated Plymouth Colony. First the *Mayflower* had returned with its hold empty in 1621, and then the returning *Fortune* had been boarded by the French, who had seized its cargo of furs, sassafras, and clapboards. When it finally reached London in February 1622, far from halving the colony's debts, it only added to the mounting financial problems of the investors. Weston hoped that the new venture would be more lucrative and would soon be shipping furs, timber, and salted fish back to England. Badly provisioned by Weston (no surprise there!), they spent the summer at Plymouth before moving on. The ill-fated colony, which they founded in the fall of that year, they named Wessagusset (now North Weymouth). This poorly provisioned, chaotically managed, and badly disciplined new colony soon angered the local tribe, the Massachusetts, through theft and high-handedness, so that a group of Massachusett warriors decided to destroy both the Wessagusset and Plymouth colonies. In March 1623, news of this reached Massasoit, who warned Plymouth. It was a warning reinforced by a man who escaped from Wessagusset and reached Plymouth with news that his fellow settlers were under constant threat of attack; they were trapped within their settlement and starving.

Alarmed, William Bradford assembled the Plymouth colonists, who decided on preemptive action: send Myles Standish with a dedicated group of eight chosen men, including the Native American Hobbomock, to Wessagusset, in order to kill the Massachusett leaders who were conspiring against the two colonies. As Myles set out, he pondered a personal score to settle, which was now interwoven with his wider duties. One of the conspirators, a warrior named Wituwamat (or Wattawamat), had earlier threatened him while the captain was trading for corn on Cape Cod. At that time, Wituwamat had boasted of how he had killed frightened French and English men.[18] It was a clear attempt to intimidate the captain, although Standish could not catch all of what the man said.

Arriving at Wessagusset, the captain found the place almost deserted, a number of settlers having given up independence and gone to live with the Massachusetts. Standish sent orders for them to return. However, it was members of the local Massachusetts who appeared, their leaders being a *pniese* named Pecksuot and Wituwamat. Both had a violent track record. Wituwamat, as we have seen, had earlier boasted of killing Europeans, and Pecksuot had instigated the brutal enslavement and murder of French traders.[19] To the captain the threat they posed to the English settlements was all too clear. Standish stated he was in Wessagusset on a trade mission. Pecksuot was not fooled and said, via Hobbomock, we "fear him not . . . let him begin when he dare, he shall not take us unawares." The stage was set for violence. Pecksuot later insulted the diminutive Standish by standing over him and mocking him, telling him,

> *Though he were a great captain, yet he was but a little man; and, said he, though I be no sachem, yet I am a man of great strength and courage.*[20]

Standish stared him out and made his plans behind eyes that gave nothing away. At the same time warriors provocatively sharpened their knives in front of Standish; and Wituwamat boasted of his knife, *"Hinnaim namen, hinnaim michen, matta cuts"* (meaning something like, 'In time it will see, in time it will eat, but it will not speak').[21] It was the second time that he had threatened Standish. There would not be a third.

The next day Standish once more arranged to meet Pecksuot and signalled peaceful intentions by inviting him to a meal. With astonishing trust, the Massachusett warrior agreed. He came with Wituwamat, Wituwamat's eighteen-year-old brother, a small group of other warriors, and some women. The result was bloody betrayal and slaughter in and around the one-roomed house assigned for the meeting. With Pecksuot and his male companions butchered and Wituwamat decapitated, Standish went in search of another enemy *sachem* of the Massachusett tribe, named Obtakiest. There was a short fight, but he escaped.

Standish released his female captives and prepared to leave. He could have traded these hostages for the three Wessagusset colonists who were still living with the Massachusetts, but he did not. He had come north for execution more than for saving these colonists' lives.[22]

Myles considered the mission accomplished. He returned to Plymouth with the severed head of Wituwamat wrapped in a bloodstained cloth. He would not threaten the captain again. And neither would the tall warrior, Pecksuot. But like a rock thrown into a pond, the ripples spread wide. Despite Standish's actions, Wessagusset was largely abandoned by the summer of 1623. Some from the settlement went to Plymouth Colony; others relocated farther north along the coast to Maine.[23] The small number of men who had gone over to the local people and had remained in their camp were tortured to death in retaliation.[24]

As news spread of the ambush that had been organized by Standish, Native Americans were horrified, and many moved inland away from the threat posed by the colonists. This was to the detriment of Plymouth's trade. But, more importantly, the killings at Wessagusset revealed a shocking and unexpected side to Standish and the godly community. The beloved Rev. Robinson (still in Leiden) condemned the action in a letter written from Leiden, in December 1623, to William Bradford,

*Oh how happy a thing had it been, if you had converted some
before you had killed any! Besides, where blood is once begun to
be shed, it is seldom staunched of a long time after.*

He went on to challenge the view that the Native Americans
deserved it, pointing out that they had been provoked by "those hea-
thenish Christians" [from Wessagusset]. And he reminded Bradford
that he personally had no authority over the Massachusetts, and that
the killings seemed out of proportion to the threat. Despite admitting
affection for Standish and the belief that he had been provided by God
as a useful member of the colony, Robinson also expressed concerns
that Standish lacked care for human life when provoked, and might be
attracted by the worldly status (but not one approved by God) of being
"a terrour to poor barbarous people."[25]

William Bradford, too, was clearly uneasy, but he felt compelled to
defend Standish. In a letter to the London investors he wrote,

*As for Captain Standish we leave him to answer for himself; but
this we must say, he is as helpful an instrument as any we have,
and as careful of the general good.*[26]

Not quite the same as saying he acted correctly!

As for the head of Wituwamat, it stood on a spike at the gate of
Plymouth with the bloody rag flapping like a flag. It was a warning to
any thinking of taking up arms against the colony.

In the middle of this violence and drama, ordinary life somehow
also carried on. Having been a widower since January 1621, Captain
Standish married Barbara Mullins in the spring of 1624. Barbara had
arrived in Plymouth in 1623, on either the *Anne* or the *Little James*.
Together they had seven children. She died in 1659, though her burial
place is unknown.

In 1625, Standish was chosen to travel to London to negotiate
new financial terms with the Merchant Adventurers. The Pilgrims
hoped to pay off their debt to the Adventurers so they could finally
allot land and decide where they would establish daughter settlements.

Unfortunately, he was not successful in these negotiations and returned to Plymouth in April 1626 empty-handed. Later in 1626, Isaac Allerton and several other leading Plymouth citizens, including Standish, tried again and were finally successful. The colonists used their freedom to finally organize a division of land in 1627. In this, Captain Standish received a farm amounting to 120 acres (49 hectares) in what became known as Duxbury, to which he relocated in about 1628. This settlement was finally accorded the status of a separate town with its own church and minister in 1637. Yet even as aspects of the colony seemed to be enjoying stability, threats to its spiritual integrity and its economic viability were looming.

In 1628, Standish was again in controversial form, in what we might today call The Merrymount Police Action. The roots of this went back to 1625, when a new group of English settlers set up a new settlement in what is now Quincy, Massachusetts. This was quite close to the failed colony at Wessagusset and about twenty-seven miles north of Plymouth. The colony was called Mount Wollaston, and its leader was named Thomas Morton. However, it soon came to be known as Merrymount, as the regime there was anything but Puritan. In fact, it came to embody everything that the Pilgrims of Plymouth opposed: copious consumption of alcohol, work and play on the Sabbath, Maypole dancing, sexual relationships with Native American women, and the selling of weapons to local tribes. It was this last activity that finally spurred the leadership of Plymouth into action, although what William Bradford described as the Merrymount habit of "frisking together" with native women probably added quite a strong ingredient to the cocktail of reasons he had for sorting out the situation of "lasciviousness" and "scandal" there.[27] It was, from the perspective of Plymouth, becoming a sink of pagan practice and sinful sexual behavior.

Governor Bradford ordered Captain Standish north to arrest Morton and bring an end to the activities at Merrymount. When the Plymouth men arrived, they found that the colonists at Merrymount had barricaded themselves in and were preparing to make a fight of it. The trouble was they were too drunk to fight. Their way of life prevented them from defending their way of life! Morton was easily disarmed by a stone-cold-sober Standish. The captain took Morton back to Plymouth as a prisoner; from there, he was sent back to England, where he was too well connected to be executed for blasphemy. The Maypole was chopped down. In 1629 other godly colonists, from Salem, raided Merrymount, seizing corn and destroying what was left of the Maypole. When Morton returned, he was rearrested and banished again.

In 1637, Morton wrote a bitter denunciation of this "police-action" by the Plymouth men. It was entitled *New English Canaan*, and in it he accused the Plymouth leadership of acting out of rivalry towards others who might contest the valuable beaver trade, and out of antagonism towards colonists who upheld the Church of England, with its Book of Common Prayer. Clearly, Morton wanted others to see it as a clash between religious fanatics and law-abiding members of the established Church. He also disparagingly dismissed Captain Standish as "their grand leader Captain Shrimp"—that matter of Myles's height again. [28] Morton also rejected what he considered a negative attitude towards "savages" and wrote, "I have found the Massachusetts Indians more full of humanity than the Christians." [29] His agitation in England found a sympathetic hearing under Charles I, causing major problems for the governing authorities in the Massachusetts Bay area. However, the outbreak of civil war in Britain intervened, and Morton, rather unwisely, returned to Plymouth Colony. He ended up being imprisoned in Boston, before being released and dying in Maine in 1647.

In 1635, Captain Standish took part in his last military action—the Penobscot expedition against the French. A French trading post, which dealt in furs and timber, had been established in 1613 on the Penobscot River (now Castine, Maine) but had been captured by English forces in 1628 and given to Plymouth Colony. However, in 1635, the French took it back. It was then that Governor Bradford ordered Standish to mount his biggest military expedition to date. Standish reflected on the demands of this task and decided to charter a ship, the *Good Hope*, and use it to bombard the French trading post. The master of the ship opened fire too early, and the available ammunition was spent hitting the coastline, not the settlement. In frustration, Standish abandoned the plan. When he reported back to Bradford, the Plymouth leadership asked for assistance from the Massachusetts Bay Colony, but this was refused: Boston did not wish to go to war to assist a rival colony. The whole enterprise ended with more of a whimper than a bang.

After this, the captain stood down from military adventures. It was time to make room for a younger man; later in 1635, Lieutenant William Holmes was appointed as Standish's assistant. When the Pequot War broke out in 1636, Standish raised the militia, but it was Holmes who led them into combat. This was the conflict that included the infamous destruction of a Pequot settlement near the Mystic River, in 1637, by New England militia, with terrible loss of life among the Native American noncombatants. In the attack, the militia were accompanied by Narragansett and Mohegan warriors allied with them against the Pequots.

After this, Standish only acted as a military adviser (although nominally still militia commander) from his farm at Duxbury. He busied himself as a surveyor of highways, as treasurer of the colony (1644–1649), and on committees overseeing boundaries and waterways.

His ally Hobbomock (part of the Standish household) died in 1642 and was buried on the Standish homestead in Duxbury. An era was coming to its close. Standish himself died, in October 1656, at his farm in Duxbury. The cause of death was strangury, painful and wrenching bladder spasms, which might have accompanied kidney or bladder stones or bladder cancer. He was seventy-two years old. Today his grave beneath the trees in the quiet green of Duxbury's Old Burying Ground (also known as the Myles Standish Cemetery) is surmounted by a stone enclosure and four 19th-century cannons. It seems a fitting memorial to the martial life of the captain.

History's verdict on Myles Standish

Myles Standish played an important role in the development and defense of the colony at Plymouth. This involved both bravery and energy—but also acts of violence on his part, which stand at odds with our image of the generally tolerant society founded there. As a result, there will always be an ambiguity in our image of the diminutive captain. This is not simply to apply 21st-century moral standards to a 17th-century figure, since there were contemporaries of the captain who were concerned at his willingness to use preemptive violence. He himself would have pointed to Pecksuot's and Wituwamat's open boasting about the killing and enslavement of Europeans, and he would have justified his actions as necessary in order to prevent impending attack.

This controversy is rather at odds with the popular image of the man, due to the fictionalized character concocted by Henry Wadsworth Longfellow in his famous narrative poem *The Courtship of Miles Standish*. This made him something of a folk hero in 19th-century America and obscured the—sometimes—brutal realities of aspects of his life in Plymouth. In Duxbury, the poem prompted the construction of monuments in Standish's honor. Between 1872 and 1898, the Myles Standish Monument was erected, the third-tallest monument commemorating an individual in the United States.[30] It is 116 feet (35.3 m) tall and is topped by a 14-foot (4.3 m) statue of the (actually diminutive) captain looking out to sea, while ospreys wheel overhead. A second, but smaller, monument was placed over the traditional site of his grave in 1893. This location was chosen after two excavations—in 1889 and 1891—to confirm his burial place. In 1930, a third exhumation occurred and resulted in Standish's remains being placed in a sealed chamber beneath the grave-site monument, in Myles Standish Cemetery in Duxbury. All that remains of his farmhouse is a depression in the ground marking where the cellar once was, now to be found in a small park, owned by the town of Duxbury. Perhaps his most enduring monument, though, was the survival of the colony itself. This he would, no doubt, have stated was what drove his most controversial actions.

12

The Lovers' Story:
John Alden and Priscilla Mullins

When Christopher Jones, the master of the *Mayflower*, selected his crew, he took on men who had some experience of the Atlantic, to make up for his own lack of experience in those challenging seas. However, it was not just seafaring practicalities that motivated him. There were also family connections influencing one of his appointments. He employed John Alden, who was probably his cousin, as the ship's cooper in charge of storing provisions. As John Alden knew from long experience, well-coopered, watertight casks could contain everything from water, wine, and beer to flour and hard biscuits. They were strong and could be rolled with ease.[1] They were the acme of 17th-century packaging. Poor work in this department could spell out disaster for everyone on board, especially as the Atlantic voyage of the *Mayflower* turned out to be a particularly long one. Weeks at sea could only be survived if the food and drink stored in the *Mayflower*'s hold were of sufficient quality to meet the demands of the journey. Hungry passengers—even those whose stomachs were frequently emptied by appalling bouts of seasickness—needed victuals of a reasonable quality to put there in the first place! Until the next heaving motion of the ship caused those stomach contents to be jettisoned over the side, some sustenance could be gained from getting down the salted and dried provisions. The crew member in charge of provisions might not have the most romantic and exciting job on the ship, but the lives of all aboard depended on him.

So it was that a family member, John Alden, was sent on ahead to Southampton to buy provisions and store them in sealed barrels in preparation for the arrival of the *Mayflower* and her temporary consort, the *Speedwell*, in that historic summer of 1620. However, this Mayflower Life would prove to be about more than hard tack and salted pork, for the story that started among the ships' chandlers and butchers of Southampton would eventually become part of the history of English settlement in North America. This was because John Alden would eventually marry a woman named Priscilla Mullins in the New World, staying there as a Stranger and transitioning into the husband of a Saint. A story whose first pages were written in Hampshire and Surrey, England, would have its later chapters written in the frontier settlements of New England.

Together, John Alden and Priscilla Mullins inspired one of the most famous poems and legends of North America, which has become a vivid human strand within the multilayered myth of the *Mayflower* and its settlements. It is a story of mutual attraction and romantic love; an aspect of the *Mayflower* story that would weave together the lives of not only John Alden and Priscilla Mullins but Myles Standish too. This was more than just the story of the barrel maker and provisions manager, and his eventual wife. This became the lovers' story. It reminds us that romance could play its part in making the new community in the New World, as well as in making the myth of that settlement, which would color later images of the Pilgrims with pastel pigments of human affection and love triangles, alongside the starker and more livid hues of sickness, hard work, and warfare.

We should not assume that romantic love was unknown in the 17th century. Although John Rolfe, at Jamestown, was not one of the Saints as we would recognize them at New Plymouth, his feelings for Pocahontas were strikingly passionate. While his recorded doubts about the idea of seeking her as his wife initially show much of the ethnic chauvinism of a 17th-century Englishman marrying an "ex-heathen" (after all, she had converted to Christianity and taken the new name of Rebecca, so why *not* marry her?), his attraction to her soon overcame the cultural and ethnic barriers. In his letter to Governor Dale of Jamestown in which he sought permission to marry, he wrote,

> *It is Pocahontas to whom my hearty and best thoughts are, and have been a long time so entangled, and enthralled in so intricate a labyrinth that I (could not) unwind myself thereout.* [2]

This is clearly love, however we might try to express it. John Rolfe knew it. And it overwhelmed his ethnic chauvinism. Rolfe was not unique in knowing such a powerful emotional attraction.

But back to the barrel maker and hard tack purchaser in Southampton and a girl from Surrey; for that is where the Mayflower Lives that became the Lovers' Story begins. . . .

Introducing the lovers

John Alden was born in about 1599, which meant he would have been about twenty-one when he sailed on the *Mayflower*. There are various suggestions regarding his English origins, [3] but nothing is entirely certain. [4] However, it is very possible that he came from a family living in Harwich, Essex, that was related to Christopher Jones. [5] It is very likely he was a cousin. Hence the assumption, followed here, that he was a relative of the *Mayflower*'s master.

Having come to New England the previous fall, John had a decision to make in 1621. After a tough sailing and a terrible winter, the voyage back offered a return to security away from the American wilderness. As he sat by the shoreline where the rough track of Plymouth's main street met the bay close to the tumbling water of Town Brook, he could see Cole's Hill, where the disturbed earth marked the graves of the winter dead; from there he could also look out to sea to where the *Mayflower* was being prepared by its much-reduced crew. What was it to be: chancing it in the wilderness? Or a return to the familiar shipyards and chandlers of Southampton, London, and Harwich? The joint-stock company of the Pilgrims offered him the option to stay on in New England or return to the England he knew so well. Given the choice between the little settlement being carved out of the wilderness or the route home, he finally chose to stay. For a skilled artisan, it was a challenging decision, since in that first period of struggle, everyone's top priority was staying alive. And so the experienced barrel maker had to become a farmer like everyone else.[6] But stay he did.

William Bradford, later writing in *Of Plymouth Plantation*, recorded that Alden

> *was hired for a cooper, at Southampton, where the ship victualed, and being a hopeful young man was much desired but left to his own liking to go or stay when he came here; but he stayed, and married here.*[7]

Perhaps it was the lure of the wilderness and the opportunity to be part of a great enterprise? Perhaps, having survived that first terrible winter, he felt he had invested a lot of himself in the struggling little colony? But perhaps that last point of Bradford's helps explain the decision? Maybe he had already set his heart on Priscilla Mullins. Maybe love had already started to grow in the American wilderness. Which brings us to the lady in question.

Priscilla Mullins (also spelled Mollins or Molines) was born in about 1602, in Dorking, Surrey. Her family was wealthy, as can be seen from the substantial property they left behind when they emigrated, and which still stands as Nos. 58–61 West Street.[8] Although they were strangers to the Leiden Pilgrims, her father had been brought to court for his unacceptable religious views, so he was clearly in sympathy with the Saints.[9] She was about eighteen years old when she emigrated to New England with her parents, William and Alice, and her younger brother, Joseph. As with many other families, the Mullinses suffered terribly during the first winter, when Priscilla lost the other three members of her family. In 1621, Priscilla found herself an orphan. An orphan, but not alone. For she was part of a new community in the New World and was about to take another big step forward in life.

Life in Plymouth Colony

Sometime between 1622 and 1623 she married John Alden. If the earlier date, then it was just about one year after John made his momentous decision to stay in Plymouth. We know they were probably married by 1623, because in that year Priscilla was not listed separately in the Division of Land. When the Division of Cattle took place in 1627, she and John were not only married but already had two children—a daughter, named Elizabeth, and a son, named John.[10] Records suggest that they lived on the hillside overlooking Plymouth Harbor, near the house of Governor Bradford, and close to the fort on what is now Burial Hill.

The competition for Priscilla's hand was fierce. By the time they married, the high rate of early female mortality (combined with more male arrivals) had left her as the only available young woman, with a choice of no fewer than eighteen bachelors![11] But it was John who succeeded in winning her love. Was it that he was the honorable but slightly retiring character who appears in later poetry (see below)? Was it his skill at crafts? Was it that he was especially handsome? Was it all these things? We would like to know. What is clear is that by the time the poet Longfellow finished with the story, they had become "America's First Couple overnight."[12] With, perhaps, Pocahontas and John Rolfe at Jamestown coming in a close second!

The growing Alden family lived in Plymouth until about 1631/1632. Through the Division of Land they gained land some distance away, on the other side of the bay. However, at first they only farmed this land, with their home remaining in the town of Plymouth. But this was inconvenient, and they, along with a number of others, decided to relocate. They joined a small group in founding the settlement of Duxbury (or *Duxburrough*, as it was then often known) to the north of Plymouth. Permission was reluctantly given by the Plymouth authorities, because the relocation broke up the coherent little community and it was hard to see something that had been so hard-won dissipate. When the move did occur, John Alden and Myles Standish were prominent among those who took part, so perhaps the legendary rivalry (see below) was based on a real friendship. Modern dendrochronological evidence from surviving wood indicates that the building of the first houses at Duxbury might have started as early as 1629. [13]

Together, Priscilla and John had ten children, but we know very little about Priscilla's married life. We do, though, know a lot more about their home. The original house itself is now located between a school's sports field and the edge of woodland, and can still be visited on its small knoll just north of the Blue Fish River. Its cellar hole can clearly be discerned in the ground. It is known as the Alden Homestead Site. The inscription on the information board at the site describes it as the "Site of the John Alden House built 1627." The date for the construction of the house has, however, been suggested (from the available excavated evidence) as being about 1632. [14] It was built on land that had originally been allocated to John as early as 1621. The main structure might have been an addition to an earlier house that had been constructed using wooden posts set directly into the ground, rather than on any foundations. The house seems to have gone out of use in the 1650s. As well as European items dating from the time of John and Priscilla—including cutlery, spoons, buckles, pipe stems, and pottery from North Devon that they would personally have handled—many Native American artifacts were also unearthed, indicating it had been the focus of settlement long before the arrival of the Aldens. A halberd, found by archaeologists in the cellar, is now on display at the Pilgrim Hall Museum in Plymouth.

The house would have had its daub walls protected from the harsh New England climate by the white oak clapboards we now associate with these houses but which were originally made from the waste left from the wooden blanks shipped back to England to be used to make barrels.[15] As distinct from weatherboards (which are made from soft woods and sawn), clapboards are made from hard woods and are riven (split in the direction of the wood's long fibers). As John Alden surveyed his new house, was he, as the skilled cooper, looking at his own variation on weatherboarding? Was this an Alden invention?[16] We might like to think so.

Having so many children took a toll on the family finances. During the 1670s, John was forced to petition the Plymouth Colony Court for assistance. As a result, he gained a number of land grants, which he distributed among his children to support them. Interestingly, John made no will, as he had given away most of what he owned to his children during his lifetime.

A short walk away from the Alden Homestead Site lies the still-standing John Alden House.[17] Alden family tradition states that this house was built in 1653, when John and Priscilla moved from their earlier, narrow, two-roomed home, although dendrochronology suggests a date closer to 1700 for the current structure. If the latter date is correct, then it was probably built by the grandson of John and Priscilla. It might have reused timbers from the original house. On the other hand, John and Priscilla enjoyed relatively high social status and must have grown tired of their cramped first property in Duxbury, so perhaps the surviving structure is somehow related to their desire to better their accommodation. The Alden home-site was acquired in 1907 by the Alden Kindred of America, who represent the descendants of John and Priscilla. Overall, the site is a remarkable example of continuity, especially given the number of early properties lost to fire over the centuries. A wheel-lock carbine, probably once owned by John Alden, was found hidden in the John Alden House during restoration work in 1924. It had been used so frequently that the rifling in the barrel had been worn almost completely away. Like the halberd found at the archaeological site, it is a physical connection with the world of John and Priscilla. Today it is part of the NRA's National Firearms Museum. It is often claimed to be the only known surviving firearm that came to New England on the *Mayflower*.[18]

Two other survivals from the Alden household, which are now in the Pilgrim Hall Museum in Plymouth, are a cupboard and John's Bible. It is particularly thought-provoking to look at the Bible, which would have been at the center of the family's devotional life.

John Alden was active in the life of Plymouth Colony. He was a useful man to have around (with his carpentry skills), and he and Priscilla had a sizeable number of shares in the enterprise, as she had inherited those of her dead parents and her brother. Based at Duxbury, he served the colony in a number of areas. He was, at various times: assistant to the governor from as early as 1631, a post to which he was frequently reelected until 1675; deputy from Duxbury to the General Court of Plymouth in the 1640s; one of the surveyors of highways; a leader within Myles Standish's Duxbury militia company; a member of the local Council of War; and treasurer of Plymouth Colony. He was also one of the freemen who purchased the company from the English shareholders in 1626, as part of freeing the colony from its debts and external control.

His involvement in the company's fur trading on the Kennebec River, in Maine, led to a crisis. In 1634, he was jailed in Boston as a result of a fight at Kennebec between traders from Plymouth and interlopers from the colony of Massachusetts Bay. The fight escalated into armed conflict and the killing of a Plymouth man, Moses Talbot, by John Hocking, who shot him in the head. The horrified Plymouth colonists then killed Hocking, also with a musket shot to the head. It was a bloody affair. John Alden played no part in this violent confrontation; however, he was the most senior member of Plymouth Colony that the Massachusetts Bay authorities could get their hands on. His arrest sparked a major row with Boston, since the leaders at Plymouth insisted that the Massachusetts Bay Colony had no legal authority to arrest and hold him. Only the timely intervention of William Bradford defused the situation and led to John's release.

So it was that John was able to return to Duxbury and continue his farming and his civic duties. The family remained based there until the deaths of John and Priscilla. The date of Priscilla's death is unknown, but probably occurred between 1651 and her husband's death in 1687. Both John and Priscilla were buried in the Myles Standish Burial Ground, in Duxbury. When John died in September 1687, at the age of about eighty-nine, he was the last (male) survivor of the signers of the Mayflower Compact and one of the last few surviving *Mayflower* passengers.[19] He and Priscilla have the most descendants today of all the Pilgrim families.

Local broadsheets printed obituaries of this "Aged, Pious, Sincere-hearted Christian." One broadsheet also included the peculiar addition of an anagram of his name, which, it stated, was (a rather cryptic): "End al on hj" Another broadsheet referred to the "great Honour due to that Honourable Servant of God and his Generation." And finally it concluded:

> *Let New England never want* [lack] *a Race Of Such as may be filld with Alden's Grace.*[20]

The legend(s) of John Alden and Priscilla Mullins

Two popular myths have grown up around the Aldens. One tradition claims that John was the first Pilgrim to set foot on the famous Plymouth Rock.[21] It was a story enthusiastically embraced by Alden descendant and sixth president of the United States (from 1825–29) John Quincy Adams.[22] This tradition clashes with the claims for Mary Chilton, and neither is possible to prove. The other is a more famous legend altogether. It involves the alleged romantic entanglement of John Alden, Myles Standish, and Priscilla Mullins. For years the Alden family passed down a tradition that Alden only won the hand of the beautiful Priscilla after first attempting to court her on behalf of his friend Myles Standish. As a result of this legend, while the names of most of the other female Pilgrims have dropped out of memory, that of Priscilla Mullins remains well known. In the legend, John comes nervously to woo the maiden, only to have Priscilla famously ask, "Why don't you speak for yourself, John?"

The legend of the love rivalry between Standish and Alden first appeared in 1814, in Rev. Timothy Alden's *Collection of American Epitaphs and Inscriptions*. But the story really became well known when it became the subject of a poem entitled *The Courtship of Miles Standish*, which was published by Henry Wadsworth Longfellow in 1858. Longfellow was a descendant of the *Mayflower* Pilgrims through his mother, Zilpah Wadsworth, which placed him in the family line of John Alden and Priscilla Mullins. He claimed to be putting a genuine family tradition into print. The jury is out on the believability of the claim.

As is the way of poets, the history gets revised for greater poetic effect. Wadsworth took a number of incidents that occurred over a number of years and compressed them into one year: 1621. This is all the more dramatic as this was the year of the appearance of Samoset, Massasoit, and Squanto; the year of the first Thanksgiving.

In this loosely structured poem, which almost edges into prose, Wadsworth created a romantic drama, rather than a heroic epic. In the poem, Standish is the muscular, tough action hero, compared with Alden, who is the scholar. Standish is a man of few words but self-important; Alden, though shy, is something of a poet. The background to the poem is a fierce Indian war of a kind that simply did not occur in the 1620s. The style of the poem varies in its emotional tone. There is both drama (disease and Indian Wars) alongside comedic aspects of the rather bumbling and eccentric love triangle, with inarticulate men contrasted with a quietly spoken but determined and insightful young woman.

To cut a rather long story/poem short . . . having lost his wife, Standish goes about seeking a bride based on biblical precepts, but without any passion. Priscilla is the only single woman, of marriageable age, and a beauty. Alden then has to set aside his love for Priscilla in order to honor his friendship with the taciturn captain. He comes to Priscilla, who is busy at her spinning wheel (despite the fact that no such item was in use in Plymouth in the 1620s). When he bluntly offers the captain's suit, he is met by a polite but firm young woman who is clearly not impressed by the captain sending a go-between. After listening to Alden's praise of the captain, Priscilla is clearly not won over, and we are told (in part 3, "The Lover's Errand"),

But as he warmed and glowed, in his simple and eloquent lan-
guage, Quite forgetful of self, and full of the praise of his rival,
Archly the maiden smiled, and, with eyes overrunning with
laughter, Said, in a tremulous voice, "Why don't you speak for
yourself, John?"[23]

Well, the cat is now out of the bag. Priscilla can tell John loves her, and she much prefers the young man to the brave but unromantic captain. Alden ponders returning to England, then there are battles with hostile natives and reports that Standish has been killed; but, needless to say, it all ends happily for John and Priscilla, and Standish and Alden are reconciled. Finally, Priscilla is led to her new family home riding Alden's snow-white bull, which sounds like a very dangerous thing to do![24]

There is no surviving documentation supporting the legend in any of the records of the colony at Plymouth.[25] All these tell us is that Rose Standish (the wife of Myles Standish) died in January 1621; Priscilla Mullins married John Alden, date uncertain; Myles Standish married Barbara Standish in 1623 or perhaps in 1624. But by a curious twist, Alexander Standish, who was the second child of Myles and Barbara, married Sarah Alden, who was the fourth child of John and Priscilla.[26]

The poem is charming and very memorable. In this way the lovers have been commended to generations of schoolchildren. Nevertheless, given the huge imbalance between the legend and evidence either for or against it, it is worth asking whether we can give any credence to this remarkable and evocative story

We explored something of the approach to married life and sexual relationships within marriage when we looked at the life of Susanna White ("The Mother's Story"), but here we are considering how such a union might happen in the first place. Generally speaking, among the godly of Plymouth (as within their society generally), love was seen as a product of marriage, not the other way around. In short, a good marriage led to feelings of love. The feelings that led to the union itself had to be expressed in cool and rational ways: "She is a good Christian . . . ," "She is thrifty, pious and industrious."[27] As a result, marriage was considered something of a social contract, a mutually advantageous alliance. This meant that most 17th-century marriages were arranged. Families looked for suitable partners for their children, made discreet inquiries, discussed arrangements. Among the Separatists this lack of marital grandeur seems particularly striking, because marriages like those between John and Priscilla were civil partnerships presided over by a magistrate (until 1686 in Massachusetts).

Looking at the details of such arrangements, it all seems very cold and formal: an agreement between families; an announcement of intention to marry made at three successive public meetings or nailing a notice to the meeting house door fourteen days before the wedding day (publishing the "banns"); sexual consummation, in order to validate the wedding (male impotence led to annulment of the marriage). This all took place within a policing of morals that caused those found guilty of fornication or adultery to be fined and/or whipped and made divorce a rarity. Between 1639 and 1692 there were just twenty-seven cases of divorce in Massachusetts.[28] The main grounds for divorce were adultery, desertion, or non-support by the husband. Public shaming of those who broke these sexual boundaries inspired Nathaniel Hawthorne's famous novel of 1850, *The Scarlet Letter*, which was based on the Puritan practice of public shaming. The main character, Hester Prynne, wears a scarlet-colored letter *A* (for adultery) while standing on the gallows before a hostile crowd, and then being condemned to wear the "scarlet letter" for life. Others who broke sexual taboos were fined, whipped, branded, and—in extreme cases—hanged. So, this area of life sounds strictly chaneled, policed, enforced, and punished. Not much room for romance there!

However, one can go too far in this assessment. Thomas Hooker (1586–1647) founded the colony of Connecticut after falling out with Puritan leaders in Massachusetts Bay over their restriction of voting rights to those freemen who had formally been accepted into Church membership, following a thorough investigation of their religious views and religious experiences. This was an exclusive approach fairly typical of the semi-theocracy that existed in Massachusetts Bay for a large part of the 17th century. Due to his more inclusive view of access to voting rights, he has been called the "Father of American Democracy."[29] As a result, some of his other views may also sound rather more accessible to 21st-century readers. Nevertheless, Hooker was no easygoing liberal, and his ideas clearly reflect Puritan ideas that extended well beyond his own circle. This makes his description of an ideal husband all the more intriguing in what it reveals about the possibility of romantic love among Puritans. Hooker wrote that such a husband is

the man whose heart is endeared to the woman he loves, he dreams of her in the night, hath her in his eye and apprehension when he awakes, museth on her as he sits at table, walks with her when he travels and parlies with her in each place where he comes . . .[30]

This is very romantic indeed and easily recognizable to modern readers. Of course, it could be objected that Hooker was describing the ideal state after marriage, not before marriage: the man and woman whose future life has been negotiated and arranged have their prescribed sexual encounter in the marriage bed. They learn to get along together in the home or enterprise and grow in affection. Love blooms. The man starts to look lovingly across the breakfast table at his wife, having dreamed of making love with her as he slept beside her, and he looks forward to spending time with her and talking with her in the day ahead.

Similarly, Edward Taylor might have been living on the wild western frontier of Massachusetts after graduating from Harvard in 1671, but this pastor and poet wrote of his love for his wife as being "a golden ball of pure fire." Another clergyman, John Pike, called his wife "the desire of mine eyes"; William Gouge described such love as being "like fire."[31] There is good evidence for saying that it was English—often Puritan—writers who took the medieval idea of adulterous and passionate courtly love and transformed it into wedded romantic love. This created the ideal of a romantic marriage.[32] That is romantic love by any definition. But, of course, it all happens *after* marriage. Not much room there for the flirtatious assertiveness of an *unmarried* woman: "Why don't you speak for yourself, John?"

But this is surely going too far in excising romance from the approach to marriage. After all, what about John Rolfe and Pocahontas? His romantic and sexual attraction towards her did not wait until after the legal bits before it bloomed. It drove the action forward. Well before marriage, Rolfe had "been a long time so entangled, and enthralled in so intricate a labyrinth . . ." And it was no cool, legal arrangement that caused Elizabeth Soule, as we will shortly see, to make love with Nathaniel Church in 1663 and end up being fined for fornication. Attraction could be as strong in 17th-century Plymouth as in the modern world. Sexual desire was certainly there. Romance could definitely exist, as John Rolfe proves. This was seen as part of the service owed to God, and as expressing a mutual desire for comfort. It was certainly not focused on erotic desire or sex for the sake of pleasure, nor was it a celebration of self-indulgence or of feelings subsuming everything else. But love and compatibility were considered reasons to desire marriage.[33] The possibility of what we call romance was allowed for. So, why should we exclude the possibility of mutual attraction and romantic love in the case of John and Priscilla? And maybe he did go to her on behalf of a tongue-tied Standish. And maybe an intelligent and determined young woman made up her own mind. Maybe they did, indeed, fall in love!

13

The Rebels' Story: the Billingtons, the Soules, and Other Challenges to Morality and Order

Thomas Granger was seventeen in 1642. He was a servant to one of the families that had moved the ten miles from Plymouth to Duxbury. He was seventeen and he stood quietly, waiting to die. Beside him the gallows was prepared and the rope strung from it. Before long he would be hanging from it; battling for breath if it took a time to die, or swiftly dispatched if his neck broke under his weight.

But it was not the rope that Thomas was looking at. His eyes were fixed firmly on the drama playing out below the rough scaffold. There stood Governor Bradford, in his role as magistrate, accompanied by the other magistrates of Plymouth Colony. And before them was gathered a strange menagerie: a mare, a cow, two goats, five sheep, two calves, and a turkey. Herded close together, the sheep bleated, the cow lowed, the calves jostled beside the cow, and the mare seemed nervous and pulled at its rope, while the turkey was held firmly and gobbled in irritation at its confinement.

It was hard to take it all in: the noise, the strangeness of the gathered farmyard animals, the hard stares of the men and women forming a semicircle around the scene. Then there was the deep pit that had been dug. Beside it men were leaning on their shovels. And beyond them Thomas could see the palisade wall around the village of Plymouth, the roofs of the houses, smoke drifting lazily upward on the still air. He took it all in, as if desperate to miss nothing, now that he knew he was seeing the familiar scene for the last time. And the juxtaposition of the familiar (the village) with the absurd (the jostling herd of animals) was so striking, so bizarre. He took in every detail of it . . . for the last time.

Then the charge was read out again. That he had had sexual relations with every one of the animals before him. He stared hard at the animals and tried not to look at the horrified and contemptuous faces of those in the crowd. One by one each animal was led forward. A passage from Leviticus was being read,

> *the man that lieth with a beast, shall die the death, and ye shall slay the beast. And if a woman come to any beast, and lie there-with, then thou shalt kill the woman and the beast: they shall die the death, their blood shall be upon them.*[1]

One by one each animal was led forward. The largest animals first, the horse and the cow. Then the others. Each was dispatched. Its throat was cut and it was heaved or tossed into the pit. Animals still living were becoming alarmed. The bleating and bellowing was like a slaughterhouse. Fear was infectious. The pace of the killing increased. Finally, the turkey, that most absurd of fowls, was killed and its limp corpse hurled in after the others.

Then they hanged Thomas Granger and threw his body into the pit. The men with the shovels piled in the soil. Soon the bodies of boy and animals were out of sight. The assembled villagers turned and walked away; the magistrates first. There was a low murmur of hushed voices from some. But most left in silence.

Rebels and deviants . . . the challenge to godly order

Not everyone at Plymouth was building a New Jerusalem of holy living and self-disciplined behavior. Not everyone was striving to keep to the narrow path that led to heaven and avoid the broad and easy path that led to destruction and hell.

This was for a number of reasons. For a start, not everyone had signed up mentally (or morally) to the Puritan ethic of hard work, sober living, disciplined family life, and sexual boundaries. There were Strangers as well as Saints on the *Mayflower*. This did not mean that every Stranger was (literally) hell-bent on doing whatever they wanted. That would be totally incorrect, since many, if not most, were decent-living and hardworking men and women who shared the same general ethics with regard to work and morality as the Saints. But some, although they had signed the Mayflower Compact, had certainly not signed up to the whole nine yards of the norms and disciplines espoused by the tightly knit Separatist congregation from Leiden. This dissonance could cover a wide range of alternative responses. There were non-separating Puritans who simply did not go along with the whole Separatist mind-set of splitting from the established Church, with the resulting creation of a tight-knit and rather inward-looking community. There were those of a more liberal (but still highly Christian) disposition who took a broader view of what was biblically acceptable and what was not. They might consider it fine to play football or tip-cat (a forerunner of rounders, cricket, and baseball) on a Sunday or make merry on Christmas Day, but in their work and morals they were as upright as any Puritan. However, these points of difference were fiercely divisive in the 17th century, and they would have been regarded as on the broad road to destruction by many of the godly.

Then there were those who were regarded as part of the godly community of Saints but who slipped due to personal weaknesses and inability to resist temptation. That, of course, might at times include even the most upright; and it might be a momentary lapse or a secret area of ongoing sin. Some of these sins were ones classified as such in the 17th century but less so today.

Finally, there were those who would be regarded as deviants in most faith communities. They got drunk, they cheated, they fought their neighbors, they stole, they committed adultery or other sexual sins. For, like any community, the one established at Plymouth included a minority whose moral compass was orientated well away from good living, as defined by most in their society or in many modern societies.

All of this means that an exploration of Mayflower Lives has to include some of these areas of rebellion and deviance if it is to really represent what life was like in a very human community, living in extraordinary times and conditions.

Straying from the narrow path

Some of the families at Plymouth were clearly characterized by their rebellions against what was expected of them. Of these difficult families, some were very difficult indeed. One such was the Billington family. The problems involved father (John), mother (Eleanor or Ellen), and their two sons (Francis and John Jr.). John Billington was one of the men who signed the Mayflower Compact, but he and his family never signed up for well-behaved living.

Even before the family had left the *Mayflower*, their son Francis nearly caused a disaster on the ship, as was later recounted in *Mourt's Relation*.

> *The fifth day* [of December, 1620] *we, through God's mercy, escaped a great danger by the foolishness of a boy, one of . . . Billington's sons, who, in his father's absence, had got gunpowder and had shot of a piece or two, and made squibs* [fireworks], *and there being a fowling-piece charged in his father's cabin, shot her off in the cabin; there being a little barrel*

of [gun] *powder half full, scattered in and about the cabin, the fire being within four feet of the bed between the decks, and many flints and iron things about the cabin, and many people about the fire, and yet, by God's mercy, no harm done.*[2]

Soon after this event, which could have jeopardized the entire company on the ship, his restless curiosity had a more positive outcome. For, not long after the arrival at Plymouth, Francis went exploring.

Monday, the eighth day of January [1621] ... *This day, Francis Billington, having the week before seen from the top of a tree on a high hill a great sea* [known today as Billington Sea, actually a large pond] *as he thought, went with one of the master's mates to see it. They went three miles and then came to a great water, divided into two great lakes; the bigger of them five or six miles in circuit, and in it an isle of a cable length square, the other three miles in compass; in their estimation they are fine fresh water, full of fish and fowl. A brook issues from it; it will be an excellent place for us in time.*[3]

They also chanced on seven or eight deserted Native American dwellings, but there was nobody around. However, they were understandably afraid, having just one musket, and beat a rapid retreat back to the settlement.

Despite these risky adventures, the entire Billington family survived that first terrible winter in Plymouth, which later must have caused some in Plymouth to ponder the mysterious workings of providence, given how many upright and godly people died during that time.

The problematic nature of the Billingtons was soon to manifest itself again. We have seen how, in March 1621, John Billington challenged the drill instructions of Captain Standish. Standish and the community were having none of it.

The first offence since our arrival is of John Billington who came on board at London, and is this month [March 1621] *convented* [brought] *before the whole company for his contempt of the captain's lawful command with opprobrious speeches, for which he is adjudged to have his neck and heels tied together; but upon humbling himself and craving pardon, and it being the first offence, he is forgiven.* [4]

However, the problems caused by the Billingtons were not at an end. In May 1621 John Billington Jr. replicated his brother's wandering and became lost in the woods that bordered the colony. William Bradford recounted what occurred in *Of Plymouth Plantation*. For five days the boy survived on berries before stumbling on a Native American village. By that time he had wandered twenty miles south of Plymouth to a place called Manomet. Eventually he was taken to the Nauset people on Cape Cod. In time, news of his whereabouts reached Plymouth, via Massasoit, and a group of colonists traveled there to collect him. [5] More details were provided in *Mourt's Relation*. There we learn that after the colonists nervously approached the tribe who had clashed with them on First Encounter Beach, the Nauset *sachem* Aspinet met them after sunset and delivered the boy to them,

behung with beads, and made peace with us, we bestowing a knife on him, and likewise on another that first entertained the boy and brought him thither. [6]

While this could be put down to nothing more than adventurousness, the overall nuisance value of the Billingtons was starting to be pronounced. This was apparent in 1624, when the head of the family, John Billington, was implicated in the problems caused by the actions of the Rev. Lyford. Billington was accused of complaining about the colony to this clergyman when he attended his meetings. However, Billington protested his innocence and so was not punished. But those who knew the man were getting the measure of him. William Bradford expressed his assessment of Billington in a letter he wrote to Robert Cushman (who was representing the colony in dealings with the Merchant Adventurers in London) in June, 1625.

Billington still rails against you, and threatens to arrest you, I
know not wherefore; he is a knave, and so will live and die.[7]

Bradford's low opinion of Billington was to be justified just five years later when he murdered a fellow colonist.

In September 1630 Billington was found guilty of the murder of John Newcomen, for which he was hanged. There was an old quarrel between the two men, and William Bradford recorded that Billington was

arraigned, and both by grand and petty jury found guilty of
wilful murder, by plain and notorious evidence. And was for
the same accordingly executed.

Despite the trouble caused by Billington, Bradford noted it was "a matter of great sadness unto them [the colonists]." Billington was about forty years old when he was executed. This was the first such execution in Plymouth Colony and the only one from the early period of its history. And it was not done lightly. Before the sentence was carried out, the leaders at Plymouth took advice from other settlers newly arrived in the Massachusetts Bay area. All agreed that Billington should be hanged. Bradford, noting it was just the latest of the offenses of the family, concluded, "He and some of his had been often punished for miscarriages before, being one of the profanest families amongst them." Recalling how the Billingtons had joined the venture from London, Bradford could not understand how they had ever been allowed to join the godly enterprise: "I know not by what friends shuffled into their [the Pilgrim's] company."

Bradford gives little detailed information about the murder, just noting that Billington waylaid Newcomen and shot him due to an old quarrel.[8] A great deal more detail was provided by a later writer in 1680, but close enough to the events to mean that this account might have contained genuine information from the time of the crime.

When this wilderness began first to be peopled by the English,
when there was but one poor town, another Cain was found
therein, who maliciously slew his neighbor in the field, as he

*accidentally met him, as himself was going to shoot deer. The
poor fellow perceiving the intent of this Billington, his mortal
enemy, sheltered himself behind trees as well as he could for a
while; but the other, not being so ill a marksman as to miss his
aim, made a shot at him, and struck him on the shoulder, with
which he died soon after.*

According to this later account, Billington assumed that he would
not be punished for the crime because he thought the Plymouth court
lacked the authority to carry out executions. Or, failing that, they
would not want to decrease their manpower in the colony. He was
wrong. Because "justice otherwise determined, and rewarded him, the
first murtherer of his neighbor there, with the deserved punishment of
death, for a warning to others."[9]

The case against Billington seems clear, and given the use of the
death penalty at the time, it is hardly surprising that Billington was
hanged. However, some of those antagonistic to the colony were quick
to challenge the legality of the execution. Thomas Morton, whose
riotous colony at Merrymount was abruptly terminated by the actions
of the Plymouth leadership, offered a very different version of what led
to Billington's execution. Referring to

[Billington] *that was choaked* [choked, hanged] *at Plimmouth
after hee had played the unhappy Markes man when hee was
purſued by a carelesse fellow that was new come into the Land . . .
Hee was beloved of many.*[10]

There seems no reason for accepting Morton's version of events
over the picture provided by other sources, and this looks very like a
deliberate attempt to interpret it in a way detrimental to Plymouth.
Billington might have been "beloved of many," but there must also
have been many more who regarded him as a dangerous—and now
murderous—deviant member of the colony.

In 1636, John's wife, Eleanor Billington, continued the family tradition of falling foul of the law when she was sentenced to be fined five

pounds, placed in the stocks, and whipped for slandering John Doane, another citizen of Plymouth.[11] Clearly, life in Plymouth could be very turbulent at times.

Another family showing alternatives to Puritan norms was George Soule and Mary Buckett. The first example was a minor one. George Soule was a Stranger and one of the indentured servants on the *Mayflower*. He married Mary Buckett, who arrived in Plymouth Colony in July 1623 as a single woman on the ship *Anne*. This by itself is noteworthy, as a young woman traveling alone defied Puritan norms, which assumed that all single people needed to be brought under the discipline of a family. Singleness by itself was regarded with real suspicion. The fact that Mary traveled alone did not inevitably imply that all was not well, but it suggested an independence of spirit that might point to trouble ahead. At first, all seemed well, as George was never accused of any crime, nor was he involved in any civil disputes. Furthermore, he volunteered to fight in the Pequot War in 1637. However, the war was over before the Plymouth militia were deployed in action.

But things started to go very wrong in the person of their son, Nathaniel (born between 1634 and 1646). In March 1668, he was summoned before the court in Plymouth to "answer for his abusing of Mr. [Rev.] John Holmes, teacher of the church of Christ at Duxbury, by many false, scandalous and opprobrious speeches." His sentence was to apologize publicly, pay a fine, and spend time in the stocks, although this was not carried out because Mr. Holmes asked for mercy to be shown. Nathaniel's father and brother paid to guarantee his future good behavior, as did Nathaniel himself. Then, in June 1671, Nathaniel was fined for "telling several lies which tended greatly to the hurt of the Colony in reference to some particulars about the Indians." We do not know further details, but this sounds intriguing. Finally, in March 1675, he was sentenced to a whipping for "lying [having sex] with an Indian woman." In addition, he had to provide quantities of corn to the woman to help maintain the child that was the outcome of this illegal union.[12] His crime would have been punished (by the lesser punishment of a fine) if he had committed it with an English woman, but there is other evidence to suggest that sex with Native Americans caused particular anxiety (hence the whipping), as it breached the racial boundaries of the Bible commonwealth itself. In their eyes it threatened to lead to a breakdown of sexual discipline such as was alleged to have occurred at Merrymount; this was linked to a fear (a fantasy by some perhaps) concerning promiscuous Native American women. [13]

This was not the only deviant behavior exhibited by the Soule children. In 1663, Nathaniel's sister, Elizabeth Soule, was fined for fornication (sex outside marriage). She then sued her sexual partner (Nathaniel Church) for refusing to marry her after they had had sex. She was awarded £10 damages and costs. She had hoped for £200, but clearly the court thought this was a bit steep. Despite this, Elizabeth did not moderate her conduct, because, in 1667, she was whipped for a second offense of fornication. Her partner this time was not named in the court records, and how the matter became public knowledge is anyone's guess. [14] These activities do not necessarily imply promiscuity on Elizabeth's part, since many in her society considered intention to marry as allowing licit intercourse. Consequently, about 20 percent of English brides at the time were pregnant at marriage. However, all shades of churchmanship officially believed that sex should wait until after marriage (whether that was regarded as a secular arrangement, as among the Separatists, or as a Church-blessed union, as in official Church of England beliefs). [15] Soon after 1667 Elizabeth married, so this might explain the second occurrence, and the first seemed linked to some kind of perceived intention to marry.

Other challenges to good behavior

The peace of the colony could also be disturbed in other ways. Edward Doty was the indentured servant of Stephen Hopkins in 1623, when the Division of Land occurred, suggesting that he was under twenty-five at that point. He was a man who got into trouble on more than one occasion. In June 1621 he took part in a sword and dagger fight with Edward Leister, another of Hopkins's servants. Some modern historians have speculated that the duel was fought over one of Hopkins's daughters, but there does not seem to be sufficient evidence to decide this one way or the other. Both men received minor stab wounds before others separated them. As a result, they were sentenced to have their head and feet tied together for an hour. Bad as this was, the original sentence was that they were to be tied this way for the whole day. Only their suffering caused the magistrates to reduce the punishment. Not that this caused Edward to adopt a more disciplined lifestyle, as he frequently appeared before the Plymouth court for a range of relatively minor offenses as varied as letting his cows wander, lack of care for a servant, and failing to pay money owed to another. But it could be more serious. Twice he appeared charged with assault,[16] once for theft, and once for slandering another colonist.[17] He also sued his own father-in-law over money allegedly owed him. In all, these amounted to about twenty-five court appearances (as either a plaintiff or defendant) in a similar number of years. This was all rather Billingtonesque. Perhaps not surprisingly, Edward was rarely summoned for public service. This was unusual but might reflect that he was not trusted by his peers.

Others were involved in rather more white-collar crime; perhaps we might term it "white-ruff crime." Isaac Allerton was finally forced out of the colony in 1631, despite having been elected assistant to Governor Bradford in 1621 and acting in that role for ten years. While tasked with negotiating, after 1627, with the London backers to gain the colony's financial independence, he seems to have gone rogue, indulging in personal deals, personally using colony income gained from fur trading, and involving the colony in unauthorized ventures. This only added to the colony's debts, which were already burdensome. In addition, it was Allerton who was active in bringing over an inappropriate clergyman (Rev. William Morrell), as well as helping Thomas Morton to return, despite his previous infamy at Merrymount. When Allerton returned from England in 1630, it was discovered that he had failed to secure essential supplies. As if this was not bad enough, he established his own fur trading post in Maine, in direct competition with Plymouth's own trading post there. He was finally replaced by Edward Winslow and left Plymouth in 1631, eventually moving to Marblehead Neck, on the coast southeast of Salem, Massachusetts. In his records for that year, a sorrowful William Bradford noted,

> *Mr Allerton doth in a sort wholly now desert them* [the Plymouth colony]; *having brought them into the briars, he leaves them to get out as they can.*[18]

Not a happy state of affairs. As one of the colony's associates in London put it, in a letter written to William Bradford in June 1633, "Oh, the grief and trouble that man Mr Allerton hath brought upon you and us!"[19]

Finally in 1634, following the death of his wife, Allerton settled in New Haven Colony and remarried. His trading activities involved the Dutch of the New Netherlands (in New York, New Jersey, Delaware, and Connecticut), Swedes at New Sweden (on the Delaware River), the English of Virginia, Massachusetts Bay, and Barbados. If this energy had been placed at the disposal of Plymouth Colony instead of for his own benefit, it would have greatly assisted the struggling enterprise there, rather than weakening it.

In addition to these striking examples, the Plymouth court records reveal a wide range of other crimes and challenges to godly society. Arthur Peach got a maid pregnant and was later executed for robbing and murdering a Native American, named Penowanyanquis, in 1638, in the company of Thomas Jackson, Richard Stinnings, and Daniel Cross. All but Cross were hanged, which sent a clear message in defense of Native American rights. This strict equality before the law collapsed in later years in New England and beyond.

Murder could also occur within a family. In 1648, a woman named Alice Bishop was hanged for the murder of her sleeping four-year-old daughter, Martha. Although some modern accounts state that she claimed no recollection of the crime, there seems no such evidence in the original records of Plymouth court, and we have no idea regarding her motivation or her mental health.

With regard to witchcraft trials—usually associated with Salem, Massachusetts, from 1692 to 1693—there were just two in early

Plymouth, and they resulted in charges of not guilty and fining the accusers. This is an important reminder that such accusations were not necessarily successful when not part of a hysterical panic.

Sexual challenges to contemporary norms were not restricted to the famous examples we have examined so far. The (then illegal) practice of homosexuality appears in the 1637 case of John Alexander and Thomas Roberts, who were convicted of "lude behavior and unclean carriage one with another, by often spending their seed one upon another." Alexander was severely whipped, branded with a hot iron on the shoulder, and permanently banished; Roberts was severely whipped and banned from owning land, but not banished. Other illegal sexual acts also appeared in court records. In 1660, Thomas Atkins was accused of committing incest with Mary, his daughter. This carried the death penalty, but he was found guilty of the lesser (though still shocking) crime of "incestuous attempts" towards the girl "in the chimney corner" while drunk.[20] He was whipped.

We have seen how sexual sin could manifest itself in the most shocking form in the case of the bestiality for which Thomas Granger was executed. He was a servant of Love Brewster, son of Elder Brewster of the Plymouth church. Granger had been caught having sex with a mare owned by Love. After he was arrested, his confession revealed that the whole story of sex with animals had occurred not only

> with that beast at that time, but sundry times before and at several times with all the rest of the forenamed [the list of animals] in his indictment.[21]

He was executed on September 8, 1642. All the animals concerned were killed along with him, although Bradford recorded that some of the sheep could not be identified from his descriptions. Consequently, they killed the ones that could be singled out from his descriptions, and also killed animals that were brought before him for identification. It seemed that the idea had been put into his head by another servant who had himself heard of it being done in England before he emigrated. The extent to which the matter occupied

Bradford's thoughts is seen in the way that he sought the opinions of three respected ministers regarding "Unnatural vice," centered on the question "What sodomitical acts are to be punished with death?" The answers ranged beyond narrowly defined sodomy (homosexuality) and extended to a wide range of sexual sins (adultery, incest, bestiality, rape) and the biblical teaching regarding judgement and punishment of these acts. These answers run to many pages in his *Of Plymouth Plantation.*[22] However, the strange double standards that could occur in New England with regard to sexual sin is revealed in the fact that in 1641, while Thomas Granger was executed for sex with animals, a year later, two men who together raped an eight- and a nine-year-old girl in their care got off with nothing worse than a fine and a whipping. The difference might have been that Granger was a servant, whereas the more socially superior of the two men who raped the girls (the second was a hired hand) was a "member of the church . . . and in good esteem for piety and sobriety."[23] This lenient sentence occurred, despite the contrary opinions of a number of church elders, because the offense was not a capital one in Massachusetts. This is shocking, given that sex with animals clearly was.

The whole matter troubled William Bradford beyond the specifics of this particular case and one of attempted "Sodomy" (homosexual sex), which he referred to in the same note for 1642. By the time he died, Bradford was becoming increasingly concerned about the moral state of the colony. The early spiritual zeal was, he felt, declining. Seeing how the work had been started by godly people, he was shocked to see how sin and depravity were being introduced into the colony by those who had followed on from the first godly pioneers. He concluded this was caused by a combination of the activities of the devil, designed to weaken the holy commonwealth, and the need for labor, causing ungodly settlers to be accepted because there were not enough of the godly willing to come. He seemed to think the problem was particularly acute with regard to the employment of servants. This might have been true, but the comment might simply reveal the condescension of the employer class: it's all the fault of the ungodly servants . . . He also pondered that perhaps it was because the growing prosperity of the colony attracted the wrong type of emigrant. In short, they were the victims of their own success.[24] But there was a wider and more general unease that troubled him as he considered the view held by some of his contemporaries "that Satan hath more power in these heathen lands."[25] Bradford himself was more inclined to conclude that the increase in abominable sin was the devil's response to the "holiness and purity" that the godly were endeavoring to establish in New England, but it was a worrying consideration that *perhaps* there was something about the place itself that made such sin more likely.

All of these activities reveal that it was no easier to create a godly community in the New World than it had been in the old. Bradford might ponder on the apparent fall from holiness of a later generation, compared with the first comers, or the sinful influence of a land of wilderness, but the reality was the constant weakness of human nature. Seeking to eradicate it was a constant battle. It was no more likely to achieve permanent success than the 1637 banning of smoking in public places, whose failure was revealed in the need, in 1640, to fine jurors who smoked and the 1669 attempt to eradicate smoking on the way to and from church. It was necessary to enforce civic responsibilities too; these could not be taken for granted. Attempts to make citizens better prepared to defend the colony made it a fineable offense to *not* bring a loaded musket to church! Failure to vote was also punished by a fine.

These legal attempts to impose godly behavior were dependent on juries of twelve men, as in the English legal system, with grand juries being summoned for more serious cases. The Plymouth court met four times a year (as well as on other pressing occasions) under the authority of the governor and his assistants, who were elected by the freemen of Plymouth to one-year terms of office.[26] These structures to enforce behavior were necessary, because it soon became all too apparent that the New Jerusalem was not easy to build in the face of human frailty.

14

The American Mariner's Story: Richard More, New World Sea Captain

In the bitter cold winter of 1620, a six-year-old boy came ashore at Plymouth. But this was not an opportunity to throw snowballs, go sledding, or build a snowman. This was life or death. There was no time or place for being a child. It is reasonable to imagine that in the killing winter of 1620 to 1621, little Richard More labored alongside the men as they strove to build the first structures in Plymouth, shelters for those who were freezing and dying aboard the *Mayflower*, which was anchored out in Plymouth Harbor.[1] Years later Richard must have looked back on these formative years, as he eventually became the last surviving male link to those first, almost mythical, days. In the transformed world of Massachusetts in the 1690s, his venerable roots were to make him something of a celebrity despite his shortcomings; he was a first comer who'd survived. Yet his survival would have seemed very unlikely at the start of that epic life voyage.

In 1620, little Richard was one of four More children, unwanted bastards sent to North America by their embittered father as a means to punish his adulterous wife and cleanse away the living evidence that he had been constantly cuckolded while away on business in London. The More children—Ellen (eight years old); Jasper (seven years old); Richard (six years old); and Mary (four years old)—were consigned to a new life, or death, in New England. Which it would be was of little importance to their legal father. He had washed his hands of them.

That first winter it would be death that claimed three quarters of the More children. The first to die was probably Ellen. She faded into sickness and died, possibly while the *Mayflower* was anchored in Provincetown Harbor, and she was buried somewhere ashore.[2] Next to die was Jasper; he too was probably laid in a grave dug from the sandy soil at the tip of Cape Cod.[3] They were two of the four passengers who died after the ship arrived at Cape Cod but before it reached Plymouth. Then little Mary died. We do not know where she was buried, but it was probably on Cole's Hill, after the *Mayflower* sailed across the bay to Plymouth in December 1620. The only one of the More children to survive the killing chill and sickness of that first winter was Richard. He alone of the unwanted Mores lived to hear the return of birdsong in March 1621[4] and feel the growing heat of that first Massachusetts summer. He was a little Stranger, who would later become one of the Saints, even if a rather salty seadog version of a Saint and one whose sanctity was open to question.

New England sea captain

Richard was assigned as a servant to the family of William Brewster, who had spiritual oversight of the colony in the absence of a minister. In this capacity Richard lived with the Brewster family in their cramped wooden homestead in Plymouth until the middle of 1627. He would have been familiar with the routines of the household. As a servant he would have rolled up his mattress each morning, helped with the chores, the repair of fences, and the toil of the family. At night he would have unrolled his mattress and lain on the mat-strewn floor by the dying embers of the fire. In this way he grew from child to adolescent in the New World as the only surviving member of his family. This lasted until his indenture expired, which coincided with his name appearing—aged fourteen—in the Plymouth Colony census as a member of the extended Brewster household in 1627.

After this, the teenager moved on. But not far. In 1628, he was apprenticed to fellow *Mayflower* passenger Isaac Allerton, and this drew the young man into the adventurous but dangerous world of Atlantic trade. So it was that he took part in fishing trips off the coast of Massachusetts and Maine. Toiling as a member of the crew, he knew the cold spray of seawater and the sharp sting of wet ropes and nets on raw, chafed skin, the stink of the sea's bounty as the silver harvest poured onto the deck. As the trade grew, Richard became familiar with the English coastal communities clinging to the shores from Virginia to Maine.

He also traveled farther afield. In the year 1635 he appears on a list of people arriving from England on a ship called the *Blessing*. What business had taken him from Massachusetts Bay to London and back is unknown. What we do know is that later that same year, he married a young woman named Christian Hunter, who had been a fellow passenger. Clearly, mutual attraction had occurred in the weeks of the voyage in the close confinement of the ship. They were married in Plymouth. The marriage to Christian was part of a wider connection with her family, since we know that Richard at this time began to work for Richard Hollingsworth, who was Christian's stepfather and who had also traveled to New England on the *Blessing*.

Once they had set up home together, Richard and Christian lived at Duxbury before selling the twenty acres of their holding there and moving north up the coast to Salem, in 1637. It seems this move was specifically to the area known as Salem Neck, a peninsula pushing out into the Atlantic. It was a fitting home for a man whose life would be intimately connected with the sea. In February 1643, he joined the fellowship of the church at Salem. It was there that he had his children baptized. Richard was no longer a Stranger. From his time there we know that he could write, as he signed documents, but Christian could not; she signed with her mark.[5]

Richard went on to become a sea captain and assisted in the delivery of supplies to various colonies, in Virginia, Manhattan, and the West Indies. From New England he sailed as far east as England and as far north as Nova Scotia. He shipped tobacco and other products of New England out, and English supplies back. Survival had honed his entrepreneurial skills, and, back on land at Salem, he applied for and obtained a permit to set up his own fishing stand in order to sell the hard-won produce of the Atlantic. We also pick up little snippets of his enterprise in other areas too. Fresh drinking water was in short supply, so, in 1645, Richard dug a well on the common land. It supplied his household and that of his neighbors. We know about this because a cow belonging to a man named Thomas Tuck came to drink at the well, fell, and broke its neck.[6]

As well as his seafaring, the mariner later branched out into the alcohol trade while based on shore. He was granted a license to keep what was called an ordinary (a tavern serving a meal at a fixed price) and there to sell beer and cider—but not wine or liquor—for a year, starting in September 1674.[7]

His seagoing exploits, though, might have made possible a scandalous accusation made against him. It has been suggested that Richard was a bigamist and that in October 1645—at St. Dunstan's, Stepney, in Middlesex, England—he married Elizabeth Woolnough. The parish register states that she married "Richard More of Salem in New England." If so, he had a wife on both sides of the Atlantic. This Richard More was in the London area until April 1646, when he made a rapid exit in order to escape punishment on the charge of being drunk in the company of a prostitute and also a child of eight (possibly his daughter).[8] This all occurred while he was still married to Christian, who did not die until 1676, back in Salem. Not all are convinced that this must necessarily have been *the* Richard More of *Mayflower* fame,[9] but the coincidence is remarkable, and, given Richard's later sexual conduct at Salem, rather believable. Indeed, he would not have been the first seafarer to have different wives in different ports.

Fighting for the New World

Richard's seafaring skills drew him into more than trade. They also drew him into war. He fought in several early naval campaigns in which the English colonists defended their interests in the face of other European rivals. So it was that he and his ship fought against the Dutch who were settled on the Hudson River (modern New York) in 1653. The expedition was not a success, but at least he had his expenses covered, for we hear that in July 1653, Captain More was paid for "ye Dutch expedition."[10] The Dutch, of the so-called New Netherlands, had been accused of having "leagued with Indians to destroy the English."[11] It was in response to this that the commissioners of the United Colonies (Massachusetts Bay, Plymouth, and Connecticut) had ordered countermeasures. Richard had never lived in Leiden, but one wonders if any at Plymouth pondered on the strange twists of events that had brought them from friendly exile among the Dutch to being bitter trade rivals in the New World. Given the Protestant nature of the Dutch Republic, it was particularly ironic that rivalry over trade brought it and the godly republic of Oliver Cromwell into conflict in the 1650s.

There was no irony, though, in other warfare involving Richard and his ship. In 1654–55 he was again in action, but this time it was against the Catholic French. Then there was no religious ambiguity as Richard's ship sailed north. It and other vessels carried militia who had been mustered to fight the Dutch but were now being redeployed against the French. Like the Dutch, the French threatened English fishing grounds, as well as trade with Native Americans. It was time to flex New England muscle. The fleet went north to Acadia (parts of what is now eastern Quebec, the Maritime Provinces of New Brunswick, Nova Scotia, Prince Edward Island, and stretching southwards into Maine as far as the Kennebec River). There they struck at the main French settlement, which was located at Port Royal, now in Nova Scotia. Captain Richard More was there when the French fort was successfully attacked and brought under English control in 1654. A bell from Port Royal was brought to Salem in the ketch apparently skippered by "Captain Moor."[12] This was used by the people at Cape

Ann Side (later Beverley), on the northern limit of Massachusetts Bay. However, other reports state that the bell-carrying captain was a certain Thomas Lathrop,[13] so perhaps Richard should relinquish this little claim to fame.

Despite these adventures, life could be tough in the New England Atlantic trade, and Richard's life was closely intermeshed with the ups and downs of coastal North America. In 1663, for example, the Staple Act was passed by Parliament in London, which outlawed the shipping of European goods to the English colonies unless they passed through the mother country. This was a hard blow to the independence of the New England traders and pushed up the price of goods in the colonies. Richard, like other captains, became skilful in the manipulation of paperwork in order to cover their tracks and avoid being brought to court. It was the start of an independent-minded mentality coming up against English domination, which would have an explosive future. In the next century, such interference from London that threatened the prosperity of the North American colonies would explode in the Revolutionary War, which would lead to independence. That is another story, but Richard's life and career played a part in the beginnings of that momentous process.

In the meantime, Richard had adventures enough. In 1665 news reached New England of the plight of colonists newly settled at Cape Fear, on the coastal plain and Tidewater region of North Carolina. The fifth-oldest surviving English place name in North America, the area had been known to the English since a 1585 expedition to Roanoke Island had resulted in a ship being trapped by the wind behind the cape. In 1663, an attempt to found a colony there from Massachusetts Bay failed; then another attempt was made in 1664, but this time from Barbados. Problems in supply (not unlike those which had plagued the Pilgrims at early Plymouth) soon threatened the survival of the colony. Richard More was involved in sailing to this dangerous area of the coast in order to bring in some much-needed supplies. Despite this, the colony did not prosper, and war with Native Americans only added to its troubles. In 1667 it was abandoned. This was not Richard's only rescue mission; when his friend Robert Starr was murdered by Native Americans in about 1680, he adopted the three orphaned children of the murdered man.[14]

King Philip's War

In the 1650s, Richard received land at Plymouth Colony in his capacity as an "Ancient Freemen," since he was one of the first comers of 1620. The land he gained had been purchased from the local Native Americans and was located near the Fall or Quequechan River (an outpost of Plymouth Colony) and in Swansea, in southeastern Massachusetts.

By the time Richard gained his new lands, many Native Americans of New England were becoming alarmed at the amount of ancestral territory that had passed into the hands of the English. And the application of English ideas about inalienable possession of the land after purchase made it clear that such land had passed out of native ownership forever. With the ever-increasing numbers of English settlers, this was going to lead to trouble. When it came, it would be in the form of perhaps the most bloody Indian War to blaze across the North American continent. It has been remembered as King Philip's War, although sometimes it is called the Great Narragansett War. In that violent conflagration, Richard More would play his part.

In 1661, the Pokanoket *sachem*, Massasoit, who had authority over the Wampanoag confederacy and was a friend and ally of Plymouth Colony, died. For forty years—a generation—his alliance with the Pilgrims had held, and peace had generally been maintained. But with his death all that was about to change. The root of the change from peace to bloody violence lay principally in the matter of land ownership. Massasoit's successor was his son, Wamsutta (known in Plymouth as Alexander). Soon the delicate relationships that had generally sufficed to ensure peace for the first generation in New England began to unravel. The colonists at Plymouth accused Wamsutta of selling land to other settlers in contravention, they insisted, of previous treaty arrangements. In a time of increasing tension between the English and native peoples, Wamsutta was further accused of conspiring with the

Narragansetts against the English. These were the tribe who had once sent Governor Bradford the arrows wrapped in rattlesnake skin. On the other hand, Native Americans complained of English-owned cattle trampling cornfields; they also feared the way the newcomers were taking more and more land with each passing year. In 1662, Wamsutta was arrested by the colonists over disputed land sales. They particularly resented the fact that he had sold land to Rev. Roger Williams, who had earlier fallen out with the settlers at Plymouth and had eventually been expelled from Massachusetts Bay for his dangerous ideas on religious freedom and liberty of conscience. It was a provocative move by the Plymouth authorities, since they had no legal authority over the Wampanoag *sachem*. But they had the muskets. After being released, Wamsutta died of a sudden and mysterious illness before he could reach home. His people believed he had been poisoned by the English. There was a bitter irony in that this son of Massasoit died after being arrested by Governor Josiah Winslow, whose father, Edward, had enjoyed such a close relationship with the previous *sachem*. Clearly, in the second generation, peace was unraveling fast. And worse was to follow. On Wamsutta's death, rule over the Wampanoags passed to Metacomet (or Metacom), known to the colonists as King Philip.

Soon after Metacomet/Philip became *sachem*, the body of another Native American was found in the frozen water of Assawompset Pond, in southeastern Massachusetts. The body was that of John Sassamon, a "praying Indian," or convert to Christianity. He had acted as a negotiator between the two communities, and now he was dead. But was it accident or murder? The authorities at Plymouth, alerted by the testimony of another Native American, arrested three Wampanoags, although they had no authority over them. All three were found guilty and executed by hanging on June 8, 1675. Other Wampanoags were furious. The fire had touched the kindling.

On June 20, isolated homesteads near Swansea were put to the torch and English colonists killed. The war had started. It would rage from 1675 to 1678, and many hundreds of people would eventually die over fourteen months that saw about twelve frontier towns destroyed[15] and huge numbers of homesteads burned. Once war broke out it rapidly spread across what is now Massachusetts, Rhode Island, and Connecticut, even reaching as far north as Maine. The Wampanoags were not the only ones who had decided that in order to ensure their tribal survival, the English had to be driven out. Native peoples of many tribes rose up. Death and destruction swept across New England. The Narragansetts, who had largely attempted to remain neutral, found they were inexorably drawn into the war. Individual Narragansett warriors had joined the fighting, but the tribal leaders attempted to hold back from the conflict. It would do them no good. In November 1675, Josiah Winslow of Plymouth led the largest militia force ever assembled against the threat which was deemed to be posed by the powerful Narragansetts. The militia came from across the United Colonies of Massachusetts Bay, Plymouth, and Connecticut. The main fortress settlement of the tribe lay on an island in a swamp in what is today West Kingston, Rhode Island. From its location, the battle there became known as the Great Swamp Fight.

Marching with the thousand-strong militia force was Captain Richard More, late of Plymouth and now of Salem. Along with them marched 150 Native American allies as a reminder that there was not a united front against the English. Old tribal rivalries sapped the strength of the opposition to the encroaching colonists, as it would in every Indian War until the end of the 19th century.

On the morning of December 19, Richard woke from a miserable night bivouacked in the freezing wilderness. Snow had been falling continuously, and his blanket had given him little protection against the crushing cold. With first light, he and his militia companions fell in, primed their muskets, and checked shot and powder. The wind rose and drove across the frozen swamp, throwing stinging pellets of ice into their faces. But they were ready and determined. With volleys of musket fire, they charged into the snowstorm against the dark shape of the wooden defenses around the Narragansett village. Indian allies on the flanks moved like shadows through the blizzard, their war cries mingling with the crash of muskets. By nightfall it was over. The fortress had fallen and the bodies of the dead defenders were scattered about it. Richard and the other militiamen burned down the houses and destroyed the food stores. Perhaps as many as one thousand Narragensetts (mostly noncombatants) died.[16] Warriors who could make their escape vanished into the dark and snow, vowing revenge for the massacre. Seventy of the militia lay contorted in the white cold.

Now that the Narragansetts were involved in the war, its intensity increased. In a late-winter offensive, the combined Native American forces drove back the frontier in the three colonies of Plymouth, Massachusetts Bay, and Rhode Island. Much of the greatest destruction of the war occurred in this phase. In March, they destroyed Providence, Rhode Island, and every colonial settlement on the western side of Narragansett Bay, despite Rhode Island's not being an official party to the conflict. Somewhere in the region of fifty towns were also raided in central and southeastern Massachusetts, and hundreds of settlers were killed.

But Native American resistance was ultimately doomed. Combining utter ruthlessness (the peaceful Praying Indians of Massachusetts Bay were interned on Deer Island to die of hunger and disease) with pragmatism (bringing friendly Native American tribes such as the Mohawk into their forces), the colonists drove their enemies back. The Plymouth militia, commanded by Benjamin Church, fought alongside Indian allies since the very start of the war; it was this force that finally killed King Philip in August 1676. By September the Native American resistance had been destroyed across southern New England; thousands of Native Americans were killed, huge numbers were sold into slavery. About six hundred colonial militia had died. Only Connecticut had survived without devastation, due to its alliance with local tribes holding firm. All in all, it was a tragic end to a relationship that had started with such promise when Samoset had first walked into Plymouth in the spring of 1621. Richard More had been there when the relationship had started *and* when it came to its bloody end.

Richard's life was further enmeshed in the bitter conflicts with Native Americans that brutally scarred the 1670s when he married Jane Crumpton in 1678, two years after the death of Christian, his first wife. Jane had previously been married to a man named Samuel Crumpton, who had been killed, in 1675, during an ambush of a wagon convoy carrying grain at Muddy Brook Bridge, in South Deerfield.[17] After the battle it became known as Bloody Brook.

The passing of the *Mayflower* generation

As we have seen, Richard's first wife, Christian, died in 1676. He then married Jane Crumpton, who died in 1686. By this time Richard was about seventy-two years old (if he was six in 1620, as is believed), yet his sexual appetite had not diminished. We know this because in 1688 the records for Salem church tell us that Richard's sexual misconduct had not ended with his earlier, apparent, bigamy.

> *Old Captain More having been for many years under suspicion and common fame of lasciviousness, and some degree at least of inconstancy . . . but for want of proof we could go no further. He was at last left to himself so far as that he was convicted before justices of peace by three witnesses of gross unchastity with another man's wife and was censured by them.*[18]

It seems that the church's elders had had cause to privately speak with him on a number of occasions but had held back from further action because of his venerable pedigree as a surviving first comer. It was difficult to confront (and embarrass) a man who had become something of a legend in his own lifetime. But enough was enough; finally his sexual behavior had become too much to ignore and there was nothing for it but a public confrontation and temporary excommunication. However, Richard made a public repentance of his sins and was restored to full fellowship of the local church in 1691. This intriguing little incident reveals the awed attitudes of later New Englanders towards the first generation of settlers. In a different situation the captain would probably have been rapidly chastised and thrown out of fellowship, possibly permanently. But that was too difficult to square with his fame and connections to the almost mythical past of the early 1620s.

It has been suggested that the clergyman who punished him was Rev. Nicholas Noyes, who knew Richard from the Great Swamp Fight.[19] It was Noyes who later served as the official minister at the Salem witch trials and whose call on Sarah Good (one of the first women to be accused) to repent before she was hanged, in July 1692, prompted her to boldly protest, "You are a liar! I am no more a witch than you are a wizard."[20] The evidence suggests that, unlike others, Noyes never regretted the part he played in this appalling tragedy. Which brings us to the events that engulfed Salem in the last years of the life of Richard More; and which offer a terrible insight into how, under certain circumstances, the kind of godly society established in North America could go terribly wrong. For one of the remarkable features of the life of Richard More is that the little boy who saw the beginning of that society at Plymouth also, at the end of his life, saw the terrible way such a society might be thrown off the rails.

When godly society imploded—the Salem witch hunt

It is a remarkable fact that Richard More, who was one of the youngest passengers on the *Mayflower*, lived just long enough to witness the Salem witch hunt, which exploded in 1692.

By this year New England had come a long way since its faltering beginnings in 1620, but some of the way it had changed could threaten its stability. Old certainties were challenged as traders like Richard More caused it to become more connected to the outside world. As it did so, some of its tight cohesion was lost and inhabitants grew less deferential to the elites. The activities of Baptists and Quakers made Puritan believers increasingly anxious about their religious communities. More conservative communities (such as at Salem Village) grew resentful of more entrepreneurial communities (such as at Salem Town) and accused them of sinful covetousness. Some in the Puritan godly colonies were increasingly on the defensive.

On top of this, there was economic disruption accompanying a British war with France in the American colonies, which broke out in

1689 (King William's War), which had reduced in intensity by 1692 but was not finally over until 1698.[21] As if this was not enough, a smallpox epidemic had recently hit the area. Old Richard More's community was experiencing tensions that would spiral into the Salem witchcraft trials in 1692.[22]

In January 1692, some young girls from Salem Village—the daughter and the niece of Rev. Samuel Parris—claimed to be possessed by the devil. They had fits and screamed alarmingly. The girls accused several local women of witchcraft. These were the Parris's Caribbean slave, Tituba, and two other women. One was an unpopular beggar named Sarah Good, the other the poor and elderly Sarah Osborne. Other girls began to show the same symptoms.

Good and Osborne protested innocence, but Tituba confessed and named other witches. The situation spiraled out of control, dragging in well-regarded local church and community members. Other local citizens involved in commercial enterprises were then accused. These were the kind of people earlier accused of worldliness. A terrible process was coming into action as unspoken spiritual anxieties led to vocal accusations.

As these accusations mounted, William Phips, the royal governor of Massachusetts, ordered the establishment of a special court to deal with the witchcraft cases. In June, the first witch was hanged. Between then and September, she was followed by eighteen others, with many others accused. One of those accused was Captain John Alden Jr., the son of Mayflower Lives John and Priscilla Alden. He was on his way home from Quebec to Duxbury when he broke his journey at Salem in May 1692. There he was accused of witchcraft and arrested. It was his alleged lifestyle that got him into trouble. The afflicted girls accused him of selling whiskey to Native Americans and having Native American wives and children. It was clearly gossip they had heard at home, but it could have cost him his life. However, the enterprising captain broke out of jail, got home to Duxbury, and went into hiding until the murderous hysteria blew over. He later left a firsthand account of the trials at Salem.

From October, the hunt began to subside. So-called spectral evidence (testimony involving dreams and visions) was no longer accepted in court, and in May 1693, those still held in prison on witchcraft charges were pardoned and released. The hysteria was over. In January 1697, the Massachusetts General Court declared a day of fasting for those who had been victims of the trials. Later, the trials were declared unlawful. Never again were any such witches executed in New England. It had been a terrible time.

The Salem trials offer a disturbing insight into how the positive intention to create a New Jerusalem and purify the godly community from sin could be hijacked and manipulated when spiritual accusations were not subjected to balanced and rational scrutiny.[23] There was always the risk of this within the intense spirituality and mutual policing among the Saints. Yet it should be recalled that in the less tightly policed community of Plymouth, no so-called witches were ever executed. What occurred at Salem held up a mirror to what could go wrong and how a different approach to community could prevent it occurring. And Richard More lived to see it all.

Richard was apparently alive in March 1694 but had died by April 1696.[24] His gravestone in the Charter Street Burial Ground, Salem, is the only one for a *Mayflower* passenger that is sited exactly where it was originally placed. As such, it is a fitting monument to this last Mayflower Life. The stone claims that he was eighty-four years old. The year 1692 was not added until the early 20th century and is a mistake. If he lived as late as 1696, he would have been the last surviving male passenger from the epic *Mayflower* voyage, way back in distant 1620.[25] He was an echo of another world; one in which a struggling little community had first sought to carve out a home for itself in what was, for them, the American wilderness.

15

Seeing the New England Forest
for the Trees

There are times, as we try to make sense of the impact of the *Mayflower* Pilgrims, that we cannot see the forest for the trees! There is so much variety and complexity in their legacy, over four hundred years, that it is sometimes difficult to see the overall shape. This seems a particularly fitting metaphor, given the woodland that covered large parts of Cape Cod and came down to the shore around Plymouth. Its depths came close to the town fence and seemed to contain so much that was unknown about the American wilderness to people who had come from Leiden or London.

Yet as we stand back and look at them through the lens of four centuries, there are things that stand out. Despite the immensity of the mass of trees, we can get some idea of the shape and size of the forest.

The first thing that stands out is their faith. It was for them the most fundamental feature of their lives and made sense of their world in all its complexities. Without doubt, they and those who came after them in Massachusetts Bay contributed a great deal to the cultural DNA of what would one day become the United States. Although they belonged to a branch of the Christian Church that sought to separate state from Church, there is no doubt about where they thought the civil government should look for its moral guidelines. Whatever modern readers might think of that outlook, it has had an immense impact on the kind of society that emerged, and still exists, in significant parts of the modern United States. The legacy of Puritan politics continues to influence outlooks in the 21st century.

The second thing that stands out is their ability to construct an inclusive community. They were both Saints and Strangers, yet men from both groups signed the Mayflower Compact. It is easy to question the strength of the thread that led from it to the constitution of the next century, but the Mayflower Compact clearly played its part. Plymouth Colony was no liberal institution, yet it was far more inclusive and far less repressive of difference than we find in the semi-theocracy that developed up the coast in Massachusetts Bay Colony. Plymouth might have been the home of those edgy extremist Separatists, but if we want examples of Quakers hanged and innocent people hounded to their deaths in witch hunts, we need to look outside Plymouth Colony. That stands greatly to their credit and is worth reflecting on in the divided world of the 21st century. It is a legacy worth celebrating.

The third thing that strikes us is their courage. For the Leiden Pilgrims and their associates, coming to North America was not quite like volunteering to be on a colonizing mission to Mars (they could get home a lot faster if they decided to), but it was comparable. And for most of them it was a one-way journey. Its dangers are evident today in the memorial to the dead on Cole's Hill and in the hardships detailed by William Bradford. In this they clearly stand in the great American tradition of the pioneer spirit, for all its complexities and controversies. The Pilgrims were impressively brave.

What finally stands out is their ability to work with the people who already lived in the land. There is something very moving about the mixed community that sat down together to eat the produce of the first harvest in 1621. It is easy to be cynical about the way this can be represented in modern, perhaps superficial, pageants. But sit down together they did! Much worse could have happened and later did happen. But not in 1621, despite the prejudices and anxieties of the new English arrivals. That this relationship broke down so terribly and bloodily in the next generation should not obscure the manner in which Pilgrims and local Native Americans generally worked together remarkably harmoniously in the early years. That does not deny the disturbing violence of the exceptional action at Wessagusset or the fact that the arrival of Europeans led to catastrophe for the indigenous peoples, but it reminds us that war and extermination were not inevitable. There were other paths possible. And we cannot hold the Pilgrims personally responsible for the terrible, but unintended, impact of European diseases.

It is not really surprising that the Pilgrims were rediscovered and celebrated by later generations of Americans. It is not surprising that the celebrations still continue. It might be said that the Pilgrims punch well above their weight when we consider the enormity of influences that have gone into the making of the United States. But if that is so, it is all the more to the credit of this terribly underprepared band of fighters that they climbed into the ring in the first place!

Towards the end of his life, William Bradford sought to express something of his life experiences in verse. One, which sums up much of the faith and fortitude, the challenges and changes faced by both the Saints and the Strangers, ends with a touching simplicity that opens a window onto the beliefs of so many we have met in these Mayflower Lives. Bradford tried to express how he felt God had guided him and the kind of person he had become as a result. It seems a fitting place to close this exploration of these remarkable people, whose lives influenced the history of a continent.

In wilderness he did me guide,
And in strange lands for me provide.
In fears and wants, through weal and woe,
A Pilgrim passed I to and fro. [1]

ACKNOWLEDGMENTS

I am very grateful to my wife, Christine, for reading and commenting on sections of this book. I was also greatly assisted by my visits to Plimoth Plantation (which provided a remarkable opportunity to "visit" the settlement as it would have been in 1627), and Pilgrim Hall Museum, Plymouth, and Pilgrim Monument and Provincetown Museum on Cape Cod, which provided additional insights into the history of the *Mayflower* Pilgrims. It was particularly moving to see actual artifacts at Pilgrim Hall that were owned by, or closely associated with, some of those whose lives are explored in this book. While visiting Plimoth Plantation, the conversation with the reenactor taking the part of Master Prence/Prince caused me to rethink some of my assessments of Myles Standish, and I am grateful for his thoughts on this subject. It was great to speak with Desiree Mobed at the Alden House Historic Site, and I am grateful for her directions to the actual site of the house of John and Priscilla Alden and for her suggestion of walking part of the trackway that they would have known, leading in the direction of Plymouth. I am also grateful for the additional material she kindly sent me regarding them and this location. I also wish to thank Robert Dudley, my agent, and Claiborne Hancock and Jessica

Case at Pegasus Books for all of their encouragement and support. In addition, the constructive advice and insights offered by Peter Mayer, when I first mooted the idea of this book, were very valuable indeed, and I am grateful for those suggestions. It goes without saying that all errors are my own.

—Martyn Whittock,
Thanksgiving, 2018.

ENDNOTES

1: The Master's Story: Christopher Jones, Master of the *Mayflower*

1   They had traveled 3,340 miles from Plymouth, England, to Cape Cod but had crossed the Atlantic at the snail's pace of an average of 2.10 mph. It had been a journey of some 1,584 exhausting hours.

2   The Pilgrims dated their actions by the old-style Julian calendar, which was ten days behind the (modern) Gregorian calendar. The dates mentioned here and throughout this book are the ones used by those on the *Mayflower*.

3   N. Bunker, *Making Haste From Babylon: The Mayflower Pilgrims and Their World: A New History* (London: The Bodley Head, 2010), 43.

4   D. A. Male, *Christopher Jones and the Mayflower Expedition 1620–1621* (Harwich: The Harwich Society, 1999), and parts reproduced at "Harwich and the Master of the Mayflower," http://www.harwich.net/ histjones.htm, accessed March 2017. This provides a very useful and accessible guide to available evidence regarding Master Jones's early years.

5   Bunker, *Making Haste From Babylon*, 44.

6   A. Ames, "The name May-Flower," ch. 1 in *The May-Flower and Her Log* (Boston, MA and New York: Houghton Mifflin, 1907).

7   C. E. Banks, *The English Ancestry and Homes of the Pilgrim Fathers: who came to Plymouth on the Mayflower in 1620, the Fortune in 1621, and the Anne and the Little James in 1623* (Baltimore, MD: Genealogical Publishing Co., 2006, originally published in 1929), 26.

8   Bunker, *Making Haste From Babylon*, 37.

9   C. H. Johnson, *The Mayflower and Her Passengers* (Bloomington, IN: Xlibris Corp., 2006), 30–31.

10   Bunker, *Making Haste From Babylon*, 37.

11   Johnson, *The Mayflower and Her Passengers*, 34.

12   R. G. Marsden, "The Mayflower," *English Historical Review*, October 1904, 677.

13   K. Caffrey, *The Mayflower* (Lanham, MD: Rowman & Littlefield, 2014), 330–31.

14   D. Lindsay, *Mayflower Bastard: A Stranger Among the Pilgrims* (New York: St. Martin's Press, 2002), 54–55.

15   William Bradford, *Of Plymouth Plantation, 1620–1647, by William Bradford, Sometime Governor Thereof, A New Edition*, ed. S. E. Morison (New York: Alfred A. Knopf, 2015, first published 1952), 78. All quotes in this book from *Of Plymouth Plantation* are taken from this engaging edition.

16   Once considered a myth but, since archaeological excavations in Newfoundland at L'Anse aux Meadows, in the 1960s, it has become clear that around the year 1000, Scandinavian explorers briefly settled in North America, sailing from Iceland via Greenland.

17   R. Cole Harris and G. J. Matthews, *Historical Atlas of Canada: From the beginning to 1800* (Toronto: University of Toronto Press, 1987), 48.

18   B. C. Campbell, *Disasters, Accidents, and Crises in American History* (New York: Infobase Publishing, 2008), 4.

19   Harris and Matthews, *Historical Atlas of Canada*, 48.

20   Campbell, *Disasters, Accidents, and Crises in American History*, 5.

2: The Asylum Seeker's Story: William Bradford, a Saint Fleeing Babylon

1   Revelation 18:2–4, in the 1599 edition of the Geneva Bible, which was used by the godly. *Geneva Bible, 1599 Edition*, with modernized spelling (Dallas, GA: Tolle Lege Press, 2006); https://www.biblegateway.com, accessed January–November 2017. All Bible quotes in this book are taken from this source.

2   Matthew 24:6–7.

3   See http://www.gordon.edu/page.cfm?iPageID=3196, accessed April 2018.

4   For a good overview of William Bradford's early life, see N. Philbrick, "They Knew They Were Pilgrims," ch. 1 in *Mayflower: A Story of Courage, Community, and War* (London & New York: Penguin, 2007).

5   Found in "The Life of William Bradford", from Cotton Mather's *Magnalia Christi Americana: or, the Ecclesiastical History of New-England*, 1702, http://www.pilgrimhallmuseum.org/pdf/William_Bradford _Mathers_Magnalia_Christi.pdf, accessed January 2018. Courtesy of Pilgrim Hall Museum, Plymouth, MA.

6   Philbrick, *Mayflower*, 7–8.

7   James was already king in Scotland, since 1567, as James VI. He ascended the English throne in 1603 as James I and ruled until his death in 1625.

8   From the middle of the 16th century, versions of the Bible, translated from the Hebrew and Greek texts, had become available in English, even though an earlier and unauthorized translation had cost William Tyndale his life in 1536. For English Protestants these early Bibles in English were the Great Bible (1539); the Geneva Bible (1560); the Bishop's Bible (1568), an early attempt to create an authorized version for use by all Protestant English speakers; and the Authorized—or King James—Version of 1611. Of these English translations,

it was the Geneva Bible that was the version used among those who considered themselves "the godly," until it eventually gave way to the (now more famous) Authorized King James Version from the 1650s onwards. But it was the Geneva Bible that traveled on the *Mayflower* to North America.

9   N. Bunker, *Making Haste From Babylon: The Mayflower Pilgrims and their World: A New History* (London: The Bodley Head, 2010), 95–121, with a useful map on 96–97.

10   William Bradford, *Of Plymouth Plantation, 1620–1647, by William Bradford, Sometime Governor Thereof, A New Edition*, ed. S. E. Morison (New York: Alfred A. Knopf, 2015, first published 1952), 8.

11   http://www.pilgrimhallmuseum.org/pdf/William_Bradford_Mathers_Magnalia _Christi.pdf, accessed January 2018. Courtesy of Pilgrim Hall Museum, Plymouth, MA.

12   Bradford, *Of Plymouth Plantation*, 10, note 7.

13   Bradford, *Of Plymouth Plantation*, 9.

14   Bunker, *Making Haste From Babylon*, 218.

15   J. W. Tammel, *The Pilgrims and Other People from the British Isles in Leiden 1576–1640* (Isle of Man: Mansk-Svenska Publishing, 1989), 57. Another record misspells his surname as "Katfort."

16   Bradford, *Of Plymouth Plantation*, 17.

17   Bradford, *Of Plymouth Plantation*, 25.

18   The failure in Maine led to the eventual demise of the Virginia Company of Plymouth (and Bristol) by 1618.

19   60 tons compared to 180 tons.

20   Ezra 8:21.

21   Bradford, *Of Plymouth Plantation*, 47. Bradford's phrase "they knew they were pilgrims" has become a very famous one and is often quoted as the prime reason why we call the Plymouth settlers Pilgrims. However, it had also been used by Nathaniel Morton, in his *New England's Memorial* (1669) and, consequently, has been in the public domain since then (Bradford's use of the phrase becoming well known significantly after this date). See J. D. Bangs "Always More Pilgrim Books—What's Next?—A Bibliographical Survey," lecture presented at the Banquet of the Triennial Meeting of the General Society of Mayflower Descendants, September 13, 2011, https://www.sail1620.org/articles/always -more-pilgrim-books-what-s-next-a-bibliographical-survey, accessed April 2018.

22   http://www.histarch.illinois.edu/plymouth/Maysource.html, accessed January 2018.

23   Philbrick, *Mayflower*, 29.

24   Although the venture cost the Adventurers somewhere in the region of £7,000, they only seem to have recouped about £1,800 in repayment of the debt.

25   The four others were Alden, Standish, Winslow, and Prence.

26   F. J. Bremer, *The Puritan Experiment: New England Society from Bradford to Edwards* (Hanover, NH & London: University Press of New England, 1995, first published in 1978), 34.

27   An excellent and accessible modern edition of this highly influential document can be found in: William Bradford, *Of Plymouth Plantation, 1620–1647, by William Bradford, Sometime Governor Thereof, A New Edition*, ed. S. E. Morison (New York: Alfred A. Knopf, 2015, first published 1952).

28   An accessible, edited, modern edition is: Bradford, William, *Of Plymouth Plantation*, S. E. Morison (ed.), used in this book.

29   S. V. James, Jr., ed., *Three Visitors to Early Plymouth* (Bedford, MA: Applewood Books, 1997, first published by Plimoth Plantation, Inc., 1963), 49.

3: The Mother's Story: Susanna White, Mother of the First Baby Born in New England

1   R. M. Sherman, R. W. Sherman, and R. S. Wakefield, *Mayflower Families Through Five Generations*, vol. 13, *Family of William White*, 3rd ed. (Plymouth, MA: General Society of Mayflower Descendants, 2006), 3. This would also seem to be the implication in N. Philbrick, *Mayflower: A Story of Courage, Community, and War* (London & New York: Penguin, 2007), 104, where her marriage to Edward Winslow is placed within the tradition inherited from the Low Countries.

2   C. H. Johnson, *The Mayflower and Her Passengers* (Bloomington, IN: Xlibris Corp., 2006), 246–247.

3   See the report on the research of Sue Allen and Caleb Johnson at http://www .mayflower400uk.org/news-blog/2017/october/new-discovery-confirming -pilgrim-origins/, accessed January 2018; also see "Mayflower Passenger List: Susanna (Jackson) White," http://mayflowerhistory.com/white-susanna/, accessed January 2018.

4   William Bradford, *Of Plymouth Plantation, 1620–1647, by William Bradford, Sometime Governor Thereof, A New Edition*, ed. S. E. Morison (New York: Alfred A. Knopf, 2015, first published 1952), 53–54.

5   Plimoth, Plimouth, Plymouth, or New Plymouth served as the capital of Plymouth Colony from its founding in 1620 until the colony's merger with the Massachusetts Bay Colony in 1691. The name New Plymouth continued to be used until 1691. Thereafter, it was just Plymouth. For simplicity, in this book we will always call it by the modern form of Plymouth or New Plymouth, not Plimoth.

6   This early 17th-century spelling survives today in the name of the reconstructed settlement known as Plimoth Plantation. Earlier, in 1605, the French navigator, cartographer, and diplomat Samuel de Champlain had sailed into what is now Plymouth Harbor, and named it Port St. Louis. That name was soon eclipsed by the name chosen for it by English explorers and, later, settlers.

7   Bradford, *Of Plymouth Plantation*, 53.

8   P. Elmer, *The Healing Arts: Health, Disease and Society in Europe 1500–1800* (Manchester: Manchester University Press, 2004), 325.

9   Bradford, *Of Plymouth Plantation*, 26.

10   D. B. Heath, *Mourt's Relation: A Journal of the Pilgrims at Plymouth* (Bedford, MA: Applewood Books, 1963). This is a well-presented and accessible edition of this primary document. All quotes in this book from *Mourt's Relation* are taken from this engaging edition.

11   Possibly in the last three days of the month; see http://mayflowerhistory.com /white-susanna/, accessed January 2018, or Peregrine may have been born in December; see http://www.pilgrimhallmuseum.org/susanna_white.htm, accessed January 2018. Courtesy of Pilgrim Hall Museum, Plymouth, MA.

12   "Eleanor Billington," http://mayflowerhistory.com/billington-eleanor/, accessed January 2018.

13   S. Hardman Moore, *Pilgrims: New World Settlers & the Call of Home* (New Haven, CT & London: Yale University Press, 2007), 100.

14   F. J. Bremer, *The Puritan Experiment: New England Society from Bradford to Edwards* (Hanover, NH & London: University Press of New England, 1995, first published in 1978), 113.

15   Josiah Winslow died in 1680, and Elizabeth Winslow died in 1698 as Mrs. Curwin.

16   *Boston Newsletter*, July, 31, 1704, and quoted in *The Mayflower Descendant*, vol. 24, facsimile reprint 1922 (Bowie, MA: Heritage Books, 1996), 128.

17   F. J. Bremer, *The Puritan Experiment*, 117, gives a succinct overview of the data and research on colonial-era Plymouth.

18   Bremer, *The Puritan Experiment*, 114.

19   Bremer, *The Puritan Experiment*, 114.

20   See Bremer, *The Puritan Experiment*, 114.

21   L. Ryken, *Wordly Saints* (Grand Rapids, MI: Zondervan, 1986), 43–45.

22   For a very balanced overview of the Puritan outlook, see D. Doriani, "The Puritans, Sex and Pleasure," in *Christian Perspectives on Sexuality and Gender*, E. Stuart and A. Thatcher, eds. (Leominster: Gracewing Publishing, published jointly with Wm B. Eerdmans, Grand Rapids, MI, 1996), 33–52.

23   R. Godbeer, *Sexual Revolution in Early America* (Baltimore, MA & London: Johns Hopkins University Press, 2002), 34–36.

24   An insight into these homes can be gained by a visit to the excellent reconstructed settlement at Plimoth Plantation, Plymouth, Massachusetts.

25   However, standing at the lower part of the reconstructed street in Plimoth Plantation gives one a remarkable opportunity to imagine the view exactly as Susanna would have seen it (with the exception that the fort she saw would not have been roofed).

26   A young cow that has not yet calved.

27   E. J. Reilly, *Legends of American Indian Resistance* (Santa Barbara, CA: ABC Clio, 2011), 5.

28   See http://www.pilgrimhallmuseum.org/susanna_white.htm, accessed January 2018.

29   Johnson, *The Mayflower and Her Passengers*, 260.

30   Johnson, *The Mayflower and Her Passengers*, 248.

4: The Adventurer's Story: Stephen Hopkins, Survivor of Shipwreck and with Unique New World Experience

1   Stephen's life has attracted the attention of a number of researchers, due to its drama and contrasts. A particularly accessible and engaging account, to which this chapter is particularly indebted, is found in C. H. Johnson, *Here Shall I Die Ashore. Stephen Hopkins: Bermuda Castaway, Jamestown Survivor, and Mayflower Pilgrim* (Bloomington, IN: Xlibris Corp., 2007). A brief overview of his life can be found at http://www.pilgrimhallmuseum.org/stephen_hopkins .htm, accessed February 2018, and a more lengthy one can be found at http://mayflower history.com/hopkins-stephen/, accessed February 2018.

2   https://www.encyclopediavirginia.org/Indentured_Servants_in_Colonial _Virginia, accessed February 2018.

3   The experience was dramatically described in a report published soon after the events: *A true repertory of the wreck and redemption of Sir Thomas Gates, Knight, upon and from the islands of the Bermudas . . .*, written by William Strachey, Esquire, and dated July 15, 1610.

4   See https://www.nps.gov/jame/learn/historyculture/john-rolfe.htm, accessed February 2018.

5   Quoted in Johnson, *Here Shall I Die Ashore*, 196. The quotation is from *Wreck and Redemption of Sir Thomas Gates, Knight*, by William Strachey, 1610 (published 1625).

6   Quoted in Johnson, *Here Shall I Die Ashore*, 196. The quotation is from *Wreck and Redemption of Sir Thomas Gates, Knight*, by William Strachey, 1610 (published 1625).

7   The events of this terrible winter were described by George Percy, who served as president of the Jamestown colony during this time, in his unpublished account, *A Trewe Relacyon*.

8   See S. Pruitt, "Evidence of Cannibalism Found at Jamestown," http://www .history.com/news/ evidence-of-cannibalism-found-at-jamestown, May 2013, accessed February 2018. The article refers to human skeletal evidence found by the Preservation Virginia Jamestown Rediscovery Project, and examined at the Smithsonian National Museum of Natural History in Washington by physical anthropologist Douglas Owsley.

9   William Strachey, in *Purchas his Pilgrimes*, published in 1625.

10   It should, of course, be remembered that the Adventurers who bankrolled the 1620 *Mayflower* voyage had their eyes on a quick return on their investment too, even if many of those tasked with delivering it had their eyes on more heavenly goals.

11   Certainly according to William Strachey, newly arrived from shipwreck on Bermuda, and described in his *Purchas his Pilgrimes* (1625), part 4, book 9, chapter 6.

12   http://www.newenglandhistoricalsociety.com/stephen-hopkins-jamestown -settler-mayflower-pilgrim-shakespeare-character/, accessed February 2018.

13   Almost certainly Atlantic right whales, now critically endangered.

14   D. B. Heath, *Mourt's Relation: A Journal of the Pilgrims at Plymouth* (Bedford, MA: Applewood Books, 1963), 16.

15   Heath, *Mourt's Relation*, xiii. It is assumed that William Bradford also contributed to this publication.

16   William Bradford, *Of Plymouth Plantation, 1620–1647, by William Bradford, Sometime Governor Thereof, A New Edition*, ed. S. E. Morison (New York: Alfred A. Knopf, 2015, first published 1952), 66.

17   Heath, *Mourt's Relation*, 31.

18   Heath, *Mourt's Relation*, 32.

19   Heath, *Mourt's Relation*, 37.

20   Heath, *Mourt's Relation*, 37.

21   http://www.capecodgravestones.com/easthampixweb/firenccove.html, accessed February 2018.

22   A loose confederacy made up of several tribes. The name was not actually used until the 1680s but is now often used to describe the earlier confederacy too; this convention is followed in this book.

23   A tavern where set mealtimes and set prices were offered to customers. See S. C. O'Neill, "Suitably Provided and Accommodated: Plymouth Area Taverns," *The Mayflower Quarterly*, vol. 77, no. 4 (December 2011), 335–336. *The Mayflower Quarterly* is published by the General Society of Mayflower Descendants, Plymouth, MA.

24   C. H. Johnson, *The Mayflower and Her Passengers* (Bloomington, IN: Xlibris Corp., 2006), 132–133.

25   http://www.pilgrimhallmuseum.org/pdf/Stephen_Hopkins_Will_Inventory.pdf, accessed February 2018. Courtesy of Pilgrim Hall Museum, Plymouth, MA.

5: The Outsider's Story: Tisquantum (Squanto), Native American

1   D. B. Heath, *Mourt's Relation: A Journal of the Pilgrims at Plymouth* (Bedford, MA: Applewood Books, 1963), 50.

2   Heath, *Mourt's Relation*, 51.

3   Heath, *Mourt's Relation*, 52–53.

4   Heath, *Mourt's Relation*, 57.

5   An accessible overview of his life can be found at http://historyofmassachusetts.org/squanto-the-former-slave/; and also at http://mayflowerhistory.com/tisquantum/, accessed February 2018.

6   N. Salisbury, "Squanto: Last of the Patuxets," in *Struggle and Survival in Colonial America*, eds. D. G. Sweet and G. B. Nash (Berkeley, CA: University of California Press), 1981, 233–234.

7   Heath, *Mourt's Relation*, 70.

8   Heath, *Mourt's Relation*, 70.

9   http://mayflowerhistory.com/tisquantum/, accessed February 2018.

10   http://www.shakespeare-navigators.com/tempest/TempestText22.html, accessed February 2018.

11   H. A. Marshall, "The Manners, Customs and Some Historical Facts About the Indians of Northern New England (Excerpts from Explorers and Missionaries, 1524–1657)," in *The Indian Heritage of New Hampshire and Northern New England*, ed. T. Piotrowski (Jefferson, NC: McFarland, 2008), 50.

12   J. S. Marr and J. T. Cathey, "New Hypothesis for Cause of an Epidemic among Native Americans, New England, 1616–1619," *Emerging Infectious Diseases* 16, no. 2 (2010), 281–286.

13   Heath, *Mourt's Relation*, 63.

14   This description is found in T. Morton's, *New English Canaan, or New Canaan*, 1637, quoted in K. Donegan, *Seasons of Misery: Catastrophe and Colonial Settlement in Early America* (Philadelphia, PA: University of Pennsylvania Press, 2013), 132.

15   C. Mather, *Magnalia Christi Americana*, vol. 1, 1702 (published edition of 1820 by Silas Andrus, reissued Bedford, MA: Applewood Books, 2009), 49.

16   http://historyofmassachusetts.org/squanto-the-former-slave/, accessed February 2018.

17   https://www.catholicnewsagency.com/blog/saint-squanto-a-catholic-thanksgiving-hero, accessed February 2018.

18   William Bradford, *Of Plymouth Plantation, 1620–1647, by William Bradford, Sometime Governor Thereof, A New Edition*, ed. S. E. Morison (New York: Alfred A. Knopf, 2015, first published 1952), 81.

19   J. H. Humins, "Squanto and Massasoit: A Struggle for Power," *New England Quarterly* 60 (March 1987), 54–70; a point explored since on a number of occasions by other historians.

6: The Teenager's Story: Mary Chilton, Reputedly the First to Step onto Plymouth Rock

1   http://www.pilgrimhallmuseum.org/mary_chilton.htm, accessed March 2018. Courtesy of Pilgrim Hall Museum, Plymouth, MA.

2   The period of time from January through March 1621, which was memorably described by the modern historian Samuel Eliot Morison as the "starving time." See William Bradford, *Of Plymouth Plantation, 1620–1647, by William Bradford, Sometime Governor Thereof, A New Edition*, ed. S. E. Morison (New York: Alfred A. Knopf, 2015, first published 1952), 77.

3   See J. G. Hunt, "Origins of the Chiltons of the Mayflower," *The American Genealogist* 38, 244–245; M. R. Paulick, "The Mayflower Chiltons in Canterbury, 1556–1600," *New England Ancestors* (Spring 2007); C. Johnson, "A New Record Relating to James Chilton," *The Mayflower Quarterly* (June 2009); R. Sherman et al., *Mayflower Families*, vol. 15, *James Chilton, Richard Moore* (Plymouth MA: The Mayflower Society 1997).

4   http://mayflowerhistory.com/chilton-mary/, accessed February 2018.

5   http://www.pilgrimhallmuseum.org/mary_chilton.htm, accessed February 2018. Courtesy of Pilgrim Hall Museum, Plymouth, MA.

6   S. A. Drake, *A Book of New England Legends and Folklore in Prose and Poetry*, illus. F. T. Merrill (Boston: Little, Brown, 1901, new and revised edition, first published by Roberts Brothers, 1884), 378–381. Digitally accessed at https://archive .org/details/bookofnewengland00dra, accessed March 2018.

7   Drake, *A Book of New England Legends and Folklore in Prose and Poetry*, 380.

8   Drake, *A Book of New England Legends and Folklore in Prose and Poetry*, 380.

9   F. Russell, "The Pilgrims and The Rock," *American Heritage* 13 (October 1962), 1.

10   http://www.pilgrimhallmuseum.org/plymouth_rock.htm, accessed March 2018. Courtesy of Pilgrim Hall Museum, Plymouth, MA.

11   B. Bryson, *Made in America* (London: Black Swan, 1998), 4.

12   See https://www.history.com/news/the-real-story-behind-plymouth-rock, accessed March 2018; and http://americanhistory.si.edu/press/fact-sheets /plymouth-rock, accessed March 2018, Smithsonian Museum.

13   See https://www.history.com/news/the-real-story-behind-plymouth-rock, accessed March 2018.

14   Quoted in J. McPhee, *Irons in the Fire* (New York: Farrar, Straus and Giroux, 2011), 200, who also reflects on the history and treatment of the rock.

15   F. J. Bremer, *The Puritan Experiment: New England Society from Bradford to Edwards* (Hanover, NH & London: University Press of New England, 1995, first published in 1978), 113.

16   For an interesting overview of the history of this traditional American holiday, see J. W. Baker, *Thanksgiving: The Biography of an American Holiday* (Lebanon, NH: University Press of New England), 2009.

17   Bradford, *Of Plymouth Plantation*, 127.

18   *Plymouth Colony Records*, vol. 8, ed. N. B. Shurtleff (Boston: W. White, 1855–61), 15.

19   http://www.pilgrimhallmuseum.org/mary_chilton.htm, accessed February 2018. Courtesy of Pilgrim Hall Museum, Plymouth, MA.

20   http://www.pilgrimhallmuseum.org/mary_chilton.htm, accessed February 2018. Courtesy of Pilgrim Hall Museum, Plymouth, MA.

21   http://www.womenhistoryblog.com/2007/07/mary-chilton-winslow.html, accessed February 2018.

22   R. C. Ritchie, *The Duke's Province: A Study of New York Politics and Society, 1664–1691* (Chapel Hill, NC: University of North Carolina Press, 2012), 105.

23   http://www.pilgrimhallmuseum.org/pdf/Mary_Chilton_Winslow_Will _Inventory.pdf, accessed February 2018. Courtesy of Pilgrim Hall Museum, Plymouth, MA.

24   C. H. Johnson, *The Mayflower and Her Passengers* (Bloomington, IN: Xlibris Corp., 2006), 118.

7: The Exiled Little Servant's Story: Mary More, Unwanted Four-Year-Old

1   A really useful and accessible overview of the matter of girls and delayed travel to the New World can be found at http://mayflowerhistory.com/girls/, accessed March 2018.

2   http://mayflowerhistory.com/girls/, accessed March 2018.

3   For a detailed exploration of the whole matter of the More children and the situation that gave rise to their going to North America, see D. Lindsay, *Mayflower Bastard: A Stranger Among the Pilgrims* (New York: St Martin's Press, 2002), which has proven very useful in the writing of this chapter.

4   D. Harris, "The More Children and the Mayflower, Part II," *The Mayflower Descendant* 44, no. 1 (January 1994), 14, 18.

5   Sir Anthony R. Wagner, "The Origin of the Mayflower Children: Jasper, Richard and Ellen More," *The New England Historical and Genealogical Register* 114 (July 1960), Boston, 165.

6   Wagner, "The Origin of the Mayflower Children: Jasper, Richard and Ellen More," 166.

7   Lindsay, *Mayflower Bastard*, 15.

8   Lindsay, *Mayflower Bastard*, 15.

9   William Bradford, *Of Plymouth Plantation, 1620–1647, by William Bradford, Sometime Governor Thereof, A New Edition*, ed. S. E. Morison (New York: Alfred A. Knopf, 2015, first published 1952), 441.

10   http://www.histarch.illinois.edu/plymouth/townpop.html, accessed March 2018.

11   Bradford, *Of Plymouth Plantation*, 78.

12   "Providence and the Pilgrim", by William Bradford (1590–1657), found at: http://www.bartleby.com/400/poem/26.html, quoting from eds. E. C. Stedman and E. M. Hutchinson, *A Library of American Literature: An Anthology in Eleven Volumes*, vols. 1–2, *Colonial Literature, 1607–1764* (New York: Charles L. Webster, 1891), accessed March 2018.

13   https://faithandamericanhistory.wordpress.com/tag/edward-winslow/, accessed March 2018, provides an overview of the demographic impact of the first winter.

14   http://www.plymoutharch.com/burials-on-coles-hill/, accessed March 2018.

8: The Man Overboard's Story: John Howland, Indentured Servant, Negotiator, and Fur Trapper

1   F. E. Grizzard and D. B. Smith, *Jamestown Colony: A Political, Social, and Cultural History* (Santa Barbara, CA: ABC-Clio, 2007), 206.

2   http://www.pilgrimhallmuseum.org/john_howland.htm, accessed March 2018. Courtesy of Pilgrim Hall Museum, Plymouth, MA.

3   http://mayflowerhistory.com/howland/, accessed March 2018.

4   "Pilgrim John Howland Society," *The Howland Homestead. Society of the Descendants of Pilgrim John Howland, of the Ship Mayflower*, 1911, 7–8.

5   A suggestion made, for example in A. Ames, *The Mayflower and her Log* (Boston, MA & New York: Houghton, Mifflin & Company, The Riverside Press), 1907.

6   For an eyewitness description see William Bradford, *Of Plymouth Plantation, 1620–1647, by William Bradford, Sometime Governor Thereof, A New Edition*, ed. S. E. Morison (New York: Alfred A. Knopf, 2015, first published 1952), 59.

7   G. E. Bowman, *The Mayflower Compact and its Signers* (Boston, MA: Massachusetts Society of Mayflower Descendants, 1920), 7–19.

8   A. R. Marble, *The Women Who Came in the Mayflower* (Boston, MA: The Pilgrim Press, 1920), 85–88.

9   N. Bunker, *Making Haste From Babylon: The Mayflower Pilgrims and Their World: A New History* (London: The Bodley Head, 2010), 233.

10   For his record of the visit, along with that provided by two other early visitors, see S. V. James Jr, ed., *Three Visitors to Early Plymouth* (Bedford, MA: Applewood Books, 1997, first published by Plimoth Plantation, Inc., 1963).

11   An excellent and accessible insight into the history and use of wampum can be found at https://indiancountrymedianetwork.com/history/genealogy/from -beads-to-bounty-how-wampum-became-americas-first-currencyand-lost-its -power/, accessed March 2018.

12   For an examination of evidence for the pre-European beaver population and its distribution, see B. W. Baker and E. P. Hill, "Beaver: *Castor canadensis*," in *Wild Mammals of North America: Biology, Management, and Conservation*, 2nd ed., eds. G. A. Feldhamer, B. C. Thompson, and J. A. Chapman (Baltimore, MD: The Johns Hopkins University Press, 2003), 288.

13   R. Fraser, *The Mayflower Generation: The Winslow Family and the Fight for the New World* (London: Chatto & Windus, 2017), 108.

14   Fraser, *The Mayflower Generation*, 112.

15   Bunker, *Making Haste From Babylon*, 11.

16   For a detailed account of this violent conflict, its effects, and eventual resolution, see Bradford, *Of Plymouth Plantation*, 262–268.

17   Fraser, *The Mayflower Generation*, 129.

18   N. Philbrick, *Mayflower: A Story of Courage, Community and War* (London & New York: Penguin, 2007), 168–169.

19   Fraser, *The Mayflower Generation*, 90.

20   See http://www.pilgrimjohnhowlandsociety.org/rocky-nook, accessed March 2018.

21   See http://www.pilgrimjohnhowlandsociety.org/rocky-nook, accessed March 2018.

22   http://www.plymoutharch.com/archaeology-of-the-john-howland-site-rocky -nook-kingston-massachusetts/, accessed March 2018.

23   See http://www.pilgrimjohnhowlandsociety.org/john-howland/articles/72 -howland-spoon-2, accessed March 2018.

24   M. C. Beaudry, *Documentary Archaeology in the New World* (Cambridge: Cambridge University Press, 1993), 86.

25   http://www.pilgrimhallmuseum.org/pdf/John_Howland_Will_Inventory.pdf, accessed March 2018. Courtesy of Pilgrim Hall Museum, Plymouth, MA.

26   For an intriguing insight into the significance of this book, see Bunker, *Making Haste From Babylon*, 60–62.

27   https://www.findagrave.com/memorial/6613808/john-howland, accessed March 2018.

28   Philbrick, *Mayflower*, 33.

29   http://mayflowerhistory.com/tilley-elizabeth/, accessed March 2018.

9: The Preacher's Story: William Brewster, Saint, Diplomat, and Preacher

1   https://www.pet.cam.ac.uk/who-was-william-brewster, accessed March 2018. Today, the village of Scrooby is bypassed and the quiet road that runs through the village and past the parish church is difficult to imagine as such a major thoroughfare, but such it once was.

2   https://www.pet.cam.ac.uk/who-was-william-brewster, accessed March 2018.

3   https://www.pet.cam.ac.uk/who-was-william-brewster, accessed March 2018.

4   http://www.pilgrimhallmuseum.org/pdf/Pilgrim_Press.pdf, accessed March 2018. Courtesy of Pilgrim Hall Museum, Plymouth, MA.

5   https:// www.pet.cam.ac.uk/who-was-william-brewster, accessed March 2018.

6   For a comprehensive list of passenger ages and occupations, see P. Scott Deetz and J. F. Deetz, "Passengers on the Mayflower: Ages & Occupations, Origins & Connections," http://www.histarch.illinois.edu/plymouth/Maysource.html, 2000, accessed October 2018.

7   William Bradford, *Of Plymouth Plantation, 1620–1647, by William Bradford, Sometime Governor Thereof, A New Edition*, ed. S. E. Morison (New York: Alfred A. Knopf, 2015, first published 1952), 75.

8   Bradford, *Of Plymouth Plantation*, 76.

9   The three versions differ slightly in their wording and more so in capitalization, spelling, and punctuation. However, the wording and content of the versions in *Of Plymouth Plantation* and *Mourt's Relation* are basically the same, with only minor differences.

10   When Thomas Prince published *A Chronological History of New-England in the form of Annals*.

11   Bradford, *Of Plymouth Plantation*, 76, note 3.

12   For an outline of Puritans and Covenants, see F. J. Bremer, *The Puritan Experiment: New England Society from Bradford to Edwards* (Hanover, NH & London: University Press of New England, 1995, first published in 1978), 18–19.

13   N. Bunker, *Making Haste From Babylon: The Mayflower Pilgrims and their World: A New History* (London: The Bodley Head, 2010), 286.

14 It was this need for educated ministers that led to the foundation of Harvard College by the colonists at Massachusetts Bay as early as 1636 (although it did not gain its famous name until 1638). And it was not a coincidence that the town in which it was based took the name Cambridge, an important university center of Puritan theology in England. Higher education was very important to the early New England Bible Commonwealths.

15 Gorges went to what is now Weymouth, Massachusetts, attempting to build his settlement on the site of the failed Wessagusset Colony but with no more success than that earlier venture.

16 See http://www.pilgrimhallmuseum.org/pdf/Religious_Controversies _Plymouth_Colony.pdf, accessed October 2018.

17 http://www.pilgrimhallmuseum.org/pdf/Religious_Controversies_Plymouth _Colony.pdf, accessed March 2018. Courtesy of Pilgrim Hall Museum, Plymouth, MA.

18 Samuel Eliot Morison.

19 Bremer, *The Puritan Experiment*, 35.

20 http://www.pilgrimhallmuseum.org/pdf/Religious_Controversies_Plymouth _Colony.pdf, accessed March 2018. Courtesy of Pilgrim Hall Museum, Plymouth, MA.

21 Bradford, *Of Plymouth Plantation*, 284–285.

22 Bradford, *Of Plymouth Plantation*, 293.

23 Bradford, *Of Plymouth Plantation*, 313.

24 A third meeting house was erected on this spot in 1744, to replace the 1683 building. This lasted until 1831, when a fourth meeting house was built. Destroyed by fire in 1892, a replacement church (the fifth meeting house) was dedicated in 1899, and it is that church which stands today as the church known as First Parish Plymouth.

25 Bradford, *Of Plymouth Plantation*, 97.

26 See M. Whittock, *When God Was King: Rebels and Radicals of the Civil War & Mayflower Generation* (Oxford: Lion Hudson), 2018.

27 http://mayflowerhistory.com/cooke-john/, accessed March 2018.

28 After 1663, the four settlements in this area were officially termed the Colony of Rhode Island and Providence Plantations, and continued a policy of religious toleration.

29 http://www.pilgrimhallmuseum.org/pdf/Religious_Controversies_Plymouth _Colony.pdf, accessed March 2018. Courtesy of Pilgrim Hall Museum, Plymouth, MA.

30 See http://www.gordon.edu/page.cfm?iPageID=3196, accessed April 2018.

31 For an overview of these events in New England within the wider context of the British Civil Wars, see Whittock, *When God Was King*, 185–201.

32 Bradford, *Of Plymouth Plantation*, 327.

33 Bradford, *Of Plymouth Plantation*, 329.

34 See http://www.gordon.edu/page.cfm?iPageID=3196, accessed April 2018.

10: The Pamphleteer's Story: Edward Winslow, Pilgrim Leader, Colony Agent, and Lobbyist

1   A fine, wide-ranging examination of his life and achievements can be found in R. Fraser, *The Mayflower Generation: The Winslow Family and the Fight for the New World* (London: Chatto & Windus, 2017).

2   J. D. Bangs, *Pilgrim Edward Winslow: New England's First International Diplomat: A Documentary Biography* (Boston, MA: New England Historic Genealogical Society, 2004).

3   See Bangs, *Pilgrim Edward Winslow.*

4   C. H. Johnson, *The Mayflower and Her Passengers* (Bloomington, IN: Xlibris Corp., 2006), 253.

5   An excellent overview of when various ships arrived at Plymouth can be found in the detailed list compiled by Anne Stevens. See https://www.packrat-pro .com/ships/shiplist.htm, accessed April 2018.

6   Edward Winslow, *Good Newes from New England*, 1624 (Bedford, MA: Applewood Books, 1996), 33.

7   N. Philbrick, *Mayflower: A Story of Courage, Community, and War* (London & New York: Penguin, 2007), 131–132.

8   William Bradford shortened his name to Squanto, whereas Edward Winslow usually referred to him by what was probably his actual name, Tisquantum.

9   Philbrick, *Mayflower*, 180–181.

10   Edward Winslow, *Good Newes from New England*, 1624, http://www.histarch .illinois.edu/plymouth/ goodnews8.html, accessed April 2018.

11   See R. A. Bailey, *Race and Redemption in Puritan New England* (Oxford: Oxford University Press, 2011).

12   See Philbrick, *Mayflower*, 183.

13   William Bradford, *Of Plymouth Plantation, 1620–1647, by William Bradford, Sometime Governor Thereof, A New Edition*, ed. S. E. Morison (New York: Alfred A. Knopf, 2015, first published 1952), 347.

14   P. H. Round, *By Nature and by Custom Cursed: Transatlantic Civil Discourse and New England Cultural Production, 1620–1660* (Hanover, NH & London: University Press of New England, 1999), 10.

15   http://www.pilgrimhall.org/pdf/Edward_Winslows_Will.pdf, accessed April 2018. Courtesy of Pilgrim Hall Museum, Plymouth, MA.

16   J. Hanc, "The Plymouth Hero You Should Really Be Thankful for This Thanksgiving," Smithsonian.com, November 21, 2016, found at: https://www .smithsonianmag.com/history/why-edward-winslow-plymouth-hero -thanksgiving-180961174/, accessed April 2018.

11: The Soldier's Story: Captain Myles Standish, Commander of the Plymouth Colony Militia

1   While this account uses imagination to convey something of the brutal execution that occurred at Wessagusset Colony, in March 1623, the groundwork

of reality is all too clear from the surviving records: the Plymouth men in the house; the number of Massachusett warriors (one of whom was a teenager); the presence of Massachusett women, later released; the stabbing, using the victim's own knife; the execution of two others in the room, the hanging of the adolescent, and then the killing of the other men outside; the whole bloody ambush over a meal of pork and corn bread, where the laws of host and guest should have guaranteed safety for those visiting the house; the decapitation of the man who had, on two earlier occasions, threatened Standish; Pecksuot speaking English. See Edward Winslow, *Good Newes from New England*, 1624 (Bedford, MA: Applewood Books, 1996), 47–50; Thomas Morton, *New English Canaan*, 1637, reprint, ed. J. Dempsey (Scituate, MA: Digital Scanning Inc, 2000), 110. No wonder people on both sides were deeply shocked in 1623.

2   http://www.pilgrimhallmuseum.org/pdf/Myles_Standish_Will_Inventory.pdf, accessed April 2018. Courtesy of Pilgrim Hall Museum, Plymouth, MA.

3   Nathaniel Morton, *The New-England's Memorial*, 1669 (Bedford, MA: Applewood Books, 2009), 154.

4   N. Philbrick, *Mayflower: A Story of Courage, Community, and War* (London & New York: Penguin, 2007, 25.

5   J. Winsor, *History of the Town of Duxbury* (Boston, MA: Crosby & Nichols, 1849), 97; J. D. Bangs, "Myles Standish, Born Where? The State of the Question," *The Mayflower Quarterly* vol. 72, no. 1 (March 2006), 133-159. *The Mayflower Quarterly* is published by the General Society of Mayflower Descendants, Plymouth, MA.

6   J. A. Goodwin, *The Pilgrim Republic: An Historical Review of the Colony of New Plymouth, with Sketches of the Rise of Other New England Settlements, the History of Congregationalism, and the Creeds of the Period* (Boston, MA: Houghton Mifflin, 1888 edn, 70, reprinted by ReInk Books, 2018).

7   Philbrick, *Mayflower*, 59.

8   This building, dating from 1899 (constituting the fifth meeting house), stands on the site of an earlier church built in 1683, which itself replaced one (the first meeting house) that was built in 1648 in a different location, on the north side of Town Square.

9   For an accessible overview of the weaponry of the Plymouth Colony, see http://www.pilgrimhallmuseum.org/pdf/Arms_Armor_of_Pilgrims.pdf, accessed April 2018. Courtesy of Pilgrim Hall Museum, Plymouth, MA.

10   Philbrick, *Mayflower*, 89.

11   For an idea of the kinds of dwellings that might have stood in this summer-season village, see https://www.plimoth.org/learn/just-kids/homework-help/building-home, accessed April 2018.

12   As recounted by John Pory, in a letter sent back from Plymouth in January 1623. See S. V. James, ed., *Three Visitors to Early Plymouth* (Bedford, MA: Applewood Books, 1997, first published by Plimoth Plantation, Inc., 1963), 12.

13   James, *Three Visitors to Early Plymouth*, 16.

14 James, *Three Visitors to Early Plymouth*, 24.

15 The Dutchman Isaack de Rasieres, writing c.1628. See James, *Three Visitors to Early Plymouth*, 76.

16 The Dutchman Isaack de Rasieres. See James, *Three Visitors to Early Plymouth*, 76–77.

17 The events at Wessagusset were described in some detail by a survivor of the colony, Phineas Pratt, who recounted the history of the doomed colony in 1662, to the General Court of Massachusetts. See http://www.pilgrimhallmuseum .org/pdf/Phineas_Pratt_Narrative.pdf, accessed May 2018. Courtesy of Pilgrim Hall Museum, Plymouth, MA. And by Edward Winslow, in *Good Newes from New England*, in 1624.

18 R. Fraser, *The Mayflower Generation: The Winslow Family and the Fight for the New World* (London: Chatto & Windus, 2017), 89.

19 The actions of Pecksuot were later reported by Phineas Pratt, who arrived in the spring of 1622 on the *Sparrow* and who provided us with the only surviving eyewitness account of what occurred at Wessagusset in the winter of 1622–23. See C. S. Chartier, "Plymouth Archaeological Rediscovery Project (PARP) An Investigation into Weston's Colony at Wessagussett, Weymouth, MA," www.plymoutharch.com, March 2011, 4–5, https://www.scribd.com /doc/50300822/An-Investigation-into-Weston-s-Colony-at-Wessagussett -Weymouth-Massachusetts, accessed May 2018.

20 Winslow, *Good Newes from New England*, 47.

21 Winslow, *Good Newes from New England*, 47.

22 Philbrick, *Mayflower*, 153; this was a view, held as early as 1637, of Standish's priorities at Wessagusset. See Morton, *New English Canaan*, 111.

23 After increasingly negative involvements in settlements in Massachusetts, Thomas Weston went on to be involved in further North American ventures in Virginia, Maine, and Maryland, before dying in London, probably in 1648.

24 http://www.weymouthhistoricalsociety.org/early_settlers.htm, accessed May 2018. See also W. W. LaMorte, "A Brief History of Weymouth, MA," http://sphweb .bumc.bu.edu/otlt/MPH-Modules/Weymouth/, accessed May 2016; and Phineas Pratt's account, http://www.pilgrimhallmuseum.org/pdf/Phineas_Pratt_Narrative. pdf, accessed May 2018. Courtesy of Pilgrim Hall Museum, Plymouth, MA.

25 William Bradford, *Of Plymouth Plantation, 1620–1647, by William Bradford, Sometime Governor Thereof, A New Edition*, ed. S. E. Morison (New York: Alfred A. Knopf, 2015, first published 1952), 374–375.

26 C. H. Johnson, *The Mayflower and Her Passengers* (Bloomington, IN: Xlibris Corp., 2006), 220.

27 Bradford, *Of Plymouth Plantation*, 205–206.

28 Morton, *New English Canaan*, 143 (and a number of other places).

29 Morton, *New English Canaan*, 113.

30 It was only surpassed by the Washington Monument (over 178 feet, 54.4 m) in Baltimore, Maryland (completed in 1829) and the Washington Monument (over 554 feet, 169 m) in Washington, D.C. (finally completed in 1888).

12: The Lovers' Story: John Alden and Priscilla Mullins

1   I am grateful to Desiree Mobed, director of the Alden House Historic Site, for drawing to my attention Jim Baker's valuable comments on the versatile products of the cooper. See J. W. Baker, "John the cooper," appendix 4 in *Alden House History: A Work in Progress* (Duxbury, MA: Alden Kindred of America, 2006).

2   https://www.nps.gov/jame/learn/historyculture/john-rolfe.htm, accessed February 2018.

3   For an overview of these, see A. Crane Williams, "John Alden: Theories on English Ancestry," *The Mayflower Descendant* 39 (1989), 111–22; 40 (1990), 133–36; 41 (1991), 201.

4   R. C. Anderson, *The Pilgrim Migration: Immigrants to Plymouth Colony 1620–1633* (Boston, MA: New England Historic Genealogical Society, 2004), 9.

5   C. E. Banks, *The English Ancestry and Homes of the Pilgrim Fathers: who came to Plymouth on the Mayflower in 1620, the Fortune in 1621, and the Anne and the Little James in 1623* (Baltimore, MD: Genealogical Publishing Co., 2006, originally published New York: the Grafton Press, 1929) 27–28.

6   See J. W. Baker, *Alden House History: A Work in Progress.*

7   William Bradford, *Of Plymouth Plantation, 1620–1647, by William Bradford, Sometime Governor Thereof, A New Edition,* ed. S. E. Morison (New York: Alfred A. Knopf, 2015, first published 1952), 443.

8   https://www.exploringsurreyspast.org.uk/themes/places/surrey/mole_valley/dorking/ dorking_ william_mullins_house/, accessed May 2018.

9   For a very interesting brief exploration of the status of the Mullins family, see Peggy M. Baker's article, "Priscilla's Choice," in *The Compact* 35, no. 1 (Spring/Summer 2014), published by the Massachusetts Society of Mayflower Descendants. I am grateful to Desiree Mobed, director of the Alden House Historic Site, for drawing my attention to this article.

10   http://www.pilgrimhallmuseum.org/john_alden.htm, accessed May 2018. Courtesy of Pilgrim Hall Museum, Plymouth, MA.

11   Baker, "Priscilla's Choice."

12   Baker, "Priscilla's Choice."

13   https://caleb-johnson.squarespace.com/alden, accessed May 2018.

14   See M. T. Mulholland, "An Interdisciplinary Study of the John Alden Houses, 1627 and 1653, Duxbury, Massachusetts: Archaeology and Architecture," in *The Archaeological Northeast,* eds. M. A. Levine, K. E. Sassaman, M. S. Nassaney (Westport, CT: Greenwood Publishing Group, 1999), 235–248. For an up-to-date study of the pottery found there, see C. Gardiner, "Life in a 17th-Century House: An Archaeological Study of Domestic Activities and Spaces at the Alden Family First Home," *Mayflower Journal* (Spring 2018), 33–47. I am grateful to Desiree Mobed, director of the Alden House Historic Site, for drawing my attention to this article.

15   The first use of the term *clapboard* to refer to house weatherproofing (as opposed to use as barrel staves) dates from 17th-century Massachusetts.

16   A possibility suggested by Jim Baker. See J. W. Baker, *Alden House History: A Work in Progress*.

17   For a history of this surviving structure, see http://alden.org/content /aldenhistory3.pdf, accessed May 2018.

18   http://www.nramuseum.com/guns/the-galleries/ancient-firearms-1350 -to-1700/case-3-old-guns-in-the-new-world/mayflower-wheellock -carbine.aspx, accessed May 2018.

19   For a detailed overview of their lives, see A. Crane Williams, "John and Priscilla, We Hardly Know Ye," *America History Illustrated* 23, no. 8 (December 1988).

20   http://mayflowerhistory.com/alden/, accessed May 2018.

21   E. Alden, *Memorial of the Descendants of the Hon. John Alden* (Randolph, MA: Samuel P. Brown (for the family), 1867), 146, quoting a tradition he knew from a reference, dating from 1865, preserved among some Alden descendants.

22   P. C. Nagel, *John Quincy Adams: A Public Life, a Private Life* (Cambridge, MA & London: Harvard University Press, 1999), 5.

23   *The Complete Poetical Works of Henry Wadsworth Longfellow. Cambridge Edition* (Boston, MA: Houghton Mifflin Company, 1914).

24   A very succinct overview of the poem can be found at https://www .tweetspeakpoetry.com/2017/08/15/childhood-poetry-history-courtship-miles -standish/, accessed May 2018. The one provided in this book is my own effort to sum up the poem.

25   http://www.pilgrimhallmuseum.org/john_alden.htm, accessed May 2018. Courtesy of Pilgrim Hall Museum, Plymouth, MA.

26   http://www.pilgrimhallmuseum.org/pdf/Courtship_Miles_Standish.pdf, accessed May 2018. Courtesy of Pilgrim Hall Museum, Plymouth, MA.

27   V. Karandashev, *Romantic Love in Cultural Contexts* (Grand Rapids, MI: Springer, 2016), 123, reflecting on the Puritan attitude towards love and attraction.

28   A. Belding Brown, "Love and Marriage among the Puritans," https://amy beldingbrown.wordpress.com/2015/08/17/love-and-marriage-among-the -puritans/, accessed May 2018.

29   A phrase found on the plaque commemorating his achievements, found near the cathedral at Chelmsford, Essex, England.

30   Belding Brown, "Love and Marriage among the Puritans," accessed May 2018.

31   L. Ryken, *Worldly Saints: The Puritans as They Really Were* (Grand Rapids, MI: Zondervan, 1990), 50.

32   Ryken, *Worldly Saints*, 51.

33   C. Kile, "Endless Love Will Keep Us Together," in *Women and Romance: A Reader*, ed. S. Ostrov Weisser (New York & London: New York University Press, 2001), 417.

13: The Rebels' Story: the Billingtons, the Soules, and Other Challenges to Morality and Order

1   Leviticus 20:15–16 (Geneva Bible).

2   D. B. Heath, *Mourt's Relation: A Journal of the Pilgrims at Plymouth* (Bedford, MA: Applewood Books, 1963), 31.

3   Heath, *Mourt's Relation*, 44.

4   Thomas Prince, *New England Chronology*, as reprinted in Nathaniel Morton, *New England's Memorial* (Boston, MA: Congregational Board of Publication, 1855), 291. See also http://www.pilgrimhallmuseum.org/pdf/ John_Eleanor _Billington_17th_Century_Documents.pdf, accessed May 2018. Courtesy of Pilgrim Hall Museum, Plymouth, MA.

5   William Bradford, *Of Plymouth Plantation, 1620–1647, by William Bradford, Sometime Governor Thereof, A New Edition*, ed. S. E. Morison (New York: Alfred A. Knopf, 2015, first published 1952), 87–88.

6   Heath, *Mourt's Relation*, 71.

7   William Bradford, *Governor Bradford's Letter Book*, as printed in *Collections of the Massachusetts Historical Society for the year 1794*, vol. 3 (Boston, MA, 1810).

8   Bradford, *Of Plymouth Plantation*, 234.

9   William Hubbard, *A General History of New England* (Boston, MA: Charles C. Little & James Brown, 1848), 101. This history was originally written in about 1680 but was not published until 1814.

10 Thomas Morton, *The New English Canaan of Thomas Morton* (Boston, MA: Prince Society, 1883), 216.

11 *Plymouth Colony Records*, vol. 1, ed. N. B. Shurtleff (Boston: W. White, 1855–61), 41, 42.

12 C. H. Johnson, *The Mayflower and Her Passengers* (Bloomington, IN: Xlibris Corp., 2006), 207.

13 For an examination of this subject (including the intense anxiety concerning sexual relationships between native men and European women), see R. Godbeer, *Sexual Revolution in Early America* (Baltimore, MD & London: Johns Hopkins University Press, 2002), especially 5–6.

14 The details of the Soules' offenses and punishments can be found in C. H. Johnson, *The Mayflower and Her Passengers*, 207–208.

15 Godbeer, *Sexual Revolution in Early America*, 3–4.

16 Some accounts say five cases, three of these against George Clark, who was twenty years younger.

17 http://mayflowerhistory.com/doty/, accessed May 2018.

18 Bradford, *Of Plymouth Plantation*, 244.

19 Bradford, *Of Plymouth Plantation*, 392.

20 http://mayflowerhistory.com/crime/, accessed May 2018.

21 Bradford, *Of Plymouth Plantation*, 320.

22 Bradford, *Of Plymouth Plantation*, appendix 10, 404–413.

23 Bradford, *Of Plymouth Plantation*, 320, note 6.

24   Bradford, *Of Plymouth Plantation*, 320–322.

25   William Bradford, *Of Plymouth Plantation*, 316. See also N. Philbrick, *Mayflower: A Story of Courage, Community, and War* (London & New York: Penguin, 2007), 186.

26   http://mayflowerhistory.com/crime/, accessed May 2018.

14. The American Mariner's Story: Richard More, New World Sea Captain

1   While the records are blank for his life in Plymouth between 1620 and 1627, it is reasonable to assume this, as the need for manpower was desperate during that first winter. Furthermore, Richard was a servant in a world where childhood was a luxury not enjoyed by the poorest in society.

2   William Bradford, in appendix 13, *Of Plymouth Plantation*, "Passengers in the *Mayflower*," says that she died "soon after the ship's arrival." However, some historians have placed her death after that of Jasper, her brother, and after the *Mayflower* moved to Plymouth.

3   William Bradford simply says that he died "of the common infection" before his master, John Carver, who died in the spring of 1621. However, some historians suggest that both he and Ellen were buried at what is now Provincetown. The Provincetown Memorial names only Jasper, of the More children.

4   First heard, according to *Mourt's Relation*, on March 3, 1621.

5   https://mayflower.americanancestors.org/richard-more-biography, accessed May 2018, New England Historic Genealogical Society, Boston, MA.

6   https://mayflower.americanancestors.org/richard-more-biography, accessed May 2018.

7   https://mayflower.americanancestors.org/richard-more-biography, accessed May 2018.

8   D. Lindsay, *Mayflower Bastard: A Stranger Among the Pilgrims* (New York: St Martin's Press, 2002), 102–104 & 123–124. See also I. Lawrence, "Mayflower Passenger Richard More—His connection to Annapolis Royal," http://anna polisheritagesociety.com/genealogy/family-histories/mayflower-passenger -richard-connection-annapolis-royal/, accessed May 2018. These conclusions, it must be said, have not been accepted by a number of other *Mayflower* historians, who are skeptical about the use of this evidence and the conclusions drawn from it.

9   https://mayflower.americanancestors.org/richard-more-biography, accessed May 2018.

10   J. B. Felt, *Annals of Salem*, vol. 2 (Salem, MA: W. & S. B. Ives, 1849), 504.

11   Felt, *Annals of Salem*, vol. 2, 504.

12   Lawrence, "Mayflower Passenger Richard More—His connection to Annapolis Royal," accessed May 2018.

13   Felt, *Annals of Salem*, vol. 2, 504.

14   According to Lindsay, *Mayflower Bastard*, 165–166.

15   Some accounts number this as high as seventeen.

16   J. D. Drake, *King Philip's War: Civil War in New England, 1675–1676* (Amherst, MA: University of Massachusetts Press, 1999), 119.

17   https://mayflower.americanancestors.org/richard-more-biography, accessed May 2018.

18   R. D. Pierce, ed., *The Records of the First Church in Salem Massachusetts, 1629–1736* (Salem, MA: Essex Institute, 1974), 171.

19   Lindsay, *Mayflower Bastard*, 191.

20   S. Jobe, "Sarah Good," http://salem.lib.virginia.edu/people/good.html, accessed May 2018.

21   https://www.uswars.net/king-williams-war/, accessed May 2018.

22   C. Fischer, "Pilgrims, Puritans, and the ideology that is their American legacy," http://blogs.berkeley.edu/2010/11/24/pilgrims-puritans-and-their-american -legacy/, accessed May 2018.

23   For an overview of Salem in the context of the settlement of New England, see M. Whittock, *When God Was King: Rebels & Radicals of the Civil War & Mayflower Generation* (Oxford: Lion Hudson, 2018), 199–201.

24   R. M. Sherman, V. D. Vincent, R. S. Wakefield, and L. D. Finlay, *Mayflower Families Through Five Generations*, vol. 15, *Family of James Chilton and Family of Richard More* (Plymouth, MA: General Society of Mayflower Descendants, 1997), 156.

25   Mary Cushman, née Allerton, daughter of *Mayflower* Pilgrim Isaac Allerton, was the last survivor of the *Mayflower* voyage when she died, aged eighty-three, at Plymouth in November 1699.

15: Seeing the New England Forest for the Trees

1   Quoted in William Bradford, *Of Plymouth Plantation, 1620–1647, by William Bradford, Sometime Governor Thereof, A New Edition*, ed. S. E. Morison (New York: Alfred A. Knopf, 2015, first published 1952), xxvii.

INDEX

ABOUT THE AUTHOR

Martyn Whittock graduated in politics from Bristol University in 1980, where his degree special study was in radical Christian politics and theology of the 17th century. He taught history for thirty-five years and recently was curriculum leader for spiritual, moral, social, and cultural education at a high school in the UK. He has acted as an historical consultant to the British National Trust organization, the BBC, and English Heritage. He is a Licensed Lay Minister, in the Church of England. He retired from teaching in 2016 to devote more time to writing. He lives in Wiltshire in the west of England.

He is the author of forty-seven books, including school history textbooks and adult history books. The latter include: *A Brief History of Life in the Middle Ages* (2009), *A Brief History of the Third Reich* (2011), *A Brief Guide to Celtic Myths and Legends* (2013), *The Viking Blitzkrieg 789–1098* (2013), *The Anglo-Saxon Avon Valley Frontier* (2014), *1016 1066: Why the Vikings Caused the Norman Conquest* (2016), *Norse and Legends* (2017 and published by Pegasus as *Tales of Valhalla*, USA, in 2018), *The Vikings: from Odin to Christ* (2018). The ... were cowritten with Hannah, his elder daughter and a Cambridge University graduate in early medieval history. *Christ: The First ... Years* (2016) was cowritten with his younger daughter, ... bridge University graduate in theology. His most recent ... *Was King*—explores the lives and beliefs of rebels and ... sh Civil Wars and Mayflower generation, both in the ... th America. He has recently completed *The Story of ...* ...ming), examining the Christian cross in history ...usand years, cowritten with Esther Whittock.

306